Lee
WULFF

Jack Samson
With the cooperation of Joan Wulff

Frank
Amato

PORTLAND

Dedication

This book is dedicated to the goals of the Atlantic Salmon Federation (ASF). An international, non-profit organization, ASF has worked for decades to promote optimum returns of the Atlantic salmon to their birth-rivers; to further Atlantic salmon research; and in the interests of the conservation and wise management of the species and its environment, to generate public sport and influence government policy.

Lee Wulff was North America's most famous, passionate, and articulate champion of the same ASF mission: the conservation and wise managment of the king of fish and its environment. Indeed, he served ASF for 20 years—as a Director and Vice-President of ASF (U.S.) and as Chairman and Honorary Chairman of ASF (Canada). A book about Lee Wulff is inescapably a book about his most beloved cause.

Tony Amato

Copyright 1995 • Jack Samson
Book and cover design • Joyce Herbst
All black and white photos courtesy of Joan Wulff unless otherwise noted
Front and back cover photos: Joan Wulff
Lee Wulff illustration on page 1 by Loren Smith
Printed in Hong Kong
Frank Amato Publications, Inc.
P.O. Box 82112 • Portland, Oregon 97282
(503) 653-8108 • Fax (503) 653-2766
ISBN 1-57188-019-4 • UPC 0-66066-00209-9
1 3 5 7 9 10 8 6 4 2

Contents

Foreword

Those who excel at their craft or art labor with passion, rarely doubting themselves or the importance of their quest.

Lee Wulff was such a person. Once having decided that he could make a living by endeavors associated with sport fishing, writing, film making, guiding, outfitting, and teaching he devoted his impressive energies to that end. Blessed with keen powers of observation, physical courage, a restless, innovative mind, a flair for the dramatic and a rugged constitution, he was, at the time of his death, the elder statesman of American fly fishers. His 148 pound striped marlin taken off Ecuador in 1967 remains the world fly rod record for that species on a 12-pound-test tippet, he was a superb trout fisherman, he was a pioneer in catching giant bluefin tuna from open boats. He was also a first-rate, dedicated upland bird and small and big game hunter.

In his 70s and 80s, Lee sought new challenges, among them catching Atlantic salmon on tiny No. 28 dry flies—better suited for one-pound trout—that had to be fished with four-pound test leaders. I was with Lee on New Brunswick's Upsalquitch River when he began this endeavor and he was still at it a year later when we were on the Ste. Marguerite in Quebec. On the Ste. Marguerite, he hooked a good salmon that, more than a half hour later, came off the hook.

In chronicling that encounter in my New York *Times* column, I carelessly wrote that the leader had parted. A few days later, I received a letter from

Lee which began: "I hate you," and then went on to explain that the hook had pulled out.

He was being humorous, of course, but it was also a matter of considerable concern to him. I had inadvertently implied that he had gotten heavy-handed in playing the fish. Most salmon fishers would have been pleased to remain connected with a salmon of that size—the guide, Lee and I had estimated its weight at about 15 pounds—on such light tackle for a minute or so, and the manner of its escape would have been of little import. Lee had refined the art of playing a salmon to such a degree that, to him, applying too much pressure on the delicate tippet was unthinkable.

Almost inevitably, given his early years of exploring Newfoundland's rivers in single-engine float planes, he became best-known for his knowledge of Atlantic salmon and how to fish for them. A lesser man would have been content with the fame that came his way for that achievement, but Lee also labored—with unflagging intensity for half a century—for conservation of the Atlantic salmon. He was the conscience and the soul of that effort.

There comes a time in the lives of sensitive and thinking fishers and hunters when bulging creels and game bags are no longer the goal, when the beloved quarry's survival as a species is the most important consideration. It is a complex affair of the heart and mind. One continues to kill an occasional salmon or trout, duck or ruffed grouse if only to re-create the visceral excitement and ambiance of the quest that was launched decades before. And then, the deed done, one is reminded, with ever-increasing intensity as one grows older, of the value and uniqueness of that which was taken. This happened to Lee with the Atlantic salmon early on. He responded to that awareness and became the salmon's champion. Without that dedication he would have been remembered as the most skilled and inventive fly fisher of this century. With it, he became truly great.

—Nelson Bryant

Introduction

At first the thought of writing the biography of Lee Wulff was mind-boggling. Even as a writer who had done several biographies of great men (Ernest Thompson Seton and General Claire Lee Chennault) I was numbed by the thought of the research involved. Lee had lived to the ripe old age of 86 and had fished everywhere.

"I admire your courage in tackling a book on Lee Wulff," wrote Henry Lyman, editor emeritus of *Salt Water Sportsman.*

But as I got into the writing and research the job became easier than I had thought it would be. In the first place I had known and fished with Lee personally. We were both deeply involved in the outdoor field—in my case Editor-In-Chief of *Field & Stream* for almost 15 years—and we knew almost everyone in the "industry."

Lee was about 15 years older than me, but we were both life-time fly fishermen. I had been a navigator/bombardier in China in World War II, but had gotten my private pilot's license in 1949—two years after Lee got his. We were both writers of outdoor books and countless magazine articles—most on fishing and hunting. Lee had gotten a start on me in salmon fishing because of his years in Newfoundland before and after the War, but I gradually began catching up to him—fishing the salmon rivers in Quebec, New Brunswick, Iceland and Scotland while with the world's largest outdoor magazine, *Field & Stream.*

And though Lee had caught big bluefin tuna off Nova Scotia early, I had caught them off Prince Edward Island and Bimini in the Bahamas—and we both were ardent saltwater flats fly fishermen. Lee had caught some Pacific sailfish on a fly and still holds the world record for a striped marlin he caught in Ecuador on 12 pound tippet back in 1967. And while that did impress me years ago, I had caught a lot of sailfish and marlin on a fly in the intervening years.

The more I learned about Lee the more I realized he was just another fisherman—like the rest of us—but what a fisherman! By the time I was deeply involved in the research of his early life I had forgotten to be intimidated by the task ahead.

But without the help of a great many people, the job would have been almost impossible. Most of the people who knew Lee in the pre-war years and in the 1940s, are no longer with us. But, on the positive side, Lee never threw away a scrap of paper on which he made notes or a letter from anyone, which—for a biographer—is a godsend. I do not envy biographers of the future—with most communication being done today either by telephone or FAX machine.

I am deeply indebted to the following for help with the research on the life of Lee Wulff: Joan Wulff, Barry Wulff, Bill Brewster, Neil Marvin, Nelson Bryant, Helen (Wulff) Clemments, Joe Cullman, Max Francisco, Hal Lyman, Jack Dennis, Charles Meyer, Gardner Grant, Ernie Schwiebert, Gene Hill, Angus Cameron, Curt Gowdy, Jim Rikhoff, Steve Sloan, Mike Leech, Ben Wright, H. G. "Tap" Tapply, Wilf Carter, Jack Fenety, Mac Francis, Keith Gardner, John Merwin, Ben Sherman, Mark Sherman, Bob Sherman, Ed Zern, Arthur Oglesby, Stan Bogdan, Jack Hegarty, Bruce and Susan Waterfall, Gary Sherman, Jim Chapralis, Bob Jacklin, Ralph Moon, Pete Kriendler, Bill Munro, Tom Paugh, Robert Bryan, Ed Janes, Wendell Sharpe, Arnold Gingrich, John Groth, Bill Piersall, John Bailey, Howard Brant, Judith Bowman, Hank Siegel, Jim Butler, Silvio Calabi, Kip Farrington, Grits Gresham, Lefty Kreh, Stu Apte, Tom Pero, John Randolph, A. J. McClane, George Reiger, Mark Sosin, Zack Taylor and Leonard Wright.

Alaska—and Points South

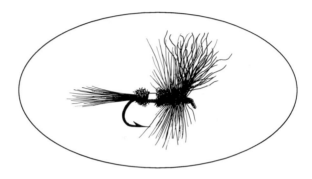

President Theodore Roosevelt was gaining international recognition for the United States early in 1905 by arranging a peace conference between Russia and Japan—trying to end a war between the two nations that had been waged since February 10, 1904. He would be awarded the Nobel Peace Prize the following year for his efforts.

But those global events were far from the minds of Mr. and Mrs. Charles Wulff of Valdez, Alaska in the early afternoon hours of February 10, 1905. Charles Wulff, a deputy sheriff of that tiny frontier town, had just heaved a huge sigh of relief as the whistle of the steamship *Excelsior* reverberated around the frozen hills surrounding the village. His wife had just safely given birth to a son—Henry Leon Wulff—at 2 p.m. on that cold, overcast day.

Though the creeks and rivers were sheathed in ice at that time of the year, it wouldn't be long before "Lee" Wulff was fishing.

As he wrote many years later for *True Magazine,* "My mother used to tell me I was fishing with a bent pin on a piece of string as soon as I could crawl the fifty yards to the 'crick' behind the house."

The Valdez area even today offers a diversity of sport fishing opportunities. Valdez supports the largest recreational fishery in Prince William Sound and the largest pink salmon fishery in Alaska. In addition there is great coho, sockeye salmon and trout fishing.

"Valdez was a great town for a fisherman's boyhood," Wulff continued in his magazine article. "The streams had great runs of trout and salmon, and there was a good smelt run in the winter. From the bay we could catch not only salmon but cod, flounder and halibut. Each fall, when the salmon and trout runs were on, every family in town wanted to salt down at least a couple of barrels of those fish, and a kid who liked to catch fish could fish endlessly and never catch more than his family and his neighbors needed, no matter how many he caught.

"There were hundreds of sled dogs in town, and if you add the needs of the dogs to the human demands in that town of 1,700 souls, the total was staggering. There were no game laws. There was only a vital need and a seemingly endless supply of fish, runs of trout and salmon that streamed into the fresh waters over and beyond the take of the canneries that operated farther out in Prince William Sound.

"Early fishing memories come back across the years when I let them. Memories of early summer days when the fields on the way to two-mile creek were covered with a mottled red blanket on Johnny-jump-ups and shooting stars. But I took only fleeting notice of the flowers. My interest was in the rivers and the fish.

Father Charles Wulff with his children in Valdez, Alaska, March, 1910. Baby Lee is held and sisters Audrey (left) and Lillian standing.

11

"In the spring there were only trout and salmon parr in the streams. This was the time when fish were few and hard to catch. We young fishermen carried some hooks and a length of line. I'd find a place where a log or tree leaned out over a pool and I'd quietly let my line down to where the trout or parr were moving in the slow current. I'd twist the line to adjust the small single hook and wait until a fish swam over it. Then I'd yank. The yank would carry the small fish right out into the air and somewhat up on the bank.

"From there on my fishing was more conventional. Now there were two eyes for bait and I'd add a sinker to the line and, swinging it over my head, send it out to the deep eddies to rest on the bottom where the bigger trout were. Each fish caught had two more eyes to take out, so the supply of bait from that point on was never ending.

"Fishing with hook and line was fun but there were other methods of catching fish that were more certain and equally entertaining once the main runs came in. These called for different gear and much more stealth and skill. I could fasten a short length of soft copper wire to the end of an alder pole. Forming the wire into a loop a little larger in diameter than that of the trout I was trying to catch, I would move it down cautiously over the fish's head and fling him out onto the bank. The trout were wild, and the problems of seeing them, then stalking carefully and finally getting the snare in place, were far more challenging and effective than the simple method of throwing a sinker and bait into the pools.

"We made gaffs with a 14/0 shark hook wired to the end of an alder or bamboo pole. In gaffing the fish we liked to see them first and, as with a snare, drift the gaff gently into position and yank it into the fish. A gaff would bring ashore bigger fish than we could take with a snare, because the soft copper wire wouldn't take the heavy weight and hard twisting. The great value of the gaff lay in its effectiveness in cloudy or turbulent waters. Even though the fish couldn't be seen, if you could read the water and if your stroke was good, you could connect with fish.

"By the time I was eight," he continued, "I was proficient with the hand line, spear, snare and gaff. I was wet to the hips all summer long, either wadding wet or soaked over the tops of any boots I wore. We'd wade down a stream, and when the trout that had congregated in the tail of the pool tried to race past us to get to safety we'd strike them with a spear or nail them with a gaff. It took a lot of judgment. We had to be able to see the fish in the twisting eddies (something most anglers never have to learn to do), then, as a trout became a fleeting shadow sweeping by at full speed, we'd strike him with a spear or gaff while allowing for the reflections and refractions and the speed of the water. As with old market gunners, once you really became skillful you were so deadly that your catch was basically limited only by the number of fish in waters you worked.

"The commonest method of taking salmon during the run was by snagging with a 3/0 treble on a heavy line tied to the end of a 15-foot bamboo pole. Such an outfit gave one a 30-foot reach, and when the fish were thick the catching was easy. Most of the citizens who were looking for their barrel or two of salmon caught them that way. I thought snagging was too haphazard and liked it even less when, in my ninth summer, I hooked a big coho on a back fin, pulled back hard, and then had the hook pull loose. The big tackle snapped back across my shoulder, looped around my neck and dragged a hook-point across my open left eye, directly over the pupil. For the better part of a year I had a slight scar there, long enough to be a good reminder.

"The year I was ten, most of my fishing was done with a character called 'Slop Jack.' He was the town indigent and handyman. Small and cheerful, he hauled garbage and did odd jobs at the saloons. He boozed a bit, never seemed to have a dime, and lived alone in a weather-beaten shack. Slop Jack's main industry, and the one that tied us together, was feeding the sled dogs in the summer.

"To most sled drivers, their dogs were just a nuisance in the summer. They required food but they couldn't be worked when there was no snow. So Jack boarded them and fed them during the summer. What better ally and companion could he have than a fishing-freak kid who'd go along just for a little gear, an occasional bag of fruit or candy, and some wonderful free lunches that came from the saloons where Jack carried out slops.

"Spearing, I think, was the prime sport of all. It was more exciting and more deadly than any other method. Anyone who has ever become good at it realizes that it became too deadly to be allowed as pressure on the fish increased. I'm glad I lived at a time when I could learn and enjoy it. Jack and I would work a stream together, sneaking upstream on the banks on each side and spearing the fish we could see from shore. Then we'd wade back down, side by side, taking as many of the fish we hadn't on the way up as possible.

"Jack was not my only older fishing companion. A friend of my father's, a guard at the local jail named Rosey Roseen, also took me under his wing. Rosey was a displaced Englishman and a devoted fly fisherman. I'll be forever grateful for the introduction he gave me to fishing with a fly.

"In my ninth and tenth summers I spent a good many hours with him, using first a bamboo pole with wire guides and waxed mason line attached to a 6-foot, three-fly silk worm gut leader. In my tenth year I had a combination lance-wood and greenheart rod and a fair assortment of flies, some of which

I'd tied under Roseen's supervision. When the big runs weren't on, I divided my time between the superb sports of spearing and gaffing with Jack and casting flies for the smaller fish with Rosey."

It was an ideal life for a youngster who loved fishing and the outdoors. Lee had lots of school friends, did well in his studies and was generally well-liked by the community. A story in the February 11, 1914 issue of the Valdez *Daily Prospector* indicates his social status.

"Birthday Party For Henry Wulff" the headline reads and the story continues—in a sub-head: "Ninth Anniversary of Valdez Boy is Fittingly Celebrated—Plenty of Eats for All."

"The ninth anniversary of his birth was fittingly celebrated by Henry Wulff when he entertained a number of his boy friends at the home of his parents on Reservation Avenue on Tuesday afternoon.

"Refreshments, consisting of fruit punch, candies, cookies, cake and ice cream were served in plenty to the youngsters. Miss Stuart assisted Mrs. Charles Wulff in entertaining the boys.

"Those present were: Jimmy Mead, Loyd Fish, Ewell Thawley, Eugene Keesler, Corny Schmidt, George Boyd, Willie Dolan, Edward Dolan, Albert Heckey, Clarence Rudolph, Henry Wulff, Lillian Wulff and Audrey Wulff."

Of course the fact that Lee's father, Charles, was the publisher of the newspaper might have had something to do with the coverage devoted to the event.

But catastrophe was just around the corner for Lee—in the form of a sudden move back to Brooklyn, New York where his parents had lived before moving to Valdez at the turn of the century. Charles Wulff had gone to Alaska to seek his fortune in the gold fields, but—like many others—went broke. He managed to earn a living, however, as a building contractor, deputy sheriff and finally as a newspaperman. Lee's mother had immigrated from Norway and was living in Staten Island, New York when she and Charles Wulff fell in love. His mother made the long voyage to Valdez a few years later to join her fiancee—no small journey for a single woman in those days.

But a coal company in Brooklyn was still owned by Lee's grandfather who died—leaving the business to his sons. The family moved back to Brooklyn to manage the business in the winter of 1915-16. One can only try to imagine the shock to young Lee at having to adjust to life in a big city—after the near-wilderness of tiny Valdez.

Lee must have been something of a novelty to his Brooklyn schoolmates. A story and photo in the June 28, 1918 issue of the Brooklyn *Eagle* must have opened a few eyes.

Below a photo of Lee holding a stick—upon which are suspended two big

Lee at nine years old with a catch of salmon and trout from Valdez.

coho salmon and four trout that would have been record-holders in New York state in those days—the story read:

"Henry Wulff, the honor pupil of the graduating class at Public School No. 154, Windsor Place and Eleventh Avenue, is an Alaska boy, who received his early education in the public school at Valdez, Alaska, and who since coming to Brooklyn two and a half years ago to live, has been an Eagle Honor Roll pupil most of the time, first at Public School No. 130 and later at Public School No. 154.

"He is the son of Mr. and Mrs. Charles G. Wulff of 567 Sixteenth St. Mr. Wulff returned to Brooklyn two and a half years ago after living twenty years in Alaska, where he owned and edited the Valdez *Daily Prospector*."

But Lee hated Brooklyn and longed for Valdez, his friends there and his dog, Rover, which he had to leave behind. Writing a poem for a school assignment in 1916, it is not difficult to fathom his state of mind:

> City life is not for mine
> housed in by sturdy walls.
> Away from the fresh air
> and where the clear Siwash falls.
>
> Away from the trout in that clear stream
> and those salmon whose scales do gleam.
>
> Away from dear old Meade Crick
> which never yet has seen a brick.
>
> I love Alaska—yes my old home far away
> and I'm coming back I say.
> —Henry Wulff

But the torture of life in a big city for an outdoor boy was not to last forever. Charles sold his interest in the John F. Schmadeke Coal Company on the Gowanus Canal in Brooklyn and the family moved west to San Diego, California in 1920. World War I had been over for two years. The presidential election of 1920 was in part a referendum on whether the United States should join the League of Nations. The Democratic nominee, James M. Cox, ran on a platform that the U.S. should join. Republicans, with Warren G. Harding as their candidate, took no real stand on the issue.

This was the first presidential election in which women could vote. They apparently voted the same way as most men and the election went overwhelmingly Republican. It seemed to indicate that most Americans wanted—above all else—to forget the recent terrible war.

Lee was jubilant at the thought of moving West. Any place, he thought, would be better than the huge, confining city.

California and Paris

San Diego was a welcome change from the crowded and smoky streets of Brooklyn. The city by the sea was still a small town in 1920—with the exotic border of Old Mexico only a few miles to the south.

Lee, already an expert at catching cod, flounder and halibut from the sea near Valdez, took to the warm southern California waters like a seal pup. At 15 years of age, he was already over six feet tall and growing. Soon tan from the sun, he and his high school friends—both male and female—spent most of their off time on the beach. A few of his classmates had small boats and the fishing near the kelp beds netted sea bass, corvina and yellowtail—among other species. Josiah Cotton remembers Lee at high school age.

"In August 1920 we moved from Boulder, Colorado to San Diego, California. In September I attended high school and met Lee Wulff—who lived a block from our house. We became good friends and would go fishing in the surrounding lakes. I remember fishing at one lake and catching many bass, but keeping only the biggest—which we took home and Lee made a plaster cast of it and when it was dry, he painted it and hung it on the wall. It looked like the real fish. Lee taught me how to tie flies. We didn't have a regular fly-tying vise, but we improvised with a pair of pliers.

"In the fall my family moved to Hollywood, but Lee and I corresponded and the next summer I visited him in San Diego and he came back to Hollywood with me. We both wanted to earn some summer money and in reading the want-ads we saw an ad for apricot pickers. So we took the Red Car to San Fernando Valley and as we were at an apricot ranch a man offered us a job loading boxes of apricots into freight cars at 40 cents an hour. We went back to my house and got blankets and a tarp and reported for work the next morning. For two weeks we loaded apricot boxes into freight cars and slept in a field next to the freight cars."

Years later Joe talked to Lee about that summer. He said Lee never said much about their fishing together.

"I asked why," Joe wrote "and Lee said loading apricots was one of the highlights of his life as he had never worked and earned money before. I remembered him writing back after he returned to San Diego that he had bought a camera with the money he earned loading apricots."

Lee as a graduate from San Diego High School.

Lee graduated from San Diego High School on January 27, 1922 and enrolled in San Diego State College. There, at 18, he played football, basketball and ran track. Discovering girls as well as sports cut down some on his fishing, but an old friend, Henry Parrish, remembers his fishing prowess even in those days. He, Lee and a student named Johnny Squires were close friends and studied engineering together.

"The three of us played football at San Diego State College in 1923 and 1924. The enrollment then was approximately 800 students.

"The three of us belonged to a national academic fraternity, P.D.Q's which often sponsored boat rides during the summer vacations. Girl friends as well as the members enjoyed the surf boards which were pulled at high speed by the boat, the *"Glorietta."* I recall one fishing trip with Lee. We had our girlfriends, who were not bad fishermen, with us. I had the dubious honor of baiting their hooks and taking the fish off their hooks—and this really kept me busy because Lake Hodges was really loaded (with bass) at that time.

"Lee asked to be let off on the shore. At the end of half an hour he signaled to be picked up. He asked me to follow him and there, the banks seemed to be alive with fish. He had been using a small aeroplane-type spinner with a fly some 12 inches above it. The wind was very strong toward the shore, but, in spite of this, Lee was able to cast some 20 feet out past the weeds and was able to catch two fish each cast. He insisted I try it, but my casts were only five or six feet beyond the weeds. Even these feeble attempts brought in one or two fish each time. Never would I have tried against that wind. I think he could communicate with those fish."

But not all his time was spent fishing. Lee was a popular student and was into all sorts of activities. His yearbook at Stanford University—where he majored in engineering—gives us a picture of Lee as a college student.

"Well, folks, line up and take a slant at this college kid who is just getting ready to step out in earnest on his life trail. He is a graduate of San Diego State College in San Diego and has one year more at Stanford before he is turned loose to paddle his own canoe. And as he is soon to be an engineer, the canoe will probably be manned and handled okay. His name is Lee Wulff and he was born in Valdez, Alaska. Query: Is he eligible for the presidency? Absolutely yes, and here's hoping he gets it if his fancy happens to turn that way.

"Lee Wulff is a little fella—six feet one, 180 and still growing. In college athletics he was a bear, being a three-letter man at State College, winning his letters in football, basketball and track. Quite a good many at college have one letter, some two, but the three-letter men are scarce because the competition is so keen and the candidates are numerous.

19

"Hunting and fishing are his favorite sports and once again let it be writ, he is a bear. Not long ago Lee took his father up to Alaska and in the company with another old sourdough the trio mushed into the game fields. Even in that faraway land the much joked about Tin Lizzie was there with tires on—patched and tired tires. Lizzie packed the trio 220 miles from Valdez, up into the Delta River country. The Delta flows into the Yukon and on the other side of the ridge from them was the Copper River. Trekking in they left gasoline at stated intervals to be picked up on the return trip, and the scheme worked like a charm. Lizzie was on her good behavior.

"The hunt was a dream come true for game was plentiful, the weather decent and good luck perched on their tent ridgepole. Lee bagged moose, caribou, sheep and goats. Lee told of the wonderful trout fishing in Alaska, where rainbows are legion and fat. One of his biggest brook trout won a prize offered by *Field & Stream*. He is a fly fisherman with considerable know-how and a great liking for the gentle game Old Ike Walton immortalized.

"In the matter of game conservation, this youngster is all right. He has been a member of the Fish and Game Protective Association since its inception and believes in safeguarding our wildlife. In the Union's Gallery of Sportsmen, Frank Northern is the oldest and Lee Wulff the youngest—a span of more than 60 years standing between them—May and December . . . Lee Wulff—really just starting. Let's all wish him good luck and lots of it."

As graduation day approached, Lee became aware he really had very little interest in engineering. This presented quite a problem in his family because he had majored in engineering to please his father, Charles, who once said he hoped Lee would be an engineer because he had seen few unemployed engineers in his life. But Lee—although he had no firm idea what he wanted to do with his life—knew he didn't want to be an engineer. This caused a serious disagreement with his father—the first break between the two. However Charles finally relented on the condition that Lee reconsider returning to a career in engineering after whatever "fling" he had after graduating. But as Lee told John Merwin for the foreword of his excellent book, *The Compleat Lee Wulff*:

"Well, I was one of two people in our engineering group who ever went to a museum or an opera or anything like that. I felt at that time that engineers mostly went out in the bush, and they didn't have any amenities—the arts and so forth—available. I felt that an artist had a wide scope. A farmer could talk to any other farmer in the world, while most people were limited to their own age group and their own income group; an artist really had no limitations. He talked with anybody. I had a little talent; so I thought, I'll be an artist."

The thirty-fifth Annual Commencement Exercises for Stanford University were held at Memorial Church on Monday, June 21, 1926. Lee was finally on his own. As he told Merwin:

"When I got out, I knew I wasn't going to be an engineer, so I just took what money I could scrape up and went to Paris to study and become an artist."

It wasn't that simple. He needed to convince his parents this was a good idea first—no mean task. His father and mother finally lent him the money—with a promise that he would repay them. A round-trip boat ticket to Paris wasn't that cheap—even in 1926. A Mr. Stanley A. Weigel, a graduate law student at Stanford, conducted an annual student excursion to Europe for Stanford graduates allowing them to see ten countries—from Germany to Rumania and Turkey, returning through Italy, Switzerland and France—for $745 for the eleven week trip. But that was a lot of money.

Paris—mysterious, romantic and fascinating to a 21-year-old American who had never before been abroad—captured Lee's imagination as had nothing else in his young life. He wandered the narrow, twisting streets that summer of 1926 and finally located a room in a boarding house near the Left Bank that catered to foreign art students.

Paris in 1926 was to most young Americans—Lee included—the city of Gertrude Stein and Ernest Hemingway. Stein had just finished writing *The Making Of Americans* in 1925—though she was famous for her short stories, *Three Lives.* A celebrated personality, she encouraged, aided and influenced—through her patronage as well as through her writing—many literary and artistic figures.

At the time Lee was living in Paris, Stein was the leader of a cultural salon, which included such writers as Hemingway, F. Scott Fitzgerald and Sherwood Anderson. She was the one who coined the phrase "the lost generation" in describing those post-war expatriates.

While working in Paris as a correspondent for the Toronto *Star*, Hemingway became involved with the circle of expatriates and spent much of his time with Stein. With the publication in 1926 of *The Sun Also Rises*, Hemingway became truly famous and Lee would have given anything to meet him. Unfortunately he was not famous enough as a painter to be noticed by Stein or well-known enough as a writer to fall under the scrutiny of Hemingway—although Hemingway might well have appreciated Lee's fly fishing ability had he known him then.

But Lee haunted the art galleries and went to as many author's signing parties as he could. He became a student at the Delacluse Art School, run by a father-and-son team, and became fascinated by his lessons.

21

"Art school is interesting because I'm interested," he wrote his father. "I chose Delacluse's because it seemed to have more of a spirit of earnestness and because the instructors spoke English and gave criticisms daily. Usually criticisms are given about twice a week . . .

"My morning class—life study—is quite crowded. There are a number of English women—some old men, many young girls and young men. About half of the class of 30 work in oils and the remainder in charcoal—with the exception of an English woman who uses pastels, and I—who have been using dark paper, charcoal and chalk."

Though Charles Wulff was interested in the letters from his son, he still assumed Lee would be an engineer and kept questioning him about his engineering status.

Lee had received a letter from the American Society of Civil Engineers in New York saying he had been elected a junior of the Society on October 1, 1926 and that notice of the election, together with the necessary papers in the matter, had been mailed to him.

"This American Society of Civil Engineers fools me," he wrote his father. "I don't know how much the dues are and I was under the impression that for juniors who applied within six months of graduation, the $10.00 fee and first year's dues were dropped.

"I will sign the necessary things and send them to you. You can hold them until I hear from someone regarding how much to send. They don't have to be in before the last of March so there is no hurry. I wish I knew whether I'd ever need the membership or not . . . " he added, hoping his father would get the point.

But as fall moved into winter and the old city grew cold under sullen skies and freezing rain, Lee became depressed. Though his art classes were going well, he couldn't seem to see where he was going as far as his future as an artist was concerned. He returned to writing poetry—something he had long been fond of doing—particularly when he was moody.

At Night

Footsteps tread by ceaselessly.
In treading by
Footsteps sear a memory
Of things that die.

Someone's footsteps pass alone
To fade away.
Sullen leather scrapes on stone.
The echoes stay.

Joyful footsteps, now and then,
Rush by like a song.
Comes the tired tread again,
The way is long.

—Lee Wulff

Lee was certainly not the first art student to feel lost in the huge and ancient city—especially in the winter. He managed to find places where other Americans gathered however.

"The Methodist Episcopal Church at 107 Boulevard Rospail, the United States Students and Artists Club," he wrote his mother. "It is organized for young Americans studying or working over here. It has a library of books and American magazines. It also serves as a meeting place for old acquaintances, and a field for bringing Americans together. American artists have exhibitions on the walls and it is one of the few places here that is kept warm. While it is strictly a men's club, on Thursday afternoons there is a tea dance and on Sunday nights a concert and community singing and dancing. On both these occasions American women of the quarter are hostesses. It is then that the club has its greatest crowds."

Lee finally began to meet girls—which both cheered him up and led him into romances that left him distraught.

Untitled

Last night I was sad
And you seemed far away.
When I kissed other lips,
lover's lips, for a day

I kissed them in passion,
In desire, to forget,
Despairing, not caring,
But loving you yet.

I forgot in a dream,
That was tendered by hell,
Forgot that I loved you
Forgot our farewell.

Thus, I come with the dawn
To kneel at the shrine.
Forgive if you can, Dear,
This straying of mine.

And, like all young men, there were times when it all seemed so futile.

Loneliness

Inside,
Something's wrong
There is no song
As there used to be;
Only this empty shell
of me.

But then there was always another day, and . . .

Lyla

When the moonlight's gifted sadness
makes me think of you
again
I can see that little twisted smile
That sparkled—now
and then

I can still but
think—and wonder
At the sadness of
good-bye

Only sit—and then
remember
That we're through
and wonder why.

With snow on the ground and a bitter wind blowing through the streets of Paris, Lee finally began to feel that if he didn't make it in the fine arts, he was learning enough to be a good commercial artist. He had been assured that commercial artists make a very good living and it was good to at least have a goal for a change. But he kept his attendance at the gallery shows. He wrote his mother about seeing the "new" modern art at The Salon des Independents.

"Throngs of Parisians are turning toward the 38th annual winter salon to keep up their knowledge of the type of painting that is being done now. There are nearly 4,000 pieces, oil paintings for the most part, but with a few sculptures, watercolors and pastels scattered through them. There is a good representation of all schools of painting from the academic type to the most advanced modern work.

"For the most part the landscapes were painted broadly soft color harmonies of bold, daring contrasts—and on the whole were marvelous. There were nudes in all the mediums and in all manners. Josephine Baker, colored star of the Follies Bergere was prominent among them.

"Since some of the modern sculpture has been carefully rubbed smooth to conceal mistakes, an ingenious artist carved a carp out of stone, rubbed it smooth and hung it over some oil, surrounded it with caviar and lemon slices. People often stopped and remarked that the fish must have been oiled.

"A picture which has caused a great deal of discussion is a life-sized painting of a very conventional Madonna industriously spanking the boy Jesus!

"One leaves the salon with the idea firmly fixed in mind that never before have so many varied schools of painting existed at one time."

But it was at just such an art show that Lee met Helen Riha—another American art student. Blonde, blue-eyed and vivacious, Helen was in her second year of art school—after graduating from the New York School of Fine and Applied Arts. Her family was from Schenectady, New York. They found they liked the same art and the same books and soon were dining in small, out-of-the-way restaurants.

As the long winter drew to a close and the first warm days arrived, Lee's art professors arranged for him to have his first one-man show at the Salon of American Artists. It was slated for the Galleries of Jacques Seligman, 57 rue St. Dominique for July 2-14, 1927.

It went very well, Lee thought. Many American art students showed up and a fairly good smattering of the general French public—plus some well-known art critics. He was promised a second show in September and set about to gather more art to display.

The second show, or exposition, was held at 107 Boulevard Raspail and was scheduled for September 1-10. Though a lot of people showed up, Lee was disappointed.

"My exposition," he wrote his mother, "was as expected. I sold practically nothing but the publicity was good. I got a lot of abuse from an English paper here—that hates Americans. My friend on the New York *Herald* couldn't help me further because the art critic was out of town on his vacation. We held the exhibition open longer—in hopes he'd come back, but he hasn't—unless there is something in today's paper, which I haven't seen yet. I'm anxiously waiting to see what publicity Dad got for me at home." His father had done very well—arranging for a story in the San Diego *Union*. Under a two-line headline reading "Former State College Athlete wins European Art Critics' Praise" the story began:

"Rather a far cry from athletic laurels to recognition as an artist, Lee Wulff of San Diego, former State College student and athletic star, is proving the possibilities of the combination with the exhibition of his work at 107 Boulevard Raspail, Paris September 1-10, inclusive.

"Wulff's exhibit of oil painting, pastels and sketches, made during his study under the French masters during the past year, includes scenes of Burgundy, France, Belgium, southern Germany, Vienna and the battlefields.

"European critics, in complimenting his harmony, technique and force, have considered Wulff among the promising young artists of the day.

"While attending State College, Wulff . . . "

Charles Wulff had not been editor and publisher of the Valdez newspaper for nothing. Lee also recognized the value of publicity at an early age.

"Now I'm wondering how things will go in New York," he wrote as he prepared to leave for the U.S. "I hope I can get off to a flying start and make lots of money, I'm all in readiness to go—with less than 24 hours left in Paris." The day was September 13, 1927. "Strange," he added, "I feel quite at home here."

A New Life

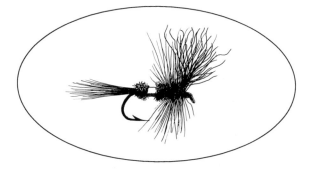

Lee arrived in New York via the Cunnard Line on September 25, 1927. He immediately went to Greenwich Village where fellow art students had told him rents were cheap and most artists lived there. He almost immediately found a room for rent at 63 W. 8th St. for $1 a day. He immediately wrote his mother.

"I'm about to start out trying to sell myself," he wrote, "or land a job. I don't know what luck I'll have, but I think I'll get by. I cashed the Liberty Bond and got an even $50 for it. I have about $100 to live on 'till I get started. I can live for about a month on that.

"It's funny to be back—with everyone speaking English. I'm going to try and sell my things—first to travel magazines, architectural magazines and book publishers. I think I can if I can get a job with an advertising agency. Thanks a lot for the publicity. Can you send me a couple of those clippings? I may want to show them! I'll be glad when I get started.—Lee"

Although New York had never been his favorite city, he was surprised to find how much he enjoyed the huge, sprawling city in the fall. The elms and chestnut trees were turning yellow in the Village and the odor of roasted chestnuts wafted down the crowded streets. The street noises were no louder in New York at night than they had been in Paris—although the police and fire truck sirens had a totally different American sound.

He kept up a running correspondence with his mother. Charles Wulff had not been well and Lee was concerned about an occasional fainting spell his father had—plus the fact that his eyes had been bothering him.

"The art game has never been as slow as it is now, they say. Just my luck to strike it that way."

For months Lee made the rounds of the employment agencies and acted on tips other young artists gave him. He managed to get a number of part-time free-lance art jobs, but it was tough going. In addition to the occasional check his mother sent him, his aunt Amanda and Uncle Fred Butterworth, who lived in Burbank, California, were able to help him out now and then with small checks. The Butterworths had lent him $300 when he graduated from Stanford so that he could buy a steamship ticket to Paris.

As the fall turned into winter the weather grew cold. Lee had also forgotten how cold New York could be when the bitter winds swept off the Hudson River and blasted down the canyons of the city. With the city locked in the grip of a week-long freeze, he wrote his mother in January.

"I've spent all night working—and I worked until 1 a.m. I've been working on two book jackets which are now nearly finished. I think I'll get checks for about $70 on this first work of the year. If all my weeks could be like this . . .

Lee after his graduation from Stanford University and a trip to Europe—1927.

27

"The great Wulff has stayed up another night. There's no use going to bed now as I have to be up by about 9 a.m. to see about the lettering on the Appleton book jacket—which is for *A Pen and Ink Passion.* Lord it's cold! I won't rest until both these jobs are settled—and the checks are in my hands. I don't think anything can happen now. It hadn't better! I've had too many of these disgustingly close calls."

But at the end of January things took a change for the better. Lee got a job at an ad agency for the magnificent salary of $50 per week—with the promise of a raise to $60 per week if his work satisfied his bosses. Now a salaried employee, he began to have more of a social life.

"Things are looking up," he wrote his mother, "I have a bank account. It is due as much to my friends as to the quality of my work. I have more friends than almost anyone I know. I'm constantly turning down engagements . . . I'm going to start drawing two nights a week and I'm going to join a gym. It looks as though I could come home for a visit next summer—and pay something back to Aunt Amanda—if I can hold the job."

By late spring he began to meet some other young men who liked the outdoors and made plans to fish some of the streams close to New York City— the Esopus and the Beaverkill in the Catskills and the Ausable in the Adirondacks. His father shipped his fly rod and flies from home and Lee was renewed by standing in a river again. He began to tie flies again and met regularly with fellow anglers—for both lunches and dinners. He felt as though his life was finally beginning to take some sort of shape—after the long year of fumbling for direction.

To his astonishment, walking along a street in the Village in the late spring of 1928, he turned a corner and came face-to-face with Helen Riha, his art school friend from Paris. The astonishment was mutual and they retired to a restaurant to celebrate the event. It turned out Helen was also working in New York and had a small apartment in the Village. Lee, delighted to see her again, made a date for dinner the next weekend.

Lee took her to Lee Chumley's Restaurant in the Village—where the art crowd met—and was surprised to find she already knew a number of people in commercial art circles. Along with the friends Lee had made, the party wound up a large, happy affair.

Helen had been in New York almost a year and had a job making a fairly good salary for a woman in 1928. By fall they had become very close friends and by the holiday season—with parties galore with mutual friends—they decided to become engaged. Lee found Helen liked the outdoors and invited her on several fishing weekends to the Catskills where several couples camped out—the women in one tent and the men in another. She was a fair fly fisherman, after Lee taught her how, and they had a lot of fun outdoors.

By spring Lee had gotten a promotion and asked Helen to marry him. They set the date at June 1st, 1929. Lee was very happy that Helen had said yes and wrote his parents as soon as the date was set. They were happy for him, but couldn't make the long trip east for the ceremony. Lee promised to come west and visit the entire family on their honeymoon. Helen thought it was a grand—and romantic—idea, never having been to the West Coast.

They had saved enough money to buy a second-hand car—a Buick touring car that had a convertible, canvas roof and side curtains that came down and were snapped to the tops of the car doors.

The marriage was a small affair in the parsonage of a church in Greenwich, Connecticut. Helen's parents, Mr. and Mrs. John Riha of Schenectady, New York attended. Lee had a friend of his from work at the agency stand as best man. Helen did not bother with a maid of honor. The two had decided they would spend at least three months on the trip so both quit their jobs. With the optimism of youth, both figured they would either get jobs on the West Coast or have no trouble finding other jobs if and when they returned to New York.

The trip was an adventure for both. Young and in love, Lee and Helen enjoyed even the small disasters that befell them. The car was constantly blowing tires and Helen remembers the trip as one stop after another at Sears & Roebuck to buy new ones. There were no paved roads west of the Mississippi River in those days and the trip took eleven days to complete. They went by the southern route—old Route 66 out from St. Louis, through Oklahoma, Texas, New Mexico and Arizona. Lee drove at night through Texas—in a steady, driving rain, to avoid the heat of the day—while Helen slept in the rear seat.

They stayed in a series of small motels—just roadside shacks—and people's homes at night. Helen said she clearly remembered staying the night in the attic of a woman's house in Tucson Arizona, while the woman sat up all night with a shotgun to keep thieves from stealing her tenants' cars.

They arrived at night in San Diego in late June. Lee's family was delighted with Helen and the newlyweds rented a small house in an artists colony close to the beach. Charles Wulff owned an interest in a grain mill on the desert over the mountains from San Diego. Before he put any more money into it, he wanted to know if Lee was interested in helping him run the business. They drove over the mountains to see the property, but Lee—after thinking it over—wanted no part of the desert climate. The temperature was hovering around the 110 degree Fahrenheit mark when they inspected the mill.

Helen loved the beach and made friends quickly with several wives in the small colony. Lee, happy to be back near the sea, went deep-sea fishing regularly. They both thought casually about getting jobs, but they were having such a wonderful time loafing that it did not seem an urgent matter. However by September their money was running low and they knew they had to do something soon. Talking it over in the tiny house by the sea, they both agreed New York was the only place where they could make any money as commercial artists. So, saying good-by to Lee's parents, they drove the long trip back to New York in mid-September—this time taking the northern route back. They went up the coast highway to San Francisco then east through Yellowstone Park and down through Wyoming and then straight east. They camped out on the good nights—sleeping in blankets under a tarp—and slept in small roadside inns and cabins on the nights when it was overcast or cold. In no great hurry, they stopped to fish at likely-looking streams and lakes. Helen remembers Lee leaving early in the morning to catch trout in the Rockies—leaving her alone to sleep until the sun warmed up the sleeping bag. He caught bass on a fly rod and popping bug from ponds in the Midwest.

They arrived in New York in late September, bone-tired but happy and relaxed—except for the fact they had no jobs. Friends helped out and by the following week Helen had a job as a sketch artist in a fashionable women's dress shop on Park Avenue at a salary of $35 per week—enough to feed them and pay rent until Lee found work.

Lee soon got a job with an ad agency at a salary of $75 a week. They were in clover, as Helen put it. Lee was designing packaging and they found an apartment in the Village where they immediately took up their social life with their many old friends.

They had no idea that disaster, in the form of the stock market crash, was about to change their lives. As the decade neared an end most Americans thought the economy would continue on its upward trend as it had since 1922, but beneath the surface were signs of trouble. On September 3rd, while Lee and Helen were still in San Diego, stock market prices reached an all-time high, but a long decline had begun.

On October 24th a sudden decline took place and bankers tried to halt the slide as best they could, but on October 29th, Black Tuesday as it was called, more than 16 million shares were traded as huge blocks of stock were dumped for whatever they would bring. Many of those ruined by the crash took their own lives—some jumping from the windows high over Wall Street. It was a frightening time and both Lee and Helen struggled through the weeks without really comprehending what was happening.

Lee, in the months prior to the crash, had been enjoying some fine fly fishing on the Ausable and Beaverkill Rivers with some friends he had recently met. One was John McDonald, who later became a writer for *Fortune* magazine, and a physics professor named Dan Bailey. Lee and Dan even started a tiny fly-tying class behind a restaurant in Greenwich Village, but the crash stopped all that.

Lee as a struggling commercial artist in New York City—1930.

Both Lee and Helen were forced to take a 10 percent salary cut following the crash and soon after that were threatened with more. People were out of work all about them and Lee suddenly was offered a commercial art job as an art director at an agency in Louisville, Kentucky. He and Helen discussed it and decided to take the job—rationalizing that they could take the position temporarily until they saved money—then return to New York.

Lee drove the old Buick down and Helen quit her job and joined him over Derby weekend. They rented a small house for $75 a month and settled in. The job was good and they made friends quickly, but Lee was not happy with Kentucky. "The fishing was terrible," Helen said later. Lee was more specific.

"Fishing has certainly affected my life," he later wrote. "In 1930 I moved to Louisville, Kentucky to be the art director at a branch of a large advertising agency. I thought of it as temporary because agency people were always moving from company to company as one moved up the ladder. It was a good job and I was getting $100 a week—a very fine salary for a young man at that time.

"I'd been there about six months when August came along. It was hot and sticky the second week of that month and there were a lot of mosquitoes in the area where we lived. Insect sprays had not been developed and in desperation I dug up a small can of Lollacapop, a fly dope paste made of tar oil, citronella, pennyroyal and a few other things. It was the standby of fishermen in the bush and I'd always used it on the northern trout streams. Smelling its familiar odor, my thoughts for that evening went back to the trout streams of New York state.

"Fishing in Kentucky hadn't been too exciting. There were a few small and shallow ponds that held bass. The Ohio River, flowing past the door, held bass too and was fun to fish, but its grayish waters were not comparable to the clean trout streams of the Catskills and the Adirondacks. Lake Herrington was in existence but the rest of the great impoundments that make today's fishing interesting weren't there yet.

"I went into the office on that August day following, and Bruce Farson, office manager of the agency, gave me the news that everyone would have to take a ten percent pay cut beginning the first of September. In my mind I smelled the Lollacapop. I saw rising trout on the West Branch of the Ausable. I said, 'To hell with the cut . . . to hell with the job. I can still get in ten days of fishing on the Ausable before the season closes.'

"So I went to the Ausable, confirmed again that the dry flies would work when those late hatching drakes were coming out and my casual streamers would take big fish. I returned to New York City tired but refreshed, bought a new suit and started to look for a job.

"The bottom had fallen out of the job market. The depression was a reality and the first areas to suffer were those in the arts and in advertising—which always take second place to production and other phases of business. I ended up taking a job with the Dupont Cellophane Company in the new Empire State Building for $35 a week. The Cellophane division was doubling its sales every six months and cutting its employee's salaries ten percent every six months too. Still, I was one of the lucky ones. What my friends in New York had to put up with to hold a job, if they had one, took the heart out of my going into business. I figured it would take someone more hard-hearted than I to be successful in the business world."

Though Lee did not realize it at the time, this exposure to the cut-throat world of business was to turn him away forever from this sort of endeavor and lead him to a life in the outdoors.

When Lee returned from Kentucky—glad to be back home—he and Dan resumed fishing in earnest and began to experiment with and seriously design new flies. The Ausable in the Adirondacks and the Esopus in the Catskills were perfect streams upon which to practice.

Lee had long questioned the design of English dry flies for American rivers. He considered them too anemic-looking for our streams—with their fine silk wrapping over quill and the delicate wire hook. It occurred to him that traditional feathers used by the British did not float long without constant dressing with a floatant like Mucelin. He reasoned that an imitation of the big mayflies that would float in spite of repeated strikes and submersions might be the answer.

He began to use bucktail instead of feathers to create his imitations of *Isonychia,* the large gray mayfly drake. He tied the wings on with dark white-tail deer hair and made the tail of the same material. The body he made of rabbit fur dubbing—a highly floatable material. For the hackle he used medium blue dun cock hackle. By the spring of 1931 he and Bailey were having spectacular success with the gray, high-riding fly during the Hendrickson hatch on the Esopus.

Lee tied up a big white-hackle fly to resemble the coffin fly—the mature stage of the green drake—and found it was invaluable for late-evening fishing in poor light. He had little use for the then-popular fan-wing coachman fly which he said had a tendency to twist when cast and kinked the leader. Also, he said, the tail—made up of a few fibers of golden pheasant tippet feather—didn't have enough strength to hold the fly up and level.

He tied the same pattern, but with bucktail wings and a bucktail tail, and it turned out very well. Lee probably would have named the three flies something like the Ausable Gray, the Coffin Fly and the Bucktail Coachman, but

The Gray Wulff, Royal Wulff and White Wulff.

Dan—already thinking about commercially-tied flies—talked him into naming them the Gray Wulff, White Wulff and the Royal Wulff. All three were later to become world-renowned as successful trout flies—and as great salmon flies in larger sizes.

Ray Bergman, a friend of Lee's listed the three patterns in his new book, *Trout* and they became popular almost instantly. Lee's friend Victor Coty also fished with Lee and Dan Bailey that summer and the next on the Battenkill, the Ausable and Catskill streams such as the Beaverkill and the Esopus— Victor concentrating on his movies which he was using to accompany his fishing lectures. Lee began to realize there was a good market for lectures on trout fishing and tried to learn as much as he could about film making from Victor.

While Lee liked dry fly fishing better than wet fly angling, he caught most of his trout on wet flies—except during the spectacular hatch time. He found he caught more trout on a plain, small grayish nymph—which he fashioned from rabbit or angora fur. It was so nondescript he was never able to interest many fly fishermen in using it and had almost no luck selling the ones he tied. He was making a good income on the side from tying flies by this time—most flies bringing 25 cents in those days. In later years these plain, small nymphs would be very popular with fly fishermen—even if they had to be "dressed-up" with a bit of tinsel or bright feather at the head to appeal to the fly fishermen (more than the fish).

This was in the days when most trout fishing meant camping out—usually in tents. That meant mosquitoes for most of the trout season and the only insect repellent one could find in those days was a combination of citronella, tar oil and pennyroyal. Leaders were made of "cat gut"—in reality silkworm gut which had to be soaked in water before knots could be tied in it. The gut came in small coils—8-12 inches long—and usually were carried in thin, circular aluminum discs lined with felt.

Fly lines were of dark silk and had to be dressed to keep them from rotting and fraying. Lines had to be dried after use and many a cabin chair was draped with drying lines in the evening.

Most rods were of lancewood until, in the 1920s, Tonkin cane was imported and split-bamboo rods were built. These stiffer rods were needed to develop line speed and coincided with the increased popularity of dryfly fishing. Lee had been using a variety of rods over the years—Heddon, Granger, Abbie and Imbrie Centennial. But one winter day in 1931 he succumbed to temptation and bought a lovely two-piece, eight-foot Jim Payne fly rod—which he had been dreaming of for years. He bought it from Max Molay of Folsom Arms in New York City and the price was a hefty $49—a fortune in those days for a fishing rod.

Lee lovingly fished with it for the following spring—taking care not to let a heavy streamer fly strike it on the forward cast or let a split shot sinker fracture the fragile bamboo. He took so much care of it that he suddenly realized he was no longer fishing relaxed. He was worrying so much about the rod being damaged that he wasn't enjoying his fishing. He sold it the following week to a friend who offered him the same price he had paid for it. He bought a three-piece Heddon fly rod for $15 and spent the balance of the money for a second-hand Hardy St. George reel, some new fly lines, a lot of hooks and fly-tying materials. He returned to casting with his usual abandon and immediately began enjoying himself again.

Lee had purchased a small Marmon coupe, with a rumble seat, and kept it in a garage a block from the 247th Street subway in the city. He and Dan (and occasionally their two wives—both named Helen) would take the subway from their Greenwich Village apartments and drive the little car to either the Catskills or the Adirondacks for weekend fishing trips.

"It is hard to imagine two more dedicated anglers," Lee wrote, "We opened the season in the Catskills even if there was snow on the banks of the Beaverkill, or the winds of the Esopus Valley froze the fly lines in the guides of our rods. We fished every free moment, and I can remember how great the fishing was.

"I remember one rain-soaked week in late June spent at the Wilmington

Notch Camp Grounds on the Ausable with our long-suffering wives. We huddled in our tents and cooked food on campfires sputtering in the rain. The river was high, of course, but we had wonderful fishing. I recall that the front half of the felt soles on my waders came loose, and I held them in place with big rubber bands made of a section cut from an old inner tube stretched around the front of each foot. That made the wading slipperier than at any other time I can remember.

"Because of the high, rushing waters we gave up on flies, except for large streamers. We fished with live stonefly nymphs most of the time—and amazed the rest of the campers with our catches. One day we left the Ausable to fish the Saranac, and each brought back a brook trout close to four pounds, having released many lesser ones."

By 1931 Lee had discovered the Battenkill—a marvelous river that wound from its source high in the mountains of Vermont and snaked its way through southwestern Vermont, into New York and finally emptied into the Hudson River near Schuylerville. He and Helen drove from New York City up to the small town of Shushan so many weekends that they decided it was cheaper and more practical to rent a small house there during trout season.

Lee first fished the great river after renting a room in the old Merritt Russell house on the river. In a story for a 1940 issue of *Country Life* Lee wrote of the river:

"When it comes to trout streams, the old 'Kill stands by herself. She starts way up in the mountains and comes sliding down, winding from one side of the flat valley to the other. Her flow is smooth and unruffled even when she strikes in hard against the steep mountains that flank the valley floor. Oaks and giant elms spread out their green to give her shade and ferns stand deep along her banks. Her flow continues steady through the dry months of summer by virtue of the height of the mountains she rises in and the timbered nature of the country she follows down. She's a big river, too, but there are no concrete highways coursing along her banks, even though she lies within two hundred miles of the largest city in the world.

"Last spring on a day in late June the river suddenly came to life after a period of dullness. In two hours of the late afternoon I netted and released ten fish—all over 13 inches and a dozen smaller ones that were all taken from a single pool. Then it was dull again for days. Those are the brown trout of the erratic feeding. When they decide to feed, the whole length of the river seems to be alive with them. And when they don't feed, it would be completely dead except for the natives. Those natives are a blessing. When the brownies have crawled into the muskrat holes and disappeared, I can go to any one of more than a dozen places and find the natives rising regularly in

36

the still, slow-flowing water and there I can spend hours catching one or two fish on my smallest dry flies with my finest leaders."

Wading the big river was never easy and one frequently slipped on the bottom and got wet. Lee devised a vest for wading, copied after the bird hunters' shooting vests. It had pockets for his aluminum fly boxes, a couple of wool patches sewn on the upper lapels in which to stick flies and a loop through which he could thrust a rod butt. With his battered felt hat askew, the vest and his waist-high waders, he became as familiar a sight on the big river as the squat figure of his friend, Al Prindle, the Shushan postmaster.

Lee made friends with a number of fishermen on the Battenkill who were later to become famous—writer John Atherton, Meade Schaeffer, the illustrator, and artist Norman Rockwell. Most lived in New York and fished weekends. Lee had begun to lecture to sportsmens clubs in the New York vicinity and was beginning to write about his fishing. He was yet to sell any magazine stories to the larger outdoor magazines, but now and then placed a fishing piece with small regional publications.

Even the small payments he received for lecturing, writing and fly-tying came in handy to supplement his illustrator's salary. The nation was truly suffering under the great Depression and Franklin D. Roosevelt's landslide victory the fall of 1932 brought a glimmer of hope that things might change for the better. Two and a half years after the 1929 stock market crash the nation's industry as a whole was operating at less than half its maximum 1929 volume.

Lee had long read about fly fishing for Atlantic salmon and had dreamed about trying it himself for years, but felt he couldn't afford it. Now—with the money he made as a free-lance writer and lecturer—he thought he would take a chance. He talked it over with Helen and they figured—with their meager savings—they might be able to spend a couple of months in the summer of 1933 in Nova Scotia. Lee figured he could recoup the money spent by lecturing on Atlantic salmon fishing—if he was lucky enough to catch any. He talked Victor Coty into coming up during that summer and taking motion pictures as well as still photos.

During that winter Lee pored over maps of Nova Scotia and talked to everyone he could who knew anything about salmon streams in the area. He finally decided he could fish the Ecum Secum—an early salmon run river on the rocky east coast of Nova Scotia but perhaps first try the Margaree River, on the northwest tip of Cape Breton Island.

Both took a leave-of-absence from their job for the summer and packing a tent, sleeping bags and cooking utensils in the coupe, they headed north.

They stayed first in the small town of Margaree—where farmers were bringing in the hay from nearby fields. Lee was a complete novice at salmon fishing—knowing only what he had read about the subject.

The Margaree is a short river, like many in Nova Scotia, but is famous for its runs of big salmon. Even in those days it was very popular with salmon anglers and was quite crowded. Lee—excited at the thought of the big fish—rigged up his trout rod and made his way down to the stream. The river was low and clear. No rain had fallen for a month and the salmon were lying in deep, dark pools waiting for the water level to rise and allow them to move upstream to their spawning grounds. Lee had only the 9 foot trout rod and decided, since the water was low and clear, to use a dry fly. He had read salmon could be taken on dries at such times.

The sun shone brightly on the rose-tinted rocks along the streambed and its rays penetrated the depths of the dark pools. Lee had spent two days in futile pursuit of fish. Not many others had taken salmon either and there was a general air of disgust at the low water conditions. Lee was standing in the gravel of the Hut Pool and casting a Bivisible dry fly up to the dark and deep water at the head of the pool. He had almost given up hope of seeing any big salmon under the poor conditions and was casting, as he said later, more for the rhythm of casting than any hope of a strike. And suddenly, as he wrote in a 1937 issue of *Field & Stream,* a miracle happened.

"Up from the blackness a long dark shape began to materialize. It drifted slowly up toward the fly. A foot below the surface the salmon was entirely visible. The sun shone on her spotted gill covers, reflecting brightly, as with infinite slowness her nose pointed upward and she sucked the fly down. This was not the famed head and tail rise I had been led to expect. There was no splash of water, no flaring of fins or tail. The fly disappeared and, with every inch of her visible, the salmon sank slowly until she was just a dark shadow again. Reality descended on me with a rush and I raised my rod.

"That movement was the signal for the wildest, fastest action I had ever had on a fly rod. The salmon swept down the pool in a magnificent run, featured by three beautiful leaps, and carried out the major part of my hundred yards of backing. Then, suddenly, she was opposite me, leaping and twisting in the fast water while I reeled frantically in an effort to get the great belly out of my line. For the next ten minutes, there were leaps and surges and a lot of vicious head shaking. It was the hard, stubborn fight of a fresh-run salmon less than five miles from salt water. After her last leap, the eleventh, I worked her close enough to see her plainly. My wrist was feeling the strain put on it in using a five-ounce rod. I was all set to bring her to gaff, when she started off again wildly on the longest run of the fight.

"This was not a steady sweep but a bulldogging series of short rushes, using the current to help her downstream. Zing-zing-zing went the reel until I wondered if she would stop short of the end of my backing. Following downstream as she went, I was able to hold even and finally gain back line. When she came into the shallow water again she was too weak to leap. She showed the silver of her side and my gaff struck home. In a few seconds she was stretched out on the pebbly bar, a twelve-pound, fresh-run female, silvery and bright, bearing the telltale sea lice, dark on the shining scales. She was really a beauty!"

A jaunty and proud Lee with his first fly-caught Atlantic salmon taken on the Margaree River of Nova Scotia in 1933.

Later Lee realized how lucky he had been on his first salmon—low water, a light rod, a dry trout fly and only 100 yards of 10-pound backing. He had never caught such a fish! He had been overwhelmed at the power and expressiveness of the great salmon. Unlike trout, the power of the salmon had built up during the fight—until the very end—instead of diminishing quickly. The memory of that fight was to stay with him until the end of his life—and sparked a long career of pursuing the great Atlantic salmon with a fly rod.

But the fishing was very slow on the Margaree and Lee had read there were more salmon in the Ecum Secum River—down the east coast of Nova Scotia, just north of Halifax. Victor Coty had joined them the second week on the Margaree and had some fine photos of Lee fishing, but they decide to head south shortly afterward.

They drove along the rocky coast until they finally saw a boy standing on a rickety wooden bridge.

"We asked him," Helen said later, 'Do you know where Ecum Secum is?' And the boy answered: 'This is it.' There was just this bridge and a small wooden house—one on each side of the road."

Because of the low water conditions, there were no salmon up in the clear water of the river, but there were a lot of salmon lying in the brackish water at the mouth of the river—waiting for the river water to rise.

"The local people told Lee he couldn't catch salmon on a fly in the brackish water, but he caught more and more each day. We gave them to the neighbors—those and all the trout Lee caught—and they canned them. They put them in big glass Mason jars and when we left they gave us canned lobster in trade."

"There was absolutely nothing for me to do there," Helen later said. "There was one small store, but it had nothing in it—only cabbage sometimes—and perhaps a chicken. I didn't have enough to eat and I was ready to go home."

By the end of August Lee realized he could catch salmon regularly and had begun to experiment with some of his own flies. He was taking good-sized salmon on his Gray Wulff and occasionally on the White Wulff—though the majority of his fish were caught on traditional double-hooked salmon patterns. He had even switched to a light trout rod and caught salmon on the seven foot rod as easily as he had on the longer nine foot rod.

But Helen had had enough of life in the tiny village of Ecum Secum and they both realized it was time to return to New York. The car was packed and Lee—reluctantly—was ready to go home. He knew he had to come back to the north country and catch more and bigger salmon. At long last he had a feeling there was a purpose to his fly fishing. He had never felt such excitement before as he did while hooking and fighting salmon. He knew if he could impart that same sense of excitement and challenge to other fly fishermen, he might be able to make a living at it.

Looking back on it, it had been a great year, Lee realized. The only dark spot had been the death of his father, Charles—suddenly, of a heart attack. It seemed inconceivable to Lee that he could no longer pick up the phone and call him whenever he wanted.

A 25 pound salmon taken in Newfoundland, August, 1937.

The North

Lee returned to his illustrating job in New York, continued his lecturing to local fishing and hunting clubs—this time with salmon fishing included—and went on with his writing for outdoor magazines. On weekends he continued to fish the streams around New York, but his heart really wasn't in it. Memories of the powerful and glistening salmon continued to haunt him. After the salmon, trout seemed so tame—even the big browns of the Battenkill.

But he made the best of it—knowing one couldn't have everything in this life. But in his dreams he saw the heavy-bodied sea-run brook trout he had caught in the Nova Scotia rivers—and salmon, salmon, salmon.

The New Deal permeated much of American life in 1934. Federal agencies increased under the administration of Franklin Roosevelt and Republicans ranted at what they considered the unconstitutionality of many of Roosevelt's moves. As the New Deal progressed and 33 new government agencies mushroomed, the national debt increased to nearly 20 percent. But the voters seemed to approve of the way the President was running the country for conditions were slowly improving.

Lee, at age 29, was mildly interested in national politics, but long before had decided nobody was going to do anything to help him but himself. His father, Charles, had instilled the work ethic in him at an early age and it had taken hold solidly. Lee was too busy with his own plans to worry much about the future of the country as a whole.

He saved enough money from his lectures, writing and fly-tying that year to treat himself to—at a discount price—a salmon fishing trip to the Little Codroy River in Newfoundland. The owner of the lodge, called Afton Farmhouse, Jim Tomkins—in exchange for a promise of a mention in a national fishing magazine—had agreed to let Lee fish for two weeks at half-price. His friend, Victor Coty agreed to come along, but to pay his own way.

Having only the Nova Scotia experience under his belt, Lee was still a novice salmon fisherman, but was not lacking in confidence. He had any number of years of trout fishing to fall back upon and a skill with a fly rod that was certainly above average, but he had yet to encounter some of the old traditions of salmon angling. He was to discover them, to his annoyance, on the Little Codroy.

To Lee's chagrin, Tomkins had instituted the old British system of rotating the pools—or "beats" as the English called them—each morning. After noon an angler was free to roam the river at will and fish any pool or stretch which was not being fished or "rested" by another angler. Lee, who had grown up fishing U.S. rivers—where an angler who was the most enthusiastic, energetic or first on the river fished the best pools—was annoyed at the old rules. Inexperienced, he did not realize the old British rules were an attempt to be fair to all anglers fishing a club.

The farmhouse looked out on a small meadow and across a narrow valley rested the bottom end of the Long Range Mountains. At the top of the valley was the lake from which the Little Codroy sprang. The river wound through the meadow and down to its mouth—only about a mile away. It was a very short river, but reputed to hold large salmon.

The best pools—Aggravation, Widow's Run, and Tomkin's Nose—were listed on a blackboard on the porch and each morning the members name who was to fish those pools was posted beside the pool's name. Lee and Victor did the best they knew how with the rotation system, but neither did very well. Lee would have far preferred to take off at dawn each day and fish the several best pools first—after the salmon had rested at night—or were replaced by fresh fish from the sea.

In the afternoon and evenings he roamed the river upstream, either with a local guide or with Victor. Newfoundland, then a colony of Great Britain, had no guide requirement for nonresidents. Lee could have come up and camped out on the river, he realized, and fished almost where he wanted. The annual fishing license in those days was $5.

He and Victor caught a few fish upriver, but Lee couldn't get rid of the feeling that all the best salmon were being fished for by other guests in the big club pools. He caught a salmon or two a day, but considered that poor fishing.

Tomkins, a tall, gangling man with the huge, callused hands of a farmer, was a fine fly fisherman himself and took a tolerant view of Lee's impatience—as he would of any young man. Sensing Lee's frustration, he suggested a side trip for Lee, Victor and himself to the Grand Codroy, a larger salmon river.

They climbed on a hand-pumped rail car and traveled to the upper pools of the bigger river—Six Birches and Seven Mile.

"The pools," Lee wrote, "were fantastic. We released salmon, and though our guides were certain they would die, we marked some with a bit of string tied loosely around the tail and proved a 100 percent release recovery on the following mornings."

But back on the Little Codroy Lee found the salmon still difficult to catch and the old resentment returned. He had not yet learned the ways of salmon and did not realize much of the fishing conditions depended upon water level.

Hoping to discover what was wrong with his fishing and realizing that his vacation was rapidly coming to an end, Lee wandered down the river until he came to the mouth—at a large pool called The Spruce. There—near a giant spruce from which the pool got its name—he cast mechanically, with little hope of a rise.

"While my thoughts had been wandering," he wrote, "the pool I was fishing had changed. The water had risen, imperceptibly, at first, until I realized it had moved up from my knees, halfway to my hips. My eyes, which had been casually keeping my dry fly under surveillance, picked up a shadow moving just beyond its drift . . . and then another. I cast just ahead and watched a long, sleek fish swim undisturbed beneath the fly. Singly and in twos and threes, salmon came in with the rising tide to cruise the pool. Some settled to form dark gray patches on the reddish gravel of the sunken bars. Others continued to cruise up into the warm, shallow flow at the head of the pool and then, turning, circled back under the shadowed spruce, testing out in each upstream circuit the discomfort and danger of the path upstream.

"I cast as swiftly as I could from one fish to another. I kept my fly over fish, the biggest I could see, for as long as possible, yet not one salmon showed any sign of interest. Darkness drew near and I gave up casting just to watch the phantom-like swimming of half a hundred Atlantic salmon. I felt a sadness at what I had just realized must come. The salmon were far more frustrated than I."

For the first time, Lee was becoming a true salmon fisherman. It is not a sport for the frantic fishing of inexperienced youth. One of the great game fish of the world, the Atlantic salmon is a prize to be sought with reverence—and patience.

"For the first time," he later wrote, in a 1974 article for *Sports Afield*, "my angling was being restricted, not by gentlemanly instincts but by hard-and-fast rule . . . I thought that because of the prevailing low-water conditions, there were very few fish in those particular pools. I know now," he continued, "it was because I was still relatively untutored as a salmon angler and had been counting on covering a lot of water instead of, as those conditions demanded, working hard over non-receptive fish. I still had not advanced to the concept of the angler-versus-salmon duels that could last for hours or days—contests where an angler works on and studies a particular salmon, or group of salmon, with knowledge that leads to success."

Though he did not catch a lot of salmon on the Little Codroy in 1935 he took a giant stride forword in understanding the sport.

Back in New York that fall he began work on his first book. He felt he now knew enough about the general fishing scene to do a handbook on the sport—for beginners—but also for the average angler who might need to broaden his knowledge. It was titled *Lee Wulff's Handbook Of Freshwater Fishing* and was to be published by J. B. Lippincott of New York.

While Lee preferred to fish with a fly rod, he nevertheless devoted considerable space to bait casting and fishing with the conventional rod and reel. Lee's friend, Raymond R. Camp, outdoor editor of the New York *Times,* did the foreword, in which he wrote:

"Having fished since my pantaloon days with an interest that increased with the years, I fancied myself something of an accomplished angler with a fair knowledge of streamcraft and lake-lore. I had fished no more than an hour with Lee Wulff before I awakened to the fact that I had much to learn before entering the charmed circle my ego had drawn. Since that fatal day I have been a willing student of a patient teacher."

Publication date for the book was scheduled for 1938—two years hence. Lee was taking particular care that the book would be highly accurate. His ambition now was to be known as a great American fisherman and he knew the book could be a stepping stone to that goal if he did it right. It is interesting that in the introduction, written by Lee, he first mentions releasing fish for future catches. The catch-and-release movement has been credited to Lee, but nowhere has anyone documented him starting it. At the end of the introduction, he writes:

"There is a growing tendency among anglers to release their fish, returning them to the water in order that they may furnish sport again for a brother angler. Game fish are too valuable to be caught only once," he wrote sometime in 1936.

But it was another fish that caught Lee's attention that summer. Always willing to try anything in the way of sport fishing, Lee suddenly discovered the huge bluefin tuna that each summer invaded the bays of Nova Scotia and Newfoundland, chasing the big baitfish schools of herring, mackerel and squid. There, Wedgeport's commercial lobster fishermen were learning to convert their 30-40 foot craft to big game fishing boats in the summer months to pursue these big "horse mackerel" as they were called then.

Lee was able to fish for these big predators on such a boat, equipped with a crude swivel chair. He was using an inexpensive 16 ounce, split bamboo rod with a hickory butt. A 12/0 reel and 800 yards of linen line that tapered down to 24-thread (72 pound test), a 12/0 hook and a 15 foot wire leader.

As Lee wrote in a July 26, 1937 letter that appeared in the *Anglers' Club Bulletin:*

"The total cost of the outfit was around one hundred dollars." He also wrote that the purpose of his fishing trip "was to prove that these great, fast fish could be subdued on reasonably priced tackle and that this fishing was not reserved for those who can afford a reel that costs as much as an automobile."

While that may have been an afterthought, it is more likely Lee used the gear simply because he couldn't afford the heavier and far more expensive equipment. At any rate, he left the port of Wedgeport one morning after four days of disappointment—two tuna hooked and lost—one about 400 pounds and one considerably larger.

"At ten after nine in the morning," he wrote, "I had a strike and off we went in the wake of a fast, shifty fish. For two hours we tried to run up on him but we were never closer to him than two hundred yards. Because of his speed, and the constant changing of his course, the boatman felt that he must be a middle-sized fish of perhaps four hundred pounds. The fog closed in on us and we were swept out to sea with the tide. Time wore on. The impenetrable blanket of fog hemmed us in. The three-hour mark was passed with the fish apparently as strong as ever, although some of the 'zing' had gone out of his runs. Occasionally the 39-thread came into the reel." The 700 yards of 24-thread line went from the reel to 100 yards of 39-thread (117 pound test) linen line that acted as a sort of heavier line leader between the wire leader and backing.

"The line was the one I had been using for some time and there was a splice in it where I had broken it across my chest, testing what appeared to be, and was, a weak spot," Lee continued.

"I had to be careful. There was also the constant danger of running afoul of some old lobster trap that had been left out. Kelp continually caught on the line. We began to see the splice quite regularly. It was thirty five yards from the end of the line.

"He was still strong, though, and the boatman began to give up hope of ever bringing him in on that tackle. He was the hardest-fighting fish they had ever seen. He stayed deep, but he was on the move. After five hours, I could stop his rushes and turn him. It looked again as if I would have my tuna.

"Then, out of the fog, we could see the waves piling higher and breaking into great white-caps. With the tide and the running of the fish, we had come into the wild, rough rip of Soldier's Ledge. For half an hour we tossed in the great waves while the fish sulked and rested on the bottom. Since the surface currents and those below were not the same, we were forced to keep running up on the fish to avoid losing too much line. In that shoal water, there was the added danger of snagging on a heavy bunch of kelp or on the bottom itself if too long a line got out.

"The tuna came up out of the tide rip refreshed and it took another half hour to wear him down to the point of exhaustion he had reached before. The water quieted down. The fish was directly below the boat, paddling slowly on its side, sending slow pulsations along the line to the rod. At last the boatmen were able to look down and see the fish. They turned and grinned at me, and stretched their arms to show that he was a big one. Ever so slowly he came up. Able hands reached the leader and up came his head. The gaffs struck home and the battle was won.

"For seven hours and forty five minutes I had worked from the swivel chair and in the end I had boated my first giant tuna." Lee and the crew had been pulled far out and headed north where they ran into the Outer Ball and met other boats headed for home. In another hour the tuna was hanging on the scales at Wedgeport wharf. It weighed 660 pounds—the second largest taken on rod and reel. It had been quite a day. Lee, exhausted, but deeply satisfied at the tired feeling of victory shook hands with the crew and posed for photographs. It would be another step on the ladder of his climb to famous angler.

It did nothing to hurt his reputation. S. Kip Farrington the famous big game angler and saltwater editor of *Field & Stream*, had been fishing the rips at Wedgeport with another well-known big game fisherman, Michael Lerner, for several years. Kip—a wealthy man from New York's Long Island—had decided to establish an annual international tuna competition at Wedgeport. With the help of Rhode Island's Julian Crandall and others, the tournament was set up, a cup donated by Boston sport fisherman Alton B. Sharp, and the date for the first match was set for September 11-13, 1937.

The first Sharp Cup consisted of two teams—one from the United States and the other from the British Empire. Most of the anglers were wealthy sportsmen and all well-known in big game angling circles. Lee had come up to Wedgeport to watch the competition and—though known by some as a good angler and one who had caught the second largest bluefin the year before—was hardly famous.

The night before the competition, three members of the British Empire team fell ill. Colonel Patrick Thompson of Nairobi, Africa came all the way from East Africa to represent his country, only to be laid low with a sprained back in practice. George Hatt of Liverpool, Nova Scotia—a well-known tuna angler—took his place. Howard Trott of Bermuda, another famous tournament angler, came down with the flu and Earl Thompson, a wealthy angler from Halifax, Nova Scotia, took his place. Duncan Hodgson, a Canadian big game angler, developed eye trouble and was forced to pull out. Tournament Chairman Farrington—to his everlasting credit—"borrowed" Lee Wulff to replace Hodgson.

The weather turned ferocious the morning of the tournament—almost forcing it to be cancelled.

"Hurricane warnings flying—no telephone or telegraph service for two of the three days—nearly half of the Nova Scotia apple crop ruined—a trawler lost on Sable Island—a schooner sunk at Shelburne—boats ashore all along the coast," Farrington wrote in his fine 1974 book, *The Trail Of The Sharp Cup.*

"These were just a few of the incidents that marked September 11, 12 and 13, 1937 when the first international tuna-angling matches were held between teams representing the British Empire and the United States."

The rest of the British Empire team consisted of Captain Louis Mowbray, Bermuda; Ross Byrne of Liverpool, Nova Scotia; Loran Baker of Yarmouth, Nova Scotia and Tom Wheeler of Toronto, Canada.

The American team consisted of Captain Kip Farrington and a consortium of other wealthy sportsmen: Ben Crowninshield, Paul Townsend, Bill Lawrence, Hugh Rutherford, Laken Baldridge, Pam Blumenthal and famed fish illustrator W. Goadby Lawrence.

"Under the circumstances," Farrington wrote, "it was remarkable that the teams were able to get out to fish at all. The tuna, and the herring they were feeding on, were driven out of the rough tide rips at Soldier's Ledge, off Wedgeport. There is probably no other place on the Atlantic coast where fish could have been taken in such a storm, and the fact that five were landed speaks volumes for Nova Scotia tuna fishing. I doubt whether anyone has ever attempted to fish under such unfavorable conditions. Besides the difficulty of fighting a fish in that sea, patches of kelp, often one hundred feet in length and half again as wide, floated all over the rip. To become fouled in it usually means, of course, a cut line and consequently a lost fish.

"The British Empire team did not muff their chance when it arrived. They caught three fish out of four hooked. Their scoring anglers were Tom Wheeler, Loren Baker and Lee Wulff. Wulff, having caught a 123-pounder on the first day, brought one in on the third day that tipped the scales at 569 pounds. This catch was one of the finest ever made in big-game angling. The motor of his boat stopped twice in the battle—which lasted an hour and fifty minutes—and the fish went under three great patches of kelp. Wulff's line was 36-thread and the rod weighed only twenty three ounces, which were the match specifications. The fact that he was fishing in competition, with more than three hundred people watching him, added to the strain. A slight error and he might have lost his fish and possibly the cup for his team."

Lee Wulff suddenly became a name in saltwater big-game fishing. The Sharp Cup went on for the next half century—with teams competing from Cuba, Chile and Mexico to France, Spain and Italy. But it is doubtful that any year's competition was more exciting than that first 1937 tournament. The weather was so dangerous the tournament was canceled. In all the teams fished 15 1/2 hours out of a scheduled 36 hours. The Board of Governors refused to let the boats go out on the final day.

Lee fighting a giant bluefin tuna during the 1937 Sharp Cup competition at Wedgeport, Nova Scotia. He caught the winning fish of the tournament.

Newfoundland

During the winter, between his two monumental bluefin tuna escapades, a son was born to Lee and Helen. The San Diego *Union* ran the story.

"A son was born February 24 in New York to Mr. and Mrs. Lee Wulff. The baby has been named Allan Lee. The good news was welcomed here by little Allan's grandmother, Mrs. Charles G. Wulff. Mr. Wulff is a successful commercial artist in New York."

The "successful commercial artist" would have far rather been a successful fisherman, writer and lecturer. He was becoming strangled by the big city and a regular job. He lived for his weekends on the Battenkill and—as Helen said—those weekends grew longer and longer.

"At first," she said, "we would drive up from New York on Friday and return late Sunday. Lee never quit fishing the river until dark so by the time we got back to the city it would be as late as three a.m. sometimes. Then we began going up on Thursdays and sometimes not getting back until Tuesday."

Helen had taken a leave from her job when her pregnancy became advanced so there was no need to get her back to work early. Lee would fish up through Tuesday and sometimes Wednesday before returning to the city. It became obvious to Helen and Lee's employer that a change had to be made.

The baby fascinated Lee. Young Allan was a beautiful baby and active from the start. One day watching the baby crawl on the floor of his studio—

after he returned from fishing in the Sharp Cup—Lee wrote this in a poem:

> "He crawled into my studio today,   Bright eyes round with wonder.
> This son of mine just ten months old, He stopped . . . and crawled . . . "
> To stare about him,

As with most fathers, the miracle of a child is almost unbelievable. Even the most minute action on the part of a baby calls for comment. The poem went on for six stanzas before ending with:

> "Grant that I may live, myself,   So that growing up may teach him
> With eyes on new and different things To be safe from hurt but never
> To be his guide   fearful
> And an example   To seek out new worlds."

Lee had formed a plan of action, but hadn't told anyone, except Helen, what he had in mind. He had written to the Newfoundland Tourist Board saying he was a professional outdoor writer and had both fished and hunted in Newfoundland. He proposed that if hired by the Bureau he would gain exposure in the American outdoor press that would greatly benefit Newfoundland. He pointed out that tourism dollars comprised a large portion of the country's income and that much additional revenue could be expected to come in if U.S. sportsmen were better informed about that country.

He had written to a number of outdoor publications of that day—*Field & Stream, Outdoor Life, Sports Afield, Country Life, Hunting & Fishing, National Sportsman, Outdoors,* and *The Spur*—querying the editors if they would be interested in stories on Newfoundland. Most of the editors answered that they would and Lee compiled a list of their answers and sent the list along with his letter. It was a longshot, he realized, but figured it could do no harm to ask. Both he and Helen knew they would have to move out of New York one day—as they had no intention of raising children in a big city. Lee remembered only too clearly how he had detested Brooklyn as a child.

As the nation moved into 1938 a slight recession took place and most people became a bit uneasy about the future of the New Deal. Congressional elections began to indicate more support for Republican candidates, but—as war became more and more likely to spread in Europe—American foreign policy began to overshadow the economy at home.

German occupation of Austria and the threat to Czechoslovakia began to fill American newspapers and radio news broadcasts. A few stories caught the public eye and provided some relief from the specter of war. Douglas G. "Wrong Way" Corrigan, unable to gain a flight exit permit to Europe, took off from New York and landed in Dublin, Ireland—claiming he had headed for California but got lost. Despite his illegal flight, he immediately became a national hero.

Attention was focused on the Spanish Civil War as Ernest Hemingway's play *The Fifth Column,* became a hit. Musical culture received a shot in the arm in 1938 as "Music Appreciation Hour" conducted by Walter Damrosch, became a weekly treat and was heard regularly by 7 million children.

Lee suddenly began to sell more magazine articles and his confidence that he could make a living at it began to soar. He sold five front-of-the-book stories—most of them on trout and salmon fishing trips—to *National Sportsman* alone. His friend, H. G. "Tap" Tapply was editor at the time and was later to become editor of *Hunting & Fishing.*

He sold stories on trout, tuna and salmon to a number of magazines and mailed clips of them to the Newfoundland Tourist Board. The tactic worked because in the early spring of that year, he received a letter from Margaret F. Godden, secretary of the Newfoundland Tourist Development Board. The letter said the board members had seen a number of Lee's stories in outdoor magazines and knew he was an ardent tuna fisherman. She said the country had an abundance of bluefin tuna in the summer months and would Lee be interested in publicizing the resource? Would he! He made arrangements to travel to the capital, St. Johns, to discuss the proposal. While there he also made a pitch to cover the salmon fishing aspects of Newfoundland—as well as the spectacular trout fishing of the region. The Board hired him and Lee immediately began to make plans for the spring season coming up—as well as the summer tuna season.

The Tourist Board agreed to hire several tuna boats from Nova Scotia to explore the tuna possibilities of a number of Newfoundland bays and promised Lee would be given access to practically any salmon river he wanted to fish the coming season. Lee was secretly delirious with joy at the thought. What a chance to learn! Included in Lee's proposal was also the idea that he would also publicize the marvelous hunting of the island—caribou, ptarmigan and moose, to name but a few game species.

That spring Lee worked hard to develop the tuna sport fishing industry in Newfoundland and between big-game fishing trips he explored many of the great salmon rivers of the huge island. Tuna were prevalent in Conception Bay near St. Johns on the east coast and plentiful at Bonne Bay on the north coast. Fishing with local crews Lee caught a number of bluefin at both locations, but couldn't seem to stir up much enthusiasm for the sport among the locals. A few of the giant mackerel had been harpooned over the years—mostly for winter dog food and food for commercially-raised fox—but nobody was interested in eating them.

The Depression had wreaked as much havoc with the economy of the big island as it had in the United States. One could hire a man to do any kind of work in those days for $1 a day. Not too many people were interested in going tuna fishing. The economy was run by a few big businessmen in St. Johns—who exported such commodities as codfish in great quantities. Everything imported from England—or elsewhere—was later sold to the inland residents of the island—for a price.

A few of these wealthy merchants tried their hand at catching tuna, but only a few succeeded in hooking one. They eventually got off and most of the anglers—like the owner of a big department store in St. Johns, Sir Cedrick Bowring—decided it was a futile sport.

But Lee had great hopes for the salmon fishing. He could see American anglers by the hundreds flocking to the rivers of Newfoundland. After all, the great rivers of the Maritime provinces of Canada, the Restigouche, the Miramichi, the St. John, the Cascapedia, the Matapedia and the like were all famous—and expensive. Most were by now either private waters—miles of them controlled by wealthy men from Canada and the United States—or water too expensive for the average man to afford. Lee felt that the public waters of Newfoundland—if handled properly—could attract those anglers of modest incomes.

But it was the salmon fishing that Lee intended to pursue first in early spring. Filled with excitement, Lee knew only a multi-millionaire would be able to accomplish what he was about to do—fish most of the 200-odd salmon rivers of Newfoundland. In addition to that, he would be fishing for bluefin tuna in the summer and making films on hunting in the fall for the lecture circuit.

His first trip was to take a train from the Channel Port-aux-Basques, on the southwest tip of the huge island, up to the town of Corner Brook. There, with a local guide, he made the 30-mile trip upstream to the great falls on the Humber River. Salmon by the thousands congregated in the big pools of the Humber, below the falls, waiting for the water to drop enough for them to jump the huge obstacle. Lee was fascinated by the hundreds of salmon trying to jump the surging waterfall.

He and the guide fished the big pools below the falls and caught at least 75 salmon, all of which they released except one which they kept for dinner. A few weeks later Lee was shocked to read in the *Western Star*, the Corner Brook newspaper, that a party of fishermen, led by Sir Humphrey Walwin, returned from the Humber Falls with a total of 400 salmon after a two-day fishing trip.

In their defense, there was no way anyone could imagine salmon being endangered in those early days. Each spring they poured up the rivers of Newfoundland by the hundreds of thousands. They were snagged, gaffed, netted and caught with all sorts of rods and reels. They were salted and shipped in barrels for export, canned, sun-dried and smoked for food and many were fed to sled dogs in the long cold winter.

Lee, however, could see the threat to these great fish even then. He remembered the huge runs of coho salmon near Valdez in his native Alaska. He had taken part in the snagging, spearing, gaffing and netting of coho in his youth and also remembered the fleets of cannery ships that lay offshore in Prince William Sound. He had been shocked and surprised when he returned to Valdez in his senior year in college to find the coho seriously threatened.

He was also later horrified to hear that a paper company had blasted a huge hole through the Humber Falls to allow easier passage for pulp-wood logs.

With local quides—who he was able to hire with approved government funds—he began to explore many of the marvelous salmon rivers of Newfoundland's west coast. He fished the Crabbs River, the Serpentine, Fishels River, Fox Island River and the Highland's River among others. In his battered felt hat, his unique fishing vest and chest wadders, he became a familiar sight on the salmon rivers of western Newfoundland that late June and July.

But, oh how much he learned about salmon! By trial and error he learned to take them on his own dry flies—the White and Gray Wulffs and the more traditional patterns like the Grizzly Bivisible and the Rat-Faced McDougall. He learned the ways of individual rivers and how to outwit and outwait moody salmon that had little interest in his first casts. He learned to read the water from watching guides who had lived on the rivers all their lives. He learned where the salmon lies were and how to spot them in the current—the almost-invisible gray shapes so difficult to see with untrained eyes. Lee never wore polarized or dark glasses—preferring to train himself to see fish with the naked eye. Nor did he wear the battered, felt hat to shade his eyes or face from the sun. He wore it to hold his coils of silkworm gut leaders which were wrapped around the band. When a few years later Nylon leaders came into widespread use, he discarded the hat and fished without one the rest of his life.

He made many fishing friends in those Newfoundland days. Most of the young men—and a lot of women—were salmon and trout anglers and the young, enthusiastic American fit right in. With his penchant for experimentation and his willingness to go anywhere and try anything, he had no lack of fishing company. There were even young women fishing guides, like Ella Manuel of Lommond, who knew the rivers close by and were excellent fly fishermen themselves. They were delighted to accompany Lee on his exploratory trips and were happy to receive the government money Lee was allowed to spend.

This day in late June was like many others. Lee and two friends had decided to take the train from Corner Brook down to the lower portion of Harry's River which emptied into St. George's Bay near Stephenville. Ray Douchette and Ed Burry and Lee had camped out on the bank of the clear river after a walk of several miles from where the tracks had bent away from the river.

Though the run had just started, the river was low and clear and the salmon were not hitting well. Douchette had suggested they award a bottle of Scotch to the one who caught the biggest salmon before 5 p.m. Though they fished hard during the morning hours, they caught only a few fish in the 8-10 pound category.

It was after lunch that Lee climbed a sloping bank over the river to spot fish. Close to the opposite shore he finally spotted three grayish shapes lying side-by-side in shallow water. Telling his companions what he had seen, he crossed the river at the shallow end of the pool and made his way up to within 40 feet of the resting fish. He cast a big White Wulff over the fish and let it make a drift of about 10 feet. None of the fish even moved.

Casting repeatedly, Lee dropped the big fly—and later smaller gray ones—ahead of the three fish for almost an hour. At one time he saw one come up slowly and drown the fly with its tail. Another time one came up and gently raised the fly from the surface with its nose. His friends, resting on the far bank, could see the action.

But, finally becoming bored with waiting, they prepared to gather their gear and move upstream. Lee, determined to take one of the fish—which he estimated at between twenty and twenty-five pounds—asked them to rummage through their fly boxes to see if they had anything bigger than his No. 4 White Wulff. While waiting for them to come up with something, he picked out a large, fuzzy, cork-bodied bass bug that his New York-based fly-tying friend, Preston Jennings, had tied for him.

He dropped the big fly with a "splat" just ahead of the fish. The fly had hardly started its float when the fish nearest Lee suddenly crossed over the other two and took the fly. As Lee set the hook the salmon turned and headed downstream. Lee was using a favorite light 7 foot rod that weighed only 2 1/2 ounces. The pool was long and deep and Lee ran down its length to keep the big salmon close to him. When it made its first leap, Ray shouted, "A twenty pounder!"

Lee's big worry was to keep the fish from cutting the leader on rocks. The salmon made three cartwheeling leaps and headed for the bottom. Lee unfastened the tailer he had designed himself, and prepared to slip it around the tail of the fish.

Lee stretched the tailer to his arm's length and leaned toward the salmon, expecting it to bolt at any second.

"If I missed him I knew how long it would take to bring him close again," he later wrote in a June, 1944 issue of *Sports Afield,* "but just how long I was yet to realize. I knew that he was still strong and capable of a wild, swift surge. But I rarely missed with my tailer and when the landing device slipped up over his tail and reached a point even with his anal fin I drew it sharply toward me and pulled the noose tight."

Lee was prepared for a sudden surge, but the fish was so strong it almost tore Lee's arm from the socket and splashed water all over him. While Lee tried to regain his balance, the salmon relaxed for a second on the surface and the tailer slipped loose and the fish slipped out. It immediately headed downstream.

Hoping the fish would make a turn at the tail of the pool Lee held the rod up, but the salmon—terrified at the encounter with the wire noose—continued downstream. Lee made for the shallow water and tried to run downstream in his heavy waders. He had 175 yards of 10 pound backing on the small 3 3/8 inch-diameter reel and was afraid of losing it all as the salmon went through the tail of the pool and into the whitewater downstream.

His friends followed him downstream—adding insults to helpful advice—until they grew weary of the battle and decided Lee was going to lose the fish in the whitewater. Two or three times Lee had to wade out into the rapids to free his line from jagged rocks or pieces of pulpwood. It was a good half hour before Lee gained enough line back so that it was finally on his reel.

"I was as hot as I can ever remember being and dog-tired from running down the shallows in heavy waders, or running more slowly but just as vigorously through water that varied in depth from hip to knee . . . whenever I closed in on the salmon he knew only too well what I had in mind and surged off again," he wrote. "At the end, with one short, shallow stretch lying between the fish and another long piece of real tough going, I took a wild gamble. The salmon had to cross a forty-foot stretch of water about a foot deep that rippled down over a gravelly bottom. He was twenty feet ahead of me and moving steadily. As he broke into that shallow water I lowered my rod, letting the line go slack, and I galloped in slow motion after him. I overtook him just as he was about to scoot into the deeper swirls, and the ghost of Old Izaak must have guided my hand because the tailer slipped over his tail and came tight. That time there was no monkey business; he was mine."

It had taken him more than an hour to subdue that salmon, but when they finally hoisted it on the pocket scale, it did indeed weighed 20 pounds—and won the bottle of Scotch.

Lee fished for tuna in Bonne Bay in late July—catching several—and then went on to Conception Bay on the east coast for August. He was able to fish the Salmonier River and the Placentia River in the St. John's vicinity before the season ended. By then he had seen a great deal of waste and needless killing of salmon and thought if he made an appeal to the Newfoundlanders, he might convince them to take some conservation measures.

Through some connections in the Newfoundland Tourist Board, he was given a chance to address the Rotary Club of St. John's in October after he finished making his films on moose and ptarmigan hunting. Lee was later to say that a friend told him it was the worst speech he had ever heard, but Lee, who said he thought he was a "fair writer" said he had gotten the message across—in spite of his poor speaking ability at that time.

A story in the St. John's *Evening Telegram* of October 14, 1938 read:

"Speaking strictly as one businessman to others, Mr. Lee Wulff, sportsman, photographer, writer and lecturer, spoke at yesterday's meeting of Rotary on the value of Game and Inland Fisheries to this country and of the absolute need for their conservation, so that our game resources will not go the way of the buffalo in the United States and become extinct.

"Rotarian Angus Reid, chairman of the Newfoundland Tourist Board, who had given Mr. Wulff an assignment to take photographs of our game resources, in introducing the speaker, mentioned that Mr. Wulff had already made movies of tuna fishing, salmon fishing, moose hunting, and partridge shooting.

"It was a long speech—somewhat rambling and probably a little "preachy" to some of the old-time Newfoundlanders, but Lee did make some good points. Also, he had seen instances of waste and misuse of resources that he could document. Among other good points made, he said:

"You, gentlemen, are businessmen, representing the businesses of your country in its many varied forms. To each of you your own business, whether it be baking, banking, or bookkeeping, is your first concern. But everything that affects your country affects each and every one of you. As your country rises and falls you rise and fall with it. If it becomes richer, you gain too, and if it becomes poorer you lose in business opportunity. And so, hunting and fishing are your businesses as well as mine . . .

"These natural resources are your country's treasures. They must be handled as carefully as any other business to give a fair return in sport and in dollars . . . I was surprised to find only one hatchery in all Newfoundland and that one is privately-owned. The time will come when your streams must be stocked. It is good business to put out small salmon parr and let the ocean send you back a crop of big salmon . . .

"Newfoundland is a country that depends on its natural resources for its existence. The main income is from pulp, fish and minerals. If your supply of those things should become exhausted, you, as a country, would be very poor indeed. The quantity of minerals in your country is fixed. You guard your pulp against fire. The fish in the ocean may be beyond your control to regulate and guard when they leave your shores, but the fish that come into your rivers will survive or perish as a result of the care that is taken of them . . .

"The near extinction of your caribou seems to have been no lesson on the saving of the salmon in your rivers. Your salmon—and I use the word advisedly because they are part of the country and belong to no man or group of men but to every Newfoundlander—are becoming fewer each year. River after river is being given the name of being spoiled as anglers and netters move on farther afield . . .

"I'd like to speak of the conditions I found while salmon fishing as an observer, with no ax to grind, no group to favor, other than to hope that through my writings and my pictures anglers will know a wider pleasure in their sport. I have seen salmon rotting on the shore at the falls on the upper Humber, dead and stinking on the bank or lying under water with the gaff wounds plainly showing, simply because there is no legal limit to the number of fish a licensed angler may take. The guides who saved them in hopes they would be able to get them out before they spoiled will be the first to lament when salmon grow scarce and they or their children have no more parties to guide. The anglers who caught the salmon should have known better. They were Americans, I'm sorry to say, and with the lesson of American game scarcity fresh in their minds they should have had enough sporting blood to release all the fish they did not need for immediate use as food.

"I have talked to salmon packers who were unanimous in admitting that each year the salmon take in their locality is growing smaller. No one denies that the salmon are going and unless something is done it will be the story of the caribou all over again. I have found that more than half the grilse in the rivers are net-marked. Yet the size of salmon mesh is big enough to allow the passage of a grilse, and anything smaller is forbidden by law. How do they get marked? Either by illegal netters or cod traps. Strangely enough, though salmon nets have a minimum mesh of 5 1/2 inches, and may not be placed nearer than a certain distance to the mouth of the rivers, the cod traps may use 3 1/3 inch mesh, and outside of a few local restrictions confined to the Avalon Peninsula, there is no restriction on their placement. I have watched the boats coming in from cod traps and what did they bring? Codfish? No, not a single codfish but grilse and salmon instead, and when the salmon run is passed these cod traps are taken up. This has been excused by some on the basis that the people are poor and they really need fish for food. It sounds like a good excuse until you consider that they were poor ten years ago, and probably will be poor ten years hence—the only difference being that if the salmon are gone they will be a darn sight poorer.

"If these poor people are starving it would be cheaper for the government to buy codfish for them than to allow them to ruin the salmon supply of any river. But usually the salmon so captured are not used for food by the men that catch them but are shipped to market and the chances are that operators of these traps are not the poorest in the community at all . . .

"There is no comparison between the amount of revenue derived by the government for each salmon that is netted as compared with that gained from a tourist for each salmon he catches. Some commercial fishermen pay only $2 for a canning license. The others pay nothing. The angler pays his license fee to the government, and his transportation, board and supplies, and other needs to the community. Sportsmen taking a few fish will provide as much revenue as the commercial fisherman taking a hundred times more, without the certainty of depleting the permanent salmon supply. On rivers where the income from tourists is as great or greater than that from the netting of salmon it looks like very poor business to allow nets to take a quantity of fish great enough to impair the salmon runs for future years. But that seems to be exactly what is going on."

The audience seemed to take it well, but Lee had no way to be sure anything would be done about the problem. But it was not long before the government put a limit on salmon—eight per day. Lee was never sure he had anything to do with it, but he certainly hoped so.

Learning About Salmon

When Lee returned to New York that fall, both he and Helen realized they had to move Allan—who was almost two years old—out of the big city of New York. They found a nice house in Chappaqua, in Westchester County, only a 45-minute drive from the city. Helen could commute on the New York Central Railroad to work. Lee, who was turning out a prodigious number of outdoor stories on Newfoundland, was able to convert one bedroom of the roomy house to a large den/studio.

He had begun to lecture—with motion pictures to accompany him—to some fairly large groups in the New York, Connecticut and Massachusetts area and as far away as Chicago. The Chicago Executive Club met regularly at the Hotel Sherman and Lee spoke to them annually. At least one thousand members each year looked forward to his illustrated lectures on hunting and fishing. He spoke to this club for 27 years.

When he could he fished the Battenkill regularly. It was the only big river near him that was even reasonably close to the size of the Newfoundland rivers. His almost constant companion those years was Al Prindle, a portly, medium-height man with a Vermont accent, who lived to fish. It didn't matter too much to Prindle what kind of fishing he did as long as he did it. If he wasn't fly fishing the Battenkill in the daytime, he would fish it at night with a bass casting rod and big plugs. Those plugs and wobbling spoons took a lot of big browns out of the Battenkill in the late 1930s and even Lee had to admit he didn't care to watch Al take all those big fish at night.

Prindle was the postmaster of Shushan, but all his fishing pals called him "Mayor"—probably because of his build and bearing. He was a colorful man and had a wonderful sense of humor. When Lee developed his fishing vest in the early 1930s, Prindle was soon seen fishing wearing an old shooting vest—with the shotgun shell loops left on. When he saw that Lee carried a small pair of scissors fastened to his vest, he showed up on the river with a foot-long pair of shears hanging from his vest.

Lee said in later years he remembered Al best for his habit of shouting "hi" each time he set the hook at the rise of a fish. He was never able to convince Prindle, however, to take it easy on setting the hook. When he hooked small fish they would come sailing out of the river—only to land far out in the grass beside the stream.

Prindle was well-read however and a fine fly fisherman. His favorite fly combination was to use three Leadwing Coachman flies in tandem. Because the post office would close at 3 p.m. each day Prindle was on the stream each day until dark during trout season. When the Battenkill was high and roily, he and Lee would fish Black Creek for northern pike on plugs or go to one of the nearby lakes and catch largemouth bass on a fly rod and popping bugs.

Lee wrote a couple of short stories about Prindle for the *Roundtable* and *Country Life*. He took a number of photos of Prindle fishing and sold them to outdoor magazines. Norman Rockwell once used Prindle as a subject for a cover of the *Saturday Evening Post.*

It was in a story that Lee wrote for *Country Life* that he told about how Al Prindle had arranged for his own funeral. He and his wife, Anna, had made arrangements with the local undertaker and had paid in advance.

"She's made the arrangements with Larry Stone, the undertaker in Salem," Al told Lee . . . "Anna at least wants me to end up dignified. In my best black suit and a white shirt and tie. But I talked to Larry, and he's promised to put an old three-fly-leader in my hand, tucked away half up the sleeve so no one can see it. I gave him the leader, and all three flies are Leadwing Coachman's. I wouldn't want to go on that trip unprepared," he said.

The clouds of war over Europe were boiling on the eastern horizon and most Americans were convinced the country was going to get drawn into the conflict. Germany had completed the dismemberment of Czechoslovakia and Hitler had turned his eyes on Poland as the next conquest. Germany and Russia had signed a non-aggression pact in August 1939 and that cleared the way for Germany to invade other European nations.

President Franklin Roosevelt, in one of his famous fireside chats, declared that the U. S. would remain neutral, but nobody really believed the country could long stay out of the conflict. By the end of the year Congress passed the Neutrality Act, which repealed the prohibition of arms shipments and authorized "cash and carry" sales of arms to warring powers.

By the end of the year Lee and Helen were discussing the idea that they might buy some land and a house on the Battenkill at Shushan, New York. Lee had been making the long five-hour drive from Chappaqua to Shushan so often it began to seem silly to live in one place and spend the majority of his time in another. Helen was pregnant again and Lee felt they could easily live on the money he was making from writing, lecturing, fly-tying, photography and the salary he received from Newfoundland as a consultant and public relations man. The Tourist Board was more than happy with the way he was publicizing the country's fishing and hunting and had indicated Lee could expect to work for the Board indefinitely. He made frequent trips to St. John's—even in winter—to discuss plans for the coming seasons and was due back to resume his exploration and photography in early spring.

Lee steering a boat on Bonne Bay, Newfoundland, 1940.

Both of Lee's first two books were published at about the same time. *Lee Wulff's Handbook of Fresh Water Fishing,* by J.B. Lippincott, $1.75 and *Let's Go Fishing* by Frederick A. Stokes, New York, $2.00, left Lee basking in the bright sunlight of authorship. Some good reviews on both coasts didn't hurt his ego any.

"This book is crammed with short bits of advice on every aspect of fish, fishing and fishing tackle," a story in the San Francisco *Chronicle* said. "Unfortunately, it is written by an easterner—about eastern problems so it isn't perfect for the land of the steelhead. It's 90 percent helpful though. Lee Wulff, who has written a great deal for the hunting and fishing magazines, is a man who knows what he is talking about. He is also surprisingly non-literary (which must have made Lee wince) which seems to be a rare quality among trout fishermen. The publishers have pulled a very fancy little extra stunt by putting each of the books in an oilskin pouch for stream wear."

The San Diego *Union* treated Lee like an hometown boy:

"Lee Wulff, formerly of San Diego," said a June 11, 1939 story, "and now of New York, has another book off the press. It has this inviting title *Let's Go Fishing.* Lee, who also illustrated the book, is one of the best-known anglers in the world. He has won an international tuna tournament and has been invited by Newfoundland to take motion pictures of fishing in full color. His first book was *Handbook Of Fresh Water Fishing.* "

Lee arrived back in Newfoundland in June of 1940 hoping to see things taking a turn for the better as far as conservation measures were concerned. He had been heartened at the decision to limit the daily salmon catch to eight fish—on the part of anglers. But he was in for a rude shock. Newfoundland was ruled by a commission of six men in those days. She was the last dominion of Great Britain and was considered a depressed area by the mother country. The six positions were Health, Justice and Education—held by Newfoundlanders. The other positions of Natural Resources, Public Works and Fisheries—the most important ones—were held by Englishmen.

Lee ran across Claude Frazier, secretary for Natural Resources, almost as soon as he arrived back in St. John's. Frazier, an Englishman who could have been type-cast by Hollywood for the part, was officious and arrogant to extremes. He immediately let Lee know that while there might be an eight-fish limit per day for anglers, no such restrictions were to be levied on commercial netters. As far as he was concerned, the economic value of commercial fishing came before the money derived from sportfishermen. Lee's connections were all with the Tourist Development Board which had been under Natural Resources, but a re-organization had shifted it to the

Public Works Department. As a result there was a lot of controversy as to where fisheries and tourism really belonged.

Lee immediately began a tour of salmon streams around the island in a small boat, looking for new salmon rivers and the best places to establish fishing camps. He was lucky enough to find a guide named Jack Young from Corner Brook who had a small boat with a cuddy cabin that would provide shelter for two men in bad weather. When the weather was good they would camp out on the streams.

The year before Lee had decided to stop fishing with his 9 foot 5 ounce salmon rod and stick with his light, 7 foot 2-1/2 ounce split bamboo rod that had served him well for trout over the years. He had caught enough salmon on it now to be convinced he could handle even the big ones—though he was yet to catch one bigger than 20 pounds.

He was learning more and more about salmon each year and seriously considered doing his next book on the fish—text with plenty of black and white photos. He was doing a lot of experimenting with new techniques and had designed a couple of new flies for salmon—some new stoneflies and the Skater. Though Lee ran across a lot of good fly fishermen while exploring new rivers, hardly any were dry fly anglers. It was very difficult to convert them to the dry fly. Decades of fishing the way they had been taught by the English years ago, were hard to forget.

Lee and a friend, Frank Silver, manager of a paper company in Corner Brook on the west coast of Newfoundland, were going to fish the Torrent and River Of Ponds for salmon in the spring of 1939. They caught the regular around-the-island steamer and were dropped off at Port Saunders the following day. They were met on the dock by Sam Shinnix, a jovial giant who was a guide on the River Of Ponds.

After first fishing the Torrent River for a few days, they moved over to the River Of Ponds where Sam was to guide them. As Lee was to write later, in an issue of *Field & Stream*, he asked Sam how the dry fly fishing was.

"I finally threw away all my dry flies," Sam said. "No, sir, you can't catch 'em on dry flies, but, mister, have you any small Jock Scotts or Silver Grays?"

"I'm going to make you eat those words," Lee told him.

Sure enough, Lee caught a fish soon after starting to fish the big river and brought it over to Sam.

"Betcha can't do it again," was all Sam said.

Three casts later Lee caught another salmon on a No. 4 White Wulff and at the end of that day Sam and a number of other guides were so impressed they killed and plucked a loon—which wasn't protected then as it is today—for feathers, from which to make more dry flies.

Lee and Joan's home at Lew Beach, New York—on the Beaverkill. Jack Samson photo.

Right: A collection of Lee's own flies on a wall behind his desk at the Lew Beach house. Jack Samson photo.

Below: A double-hooked fly tied by Lee for big ocean fish. Jack Samson photo.

Right: The Beaverkill in fall. Jack Samson photo.

Lee with a 30 pound Atlantic salmon on the Moisie River (Quebec). Lee Wulff photo.

*Lee and his long-time, close
friend Joseph Cullman.
Jack Samson photo.*

*Lee and grand-daughter
Dana Rose Lee in pastel
and charcoal by Dana's
mother, Leslie Enders.
Joan Wulff photo.*

The "Ultimate" reel designed by Lee Wulff. Frank Amato photo.

Lee fighting a salmon in Alaska. Jim Repine photo.

First salmon on Nordura River, Iceland. Lee Wulff photo.

Lee and Larry Cronin dwarfed by an iceburg in Notre Dame Bay, Newfoundland, 1970. Joan Wulff photo

Frank wrote Lee a few months later saying Sam had come down to Corner Brook on business and had spent the day going through fly shops trying to find dry flies. He said to tell Lee to come back to fish as soon as he was able—and to be sure and bring some dry flies with him.

The rest of that summer was spent exploring new rivers up the Great Northern Peninsula and catching salmon. Lee began to feel as though he understood the life cycle of this great fish by careful observation and by spending countless nights around campfires with guides who had been around salmon all their lives.

On his knees beside the headwaters of several rivers, Lee watched as tiny salmon broke from their eggs in gravel beds. In the palm of his hand he watched as the tiny tail first broke through the skin of the egg—to become a big-eyed baby alevin, less than an inch long. The tiny fish had huge bellies formed by the egg sac from which they were hatched.

For more than a month, as Lee watched, the tiny alevins lived on nourishment from that dwindling egg sac as they swam close to the banks in calm water. When the last remnants of the sac were absorbed, the tiny fish looked like other small minnows as they lived on the microscopic food found in the headwaters of the stream.

As the little fish grew, they began to resemble the small trout with which they shared the stream. Their back was transversed with black markings and their sides—silverish—contained small red dots. They feed much like trout—insects on the surface and on the bottom—plus other smaller fish they can catch. But their growth rate is slower than that of the trout, Lee saw. The parr, as it is now called, takes three or four years to develop and, when fully developed, are from 5 to 7 inches in length. By this time milt can develop in the small male parr.

These small predators are fully capable of taking a fly and it hurt Lee to see them impaled upon a big dry fly. He took great care to release them unharmed. They were strong for their size and could leap high above the surface while feeding. Lee was amazed to see the parr leap and attack large insects the size of moths and butterflies, knocking them to the surface and finally pulling them underwater.

At this time of their lives the little salmon are vulnerable to attack from a number of predators, ospreys, mink, otters, kingfishers and mergansers. They are eaten by the hundreds—and probably thousands—in those early years, but the female salmon lay millions of eggs and the loss is all part of the balance of nature, Lee knew.

About the third year—in early spring—these parr begin to lose the dark back color and the markings gradually fade. The red dots on the sides fade and the fish turns silver on the sides and belly and the back takes on a dark bluish color. The parr is ready for its journey to the sea.

Lee marveled at the timing. Nature saw to it that this change to the silvery color coincided with the spring freshets and the parr were more easily able to float down the river to the sea on high water conditions. In this new condition the little salmon were called smolts—now camouflaged against the many enemies they would meet in the sea.

It took Lee a few years to understand why all parr did not change to this silver color and leave for the sea at the same time. Old guides explained to him that this is nature's way of ensuring the salmon stock will survive. If any one of a multitude of disasters were to occur, an exceptionally deep ice freeze one year or a great loss of parr to predators, there would still be enough parr in the river to ensure more going to sea the following year—or the next.

It takes several days for the smolts to adjust to the shock of salt concentrations in the water. Floating in and out with the incoming and outgoing tides at the river mouth, gives the little silvery fish time to acclimate to their new environment. But already, Lee noticed, as he waded the river mouths, predators in the form of both fish and birds gather at the river mouths at this time of the year just to prey on the small salmon. Even as they head for the deep waters offshore, the small salmon are food for such bottom-feeders as codfish.

Lee, perched on a large rock at the sea's edge wondered where the salmon went when they left the shore. The ocean is so huge and filled with so many species of fish—how could one keep track of the salmon? From net catches, commercial fishermen knew salmon stayed close to the bottom. But how long do they stay down there? How far do they migrate? To what great far-away seas do they swim? Little did Lee know then that Atlantic salmon netted by commercial fishermen off Greenland had come from as far away as rivers in New Brunswick and Scotland.

Mature salmon do show up at certain spots while at sea, however. Residents of Newfoundland have seen them just offshore during the winter months along the north shore and off the Labrador coast. But only by studying the growth rings on a salmon's scales do scientists get any sort of scientific data. These growth rings are like those of a tree. When they are far apart, they indicate a salmon has grown rapidly and when narrow, just the opposite.

Salmon spend from one to four years at sea, commercial netters told Lee, and when they come back can weigh anywhere from 10 to 60 pounds—long, sleek, silvery and with a large body and small head. The netters said they regularly catch salmon just offshore with their bellies stuffed with herring, capelin and other small school baitfish.

It was a mystery to Lee, at first, how the salmon knew which home rivers to ascend. It seemed inconceivable that the fish—out of all the rivers pouring down into the vast sea—chose the right one. But the more he thought about it, he realized that the parr had spent at least three years in their home river and by that time the taste of water in its native stream had become as familiar to it as say the smell of air would to an animal or human. He realized he would recognize the odor of the forests and fields around his beloved Battenkill.

Though Lee could not guess it at the time, scientists later found that salmon find their own home rivers strictly by taste. A scientist at the University of Wisconsin, Dr. John Hasler, found the fish smells its way back to its own spawning river like a foxhound. The scent in the water is produced by dissolved organic water from plants, trees and sediment in the tributary and may vary from one tributary to another only in the slightest degree. Downstream it is rapidly reduced to extremely low concentrations. To detect such traces, a fish must have fantastic ability to pick up odors and tell them apart. The salmon has such an ability. It can perceive dilutions of one part in a billion. If this sounds unbelievable, scientists have proven that eels can detect alcohol in proportions equal to a teaspoonful in Lake Superior!

Salmon return to the spawning rivers filled with energy from heavy feeding. Most of them swim against the heavy currents of the spring run-off rather than wait for slower water. Lee earlier had known that very young salmon—those that returned to their home rivers after one year at sea—were different from the older and bigger salmon. But it was not until he had watched them and learned from the older guides that Lee learned they were called grilse.

These "teen-age" salmon are full of energy, amazingly swift and are great jumpers. They weigh from two to seven pounds and have the same urge to spawn as the older salmon—but they will be driven away from the spawning grounds by the older male fish.

Guides told Lee that the size of salmon varied with the rivers from which they came. Certain rivers are known for large salmon and others for small. Also these runs of salmon are comprised of fish of different ages—swimming side-by-side. No two rivers will see salmon of uniform growth. A fish which has been in the sea for two full years may weigh anywhere from 8 to 15 pounds while a fish at sea for three years may weigh 25 pounds.

Lee found that a huge 40 pound salmon may have been at sea for four years and returned to spawn for a second time. Early season salmon may enter their river with eggs and milt just beginning to develop. Fish returning later in the season may come in heavy with ripe milt or roe. The later fish will try to push rapidly up the river, eager to reach the gravel beds by spawning time in late October. Unlike the Pacific salmon species which die shortly after spawning Atlantic salmon may live to spawn two or three times.

Though a salmon may take a fly, or a bright spoon as it heads upstream, the fish enter the river with no hunger. If it did not the salmon would soon clear everything edible from the river as it swims upstream—insects, frogs, trout and even its own parr. Once in fresh water a chemical change takes place that shuts off the feeding urge. Lee spent hours on a bank tossing objects at salmon lying in the current—worms, leeches, floating insects of all kinds, to see if he could interest the salmon in feeding all to no avail. But a restlessness seemed to overtake the fish at times and they would rise and take insects, even pieces of wood, in their mouth—only to hold them for a moment, then spit it out. He guessed the fish was reacting to the floating objects the way they did as parr—acting as though the objects dimly reminded them of long-passed feeding habits.

Far up in the headwaters Lee would watch the salmon reach the gravel beds in late October. The males fought each other for territory—beds in the gravel, or redds which the females had scooped out. Trout and eels have to be driven away before the female deposits eggs in the depression and the male—wriggling on its side—covers the eggs with milt.

The longer the salmon takes to ascend the river, the darker its color will get. The silvery shine of the sea gradually turns dull and bronze-colored to blend with the mottled bottom. The salmon looks grayish from above as it rests against a rock-strewn bottom. Salmon fresh from the sea will have small, blackish sea lice clinging to their sides and bottom. These will in time drop off or be brushed off on rocks. Guide Ella Manuel told Lee that salmon jumping regularly just after entering a river were sometimes trying to get rid of the sea lice.

Salmon seemed to travel more at night than in the daytime on the way to spawn. Lee figured that, over the centuries, the fish learned they were less vulnerable to their worst enemies—otters, seals, ospreys and bears—in the dark. What fascinated him most, as an angler, was how salmon seemed to rest at the same places each year in any given river. Experienced guides could look at a familiar river and point out each traditional "lie" to Lee. He gradually learned how to read such water and to guess where the fish would be holding.

Lee would lie on his stomach on a bank for hours watching salmon holding in the current—their fins seeming not to move. Some would drop to the bottom to rest on their broad, strong pectoral fins with their bodies stretched out behind, ready for an instant getaway. After holding and releasing a great many salmon, Lee could understand and appreciate how the salmon so beautifully streamlined and so powerful, with a slick covering of slime, offered almost no resistance to the swiftly-moving current.

Lee with the fishing vest he sewed himself, circa 1939.

When the water level dropped in the river—usually because of lack of rain—salmon would gather in the larger pools and wait for the water to rise again before they would continue upstream. The longer they stayed in the pool the darker they became and the less they were interested in flies. Lee would try everything in his fly box until, disgusted, he would give up on such salmon. But he did find out that repeated casts of big dry flies to salmon lying in a holding spot sometimes resulted in a strike, after a long period of time.

Watching salmon spawn, Lee found out that when either milt or roe was left over after a pair of fish had spawned, either the male or the female might move to another redd and choose a new mate with which to complete the spawn. Though salmon ready to spawn usually paired-up with a fish of approximately the same size, now and then a pair could be of vastly different size. At times even a small grilse would slide up and fertilize the roe of a large female.

Though some guides told Lee that most of the salmon went back to the ocean and spawned again, his observations led him to believe a great many— probably a large majority—of the spent salmon died after spawning. He noticed that the fish lost nearly half their weight spawning and wondered how they could make it back to the sea in the late fall and winter when they were so thin. He learned these spent fish did not all go back to the salt after spawning but many just dropped back to large pools and spent the winter under the ice. Their metabolism slowed down to almost nothing and they ate almost nothing until the ice broke up the following spring. Others facing upstream while floating down with the current are called "black" salmon and are lucky to reach the sea before the rivers freeze. This descent to the sea is critical, Lee learned. Rivers with easy returns to the sea have a better survival rate. But those who make it back to the salt mend quickly and usually within a year are back to spawn again.

By the end of summer, Lee felt he had learned enough about these mysterious fish to write a book about them.

Newfoundland Rivers

Filled with thoughts of salmon and salmon fishing, Lee, when he arrived back in Chappaqua, New York in late September started immediately on his book. He had accumulated a number of fine black and white photos of Newfoundland and Nova Scotia salmon rivers taken by himself and Vic Coty. In addition he had learned a great deal in the last two summers about the Atlantic salmon—enough to be considered an expert by American standards.

Doing his own illustrations, Lee turned the book in by the first of the year. *Leaping Salmon* was a thin, but well-done treatise on the sport of salmon fishing with a fly, as well as a thorough profile of the fish itself. Lee dedicated the book to the many salmon guides he had known and from whom he had learned so much.

When eighteen years later he was to write his classic *The Atlantic Salmon*, Lee tended to look back on his first salmon book as a somewhat amateur effort compared to his larger work, it nevertheless was an excellent book for the time. Most American anglers knew next to nothing about fly fishing for salmon and it filled a niche that long needed filling in U.S. fishing literature.

At just about the time the book was completed and given to the New York publisher, Helen gave birth to their second son, Barry Lee Wulff. Lee suddenly realized that not only had he been born in February, but so had both his sons.

War seemed inevitable to the American people. When Lee arrived back

71

in Newfoundland in June, all talk was of the coming conflict. The U.S. had traded a number of over-age destroyers to England for several bases in Newfoundland—an air base at Stephenville and another at Gander. Construction had begun at the bases and on an 8 million dollar telephone line between the west coast and St. John's had started. Work on the telephone line had jumped wages in Newfoundland and secretaries who, a year before, had been drawing $6 per week were now making the unheard of salary of $35 a week. Anyone who wanted work could get it cutting and carting trees for the many telephone poles that would be needed for the long phone line.

Lee went back to his exploring of the salmon rivers and his photography and writing.

In addition to catching a 30 pound salmon that spring on the Serpentine River with his fragile 7 foot 2-1/2 ounce fly rod, Lee had two spectacular fishing trips which he later wrote about in his excellent 1972 book, *Fishing With Lee Wulff*. One was a trip he and a fishing friend, Ralph O'Brien—accompanied by long-time guide friends, Plus Parsons and Walter Hynes—took to the Fox Island River in search of both salmon and big sea-run brook trout.

Lee had heard rumors from his guide chums that very big trout were found in the river in June and July, after coming in from the salt in May. The party was joined after the first day by Lee's old St. John's friend and insurance broker Jack Meehan.

The weather was lovely with the new green shoots of alder along the river banks set against the dark evergreens. Whiskey jacks scolded from low branches as the men surveyed the clear river. Like Pacific Northwest steelhead, sea-run brook trout take on the silvery sheen of the ocean fish before entering rivers to spawn. By the time they are ready to spawn in the fall, these same fish will have reverted to the worm-like back markings on a dark green background and the sides again contain spots and the red belly of fresh water brookies.

But, the guides had told Lee, the winter months these fish spend at sea make them monsters. Their food consisted mainly of capelin—a fish about six inches long, that was coming to the beach to spawn. While most people came to the Fox Island River to catch salmon, the guides told Lee the trout fishing was excellent. Lee, who had fished the Russian River in Alaska for rainbows, would never have believed another river could be as good for trout.

In the low, clear water conditions the dry fly was very effective and the fishermen caught plenty of trout in the 4 to 5 pound category—big trout for any river in Newfoundland. Lee was intent on making a motion picture film on the sea-run trout while the rest were content to catch salmon.

On the morning of the fifth day it began to rain and the crew was forced to take shelter in a cabin at the mouth of the river. They were confined to the cabin for three days as the rain fell in torrents and Fox Island River became a muddy flood with trees and branches floating down its roily length. Forced to read or play cards, Lee talked to the guides about fishing. Plus Parsons said he had heard the trout sometimes went downriver with such floods and could be caught at the mouth occasionally. Ready to try anything after being cooped up for days, Lee took a casting rod and a red-and-white plug with him to the wide river mouth as Ralph came along with a fly rod.

Standing on the north side of the river as it poured its muddy waters out into the sea, Lee figured since the water turned south when it entered salt the best place to fish would be on the south side. Crossing in a dory, he walked into the water and cast the plug. On the next ten casts he caught ten big sea-run brookies. Leaving Ralph there he rushed back to the cabin to get his fly rod.

As the astounded guides stood and watched, Lee and Ralph hooked and released nearly 50 trout in the next few hours. Some weighed more than seven pounds. All fought frantically in the cold sea water. It didn't seem to matter much which fly was used. With the wind whipping their rain garments and the rain slanting down, there was no need to cast. One just let the fly whip downwind and when it hit the surface a trout would take it. They took and released more than 100 trout before they quit the next day.

Before leaving, Lee prepared a petition for the local people who lived in the small settlement of Fox Island asking the government to impose a two fish per day limit and extend the fly fishing only to an area to run for a half mile down and up the shore from the river's mouth. Lee reasoned that the fishing was so good it would soon be spoiled if people discovered it.

He was right. Not only did the government ignore his suggestion, but by a decade later a 12-inch trout was considered a good-sized fish on the Fox Island River.

Before leaving for the States in late September, Lee and Harold Smith, another Tourist Bureau employee, were asked to survey the Serpentine River and take some photos of the fishing there. The river on the west coast was difficult to reach. Lee had long considered it the most beautiful river on the island. The long, sheer-sided valley at that time was uninhabited from Serpentine Lake through the twelve miles of river that flowed from it to the sea. There were no harbors along the rugged coast within 20 miles of the river mouth. Sheer mountains rose to the sky behind the big lake, from where the river winds down through a thickly wooded valley until it plunges over a falls six miles below the lake. After that it rushes rapidly downhill the last six miles to the sea.

Harold, Lee and two guides, Jack and Francis, slogged the 12 miles from the sea to the lake on a trail that was muddy, rocky, wet and slippery at the very best. They were delighted to see the lake in late afternoon—laden as they were with bedrolls, grub, cameras and tackle. They found the salmon had already reached the lake on their spawning run, but it was too early to spawn. Most of them milled about the home pool at the lake outlet.

Anglers and guides camped in the cabin near the lake outlet and Lee and Harold each took a ten pound fish from the home pool before darkness shut them down. The following morning Jack took Hal and Lee downstream in a canoe that was kept at the cabin. A few hundred yards downstream they began to hit large and deep pools and Lee switched to streamer flies and had Hal do the same thing. Fishing under overhanging ledges and near sunken logs—places salmon don't hold—they caught sea-run brook trout up to five pounds on nearly every cast.

Downstream, at a deep bend of the river, they came to Grant's Pool, more than 200 yards long and 50 yards wide. There was a slow, steady flow in the big pool and riffles on top indicated the uneven rocks on the bottom. Using a gray bucktail floater in size 10, Lee and Hal caught four mature salmon and a couple of grilse in short order. Before they left the big pool and poled back to the lake they had taken six salmon, sixteen grilse and twenty-seven big sea-run brookies—a fine day indeed.

Lee was fishing for salmon and trout. He had tied up a couple of white marabou streamers with silver bodies and . . . some yellow and scarlet to give them color. They were four inches long but were tied on No. 4 low water salmon hooks. He gave one to Hal to use while he used a White Wulff dry fly himself.

Hal hooked up with a big trout and played it until Lee netted it and Lee switched to the same big streamer. He used it with no success but left it on as they poled back up the river to the big home pool near the cabin. It was growing dark but Lee couldn't resist the temptation to make one last cast in the big pool.

He stripped the big streamer fly for trout and was rewarded with a solid smash from a big fish. A big salmon had been swimming around in the trout pool. Lee had never taken one on a streamer and certainly not in almost total darkness. It is one thing to play a salmon in a river on a light 7 foot rod and another to play one in wide open water where one cannot see where there are snags or rocks. With 50 to 60 yards out the rod would be pointing in one direction and the salmon swimming, or jumping, in another. Lee said some-times, in the darkness, two fish would jump at once and he wondered which was the one he was hooked to.

But he finally brought the shining fish—fresh from the sea—to the tailer after a long, thrashing and jumping battle. In the darkness he released the salmon to swim away—a fitting ending to a great day. Later, around a fire with hot tea to warm the body and a welcome hot meal, there were the stories of the day and . . . finally sleep on the spruce-bough bunks as the fire slowly turned to embers in the huge stone fireplace.

Lee had a feeling as he returned to New York state that fall that he had had his last salmon fishing trip before the war changed all their lives. The Selective Service Act was passed by Congress on September 16, 1941—meaning every American man between the age of 20 and 36 must register for the military draft. Lee registered, but felt because of the two boys he was not likely to be called up in the near future. Length of military service was one year.

Realizing the country was facing a crisis, Roosevelt decided to run for an unprecedented third term against the Republican candidate Wendell L. Wilkie, whose plain-spoken manner made him a strong contender. At some other time he might have been elected, but the majority of those voting apparently decided it was not the time to change leaders. Roosevelt was re-elected and the Democrats kept a majority in Congress.

Helen had gone back to work in the city and Barry was under the care of an Algonquin Indian girl called "Didda." Lee was hard at work writing stories on Newfoundland and putting together his motion picture films on Serpentine, Fox Island River and River Of Ponds salmon and trout fishing. He took several days off to hunt grouse with his friend and editor Tap Tapply near Tap's home in Alton, New Hampshire. Amid the glory of falling scarlet, tan and yellow leaves—following Tap's old reliable setter, Duke—he thrilled to the thundering takeoff of his favorite upland game bird.

"He stalked the woods like a god," Tap said years later, remembering. "knocking down almost every bird that flushed near him, or so it seemed to one who felt lucky enough to hit one in five."

And as he had done every year since moving back East, he hunted deer in New Hampshire.

The family was at home with a few of Lee's fishing friends as guests for Sunday dinner on December 7th that fall of 1941. Barry was almost two years old and Allan nearly five. The radio announced the Japanese bombing of Pearl Harbor. Everyone was stunned and almost nobody knew where it was.

"I remember it very distinctly," Helen said recently. "One of Lee's fishing friends, John Easton, said he would enlist the very next day. He was in the reserves."

No one's lives would be the same from that day forward.

The War Years

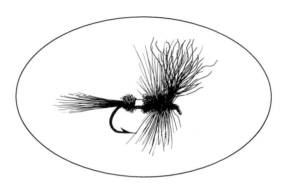

The American people—after several years of debating the fact that the United States was a neutral power—suddenly became united. "Remember Pearl Harbor" became a national slogan, even as U.S. military forces suffered embarrassing defeats in the Pacific. The Japanese took Bataan and forced American prisoners on the long Death March—only to take Corregidor in Manila Bay a month later.

By February U.S. naval forces suffered a major defeat in the battle of the Java Sea and the next month General MacArthur was ordered to withdraw to Australia by presidential order. On the European front, plans were being made in Washington for an invasion of North Africa later in the year.

Lee and Helen decided to move up to Shushan from Chappaqua—Lee to be closer to his beloved Battenkill. Rationing of gasoline, tires and cigarettes had already begun and Lee felt living in a small country town would be cheaper and better for Helen and the two small boys. Helen no longer needed to work—especially in New York City during a war. Everyone was cutting back on everything and the dress business was certainly not considered essential to the war effort. Women's fashions, reflecting the general air of restraint, kept to subdued colors and inconspicuous lines. An embargo on Japanese silk sent the silk stocking market into a frenzy and women bought up the few remaining pairs left.

Helen and the boys had been spending several summers at Shushan—in a small house Lee had rented close to the Ashworths, who owned the mill by the dam on the Battenkill—while Lee spent the summers in Newfoundland. Lee bought 15 acres of land on the river and planned to build a house close to where they had rented. But it was no time to build. Materials were scarce so they decided to buy a small house that perched on a hillside just above the land Lee bought.

It was Helen's idea to move the house from the hillside down to their land by the river, but it was no easy task. A group of men helped Lee slide it down on greased railroad ties after county workers came and removed all the telephone wires in the way. But the Newfoundland Tourist Board suddenly notified Lee he was wanted in St. Johns to discuss being on loan from the government to the U.S. military. He was to oversee the Army's recreational program—primarily salmon and trout fishing—and would be assigned to military bases as an advisor/instructor.

Helen was left on her own to supervise the rest of the move and the renovation of the small house. The house was set on a level plot close to the river, but it had suffered minor damage in the move. The roof needed repairing and it fell to Helen to drive miles to obtain slate tiles for the roof. She and the boys stayed in the rental house while a carpenter, John Westenberg, worked on the moved house all spring and summer. Because of the move nothing seemed straight, Helen recalled later—doors wouldn't shut properly nor would windows slide up and down. As annoying as it was to Helen to have a carpenter in the house all day, it was a picnic for the boys—ages five and two. Rooms were added and a barn was moved from Shushan to the house to serve as a two-car garage. A picture window was put into the living room—providing a view of the Battenkill. Later Lee was to plant fruit trees and shrubbery and Helen put in a Victory Garden as they were called during the war.

The U.S. Army Air Corps had taken over both Newfoundland military bases at Stephenville and Gander and used them as ferrying bases for U.S. and Canadian planes coming to and from the war in Europe. Lee was assigned to Special Services and his main job was to keep fishing gear in shape and to develop a recreational fishing program for the military—both based there and passing through. As is usual with the military anywhere, most of the recreational trout and salmon fishing fell to the officers. Most enlisted personnel did not have the time off for such sport.

Lee was still being paid a salary by the Newfoundland Tourist Board, but his job now was to cooperate with the U.S. military. He still had plenty of time, however, to hunt and fish on his own time and to both photograph and write. His long-time friend, Tap Tapply, who had for years been buying stories from him for *National Sportsman,* took over the editorship of *Outdoors* magazine in July, 1942. Not only did he put Lee on the masthead as his fishing editor, but bought ten feature stories from him shortly afterward. The money certainly came in handy for Lee—as repairs on the Shushan house had been costing quite a bit.

He was learning more each season about salmon and fly fishing and went through a number of experiences in these years that he was to write about later. Still using his light 7 foot fly rod, he realized somewhere along the line that reeling with his left hand made a lot more sense in fighting salmon than the customary and traditional right-hand system he had been using for years. In an article he wrote for *Outdoors* in 1946, for Tapply, he wrote:

"Being right-handed, I hold the fly rod in that hand while casting. It's not that I can't cast left-handed; I just do it a lot better and more easily with my right. That makes sense. When it comes to playing a fish, the strength required to hold the rod is far greater than that required to turn the reel handle, so I use my stronger arm for the job requiring more strength. That makes sense too.

"However, most fly rod anglers switch their rods from their right hands to their left when playing a fish in order to reel with their right hands. They do this because their left hands are clumsy and aren't trained for the manipulation of small things like reel handles. This idea has some logic behind it because it saves the necessity of training the left hand to reel, but it means that when playing a big fish, the left hand tires easily and because of that the fish may be lost. It also means that the rod must be changed from hand to hand whenever a fish is hooked. In contrast, with left-hand reeling, the rod always remains in the right hand—the strong hand, where it belongs."

In those days nearly every fly fisherman alive reeled with the right hand—if he or she were right-handed. The idea at that time was received with skepticism, but 50 years later most fly rodders—particularly saltwater ones—reel with the left hand while fighting big fish.

Lee also discovered an innovative way to fish a wet fly—one that was long-known to a handful of Newfoundlers, but nowhere else. He was later to write about it in a 1952 issue of *Outdoor Life*.

It was while fishing Portland Creek on the west coast of Newfoundland—after having flown in on a Grumman Goose with some military personnel—that Lee ran across the Portland Hitch. The river is a short, broad one on the northwest coast where the salmon ran large. The party was fly fishing when an old lobster man named Arthur Perry showed up. He advised Lee and friends that if they used what he referred to as an "itch" on their flies they would catch a lot more salmon.

Lee, used to the vagaries of Newfoundlers by this time, was unimpressed, but watched as Perry put a loop in Lee's leader, just in front of the fly, and followed that by tightening it to form a half hitch around the shank of the hook at the base of the head. Then he did a repeat, tightening the second knot just beyond the first. Handing it back to Lee, he said:

"Now, Sir, it will rivvle and I believe you'll catch a salmon."

The old English fishermen who had long ago settled on the island pronounced their f's like v's and dropped their h's, so "hitch" became "itch" and "riffle" became "rivvle."

Lee had fished a lot of Newfoundland salmon rivers at that time and considered himself quite an expert. Carefully he undid the knots and went back to his fishing, saying:

"Arthur, the Turle knot has been working satisfactorily for a long time. We'll try it that way."

Arthur shook his head sadly—leaving Lee to fish, but he trailed along as a guide.

The fishing was poor and when they finally reached the Low Rock Pool where the river empties into the sea, Lee decided to try the knots himself. When the fly came back on the retrieve, it slid across the surface—leaving

U.S. Army Air Corps Commanding General "Hap" Arnold fishing for Atlantic salmon on a Newfoundland river with Lee Wulff, 1944.

a V-shaped wake behind it. The water parted as a big salmon rushed at the fly and engulfed it. Lee had hooked his first salmon on the riffling hitch or the Portland Creek Hitch as he named it.

Nobody knows for sure where the unique method of tying the knot to the fly came from, but the most acceptable version is that officers from the old British Navy ships that first came to the land used to come ashore to fish for salmon—as they had done for centuries in their native country. They gave old flies to the Newfoundlanders and the leaders finally wore out. The hardy fishermen probably tied several knots in the leaders when they grew worn—to keep from losing fish—and more than likely didn't care how the flies rode in the river. Portland Creek is not a deep river and most salmon lie just below the surface—making it easy for them to see the skidding flies just above them.

But it is not just on Portland Creek that the unusual system of fastening the fly works, as Lee found out. Perry's version of the hitch was so that the gut or mono pulled from under the turned-up eye at the throat. This made both single and double-hooked flies ride properly—that is with the hook down on the retrieve. This works fine if the eyes turn up, but Lee found it is better to shift the hitch 45 degrees to one side or the other with his favorite single-hooked flies—depending upon which side of the current he cast from. With this retrieve, on a cross-current pull, the fly would always ride with the hook downstream. This position always seemed to be better for the way the fly rode and worked for better hooking.

Lee found he could hook salmon just as well on the Humber and River Of Ponds with the hitched fly as he did on Portland Creek. Not only did salmon hit the sliding fly on the surface, but brook trout took it and even some big browns on the Battenkill rose and took the fly. Lee reasoned that fish on such heavily-fished rivers as the Battenkill probably took the riffled flies because of the novelty of the presentation. He later advocated using the riffle hitch on wary brook trout that had been much fished-over.

As the war ground on into 1944 with an invasion of Europe imminent and U.S. forces in the Pacific invading New Guinea and gaining footholds on scattered Pacific islands—Lee continued finding rivers in Newfoundland. Being able to fly in military planes made exploration easy and he was able to take some high-ranking officers to productive new locations. His fame as an angler had spread by then and many a field-grade officer passing through Newfoundland on the way to or from Europe, managed to take a few days off to fish with him.

Lee made a lot of friends in the military that were to stand him in good stead after the war. On one memorable morning in June of 1944, just prior to the Normandy Invasion, Lee awoke to find it another humid and gray day at

Stephenville. Low-hanging clouds stretched to the horizon out over St. George's Bay and it looked like more rain. The commanding officer of the big base, Colonel H. H. Maxwell, had phoned Lee the day before at Corner Brook asking if Lee could come down and take "a couple of men" fishing the following day. Since it was part of his contract with the Tourist Board, Lee came down on the train.

He had just finished a big breakfast of bacon, eggs, toast and coffee at the transient mess hall and had picked up a Newfoundler, Jim Sullivan, who worked at the base and now and then was put on detached service to act as a guide with Lee. Fishing had been poor as it had rained for weeks and most rivers—at least on the west coast—were muddy and high.

They were told to walk out to a railroad spur and wait there for the fishing party to show up. To Lee's and Jim's utter astonishment, a phalanx of high-ranking Army generals arrived in two railroad cars—headed by Chief of Staff of the Army General George Marshall and head of the Army Air Corps, General "Hap" Arnold.

Lee said later the first thought that crossed his mind was to wonder why both men were traveling in the same plane back to Washington from meetings in Europe. Having one killed in a plane crash, he thought, would be bad enough. The two generals—with the weight of the invasion heavy on them, had both decided that half a day's salmon fishing would be the best form of relaxation they could ask for.

The party rode only a short way in the railroad car—pulled by a small engine driven by the base commander—until they reached the bank of a small, unnamed tributary that held salmon. The base had no suitable fly tackle for the generals so General Arnold was given Lee's spare outfit—his 9 foot fly rod with a 3 1/8-inch diameter reel with 100 yards of 10 pound braided nylon backing. Jim spliced an end loop on a new line for General Marshall.

They made their way down the slippery banks to the small, muddy stream and Lee later said he was disconsolate that when he wanted conditions just right for salmon, it never happened. The mist settled down on the river and it began to rain heavier. The generals, dressed in heavy raincoats with hoods over their heads, nevertheless seemed to be having a good time. General Marshall was the first to hook up and brought in a grilse close to the railroad embankment. Colonel Maxwell put the grilse on a stringer for Marshall.

Lee and Hap Arnold went downstream and fished every stretch Lee thought would hold salmon. Where, only a few days earlier, there were holding pools, now there was only muddy, rushing water. Lee was using a Silver Gray and had rigged up General Arnold with a colorful Jock Scott—hoping the salmon could more easily spot it in the murky water.

But the fishing remained slow and neither Lee nor General Arnold caught any salmon until they moved back upstream where General Marshall's party had been earlier. Lee switched the general's fly to a size 6 Silver Gray and used a size 8 Blue Charm himself. Suddenly there was a boil behind the general's fly and Lee advised him to keep casting to the same spot. A few casts later a 10-pound salmon—fresh from the sea—took Arnold's fly and somersaulted into the air.

Arnold played the salmon well and after a 15 minute fight he had the shining fish in shallow water and Lee was readying the tailer when the fish made a last spurt and the leader parted.

"I guess," Lee wrote later, Arnold said, "that fish deserves to get away."

"I saw no traces of anger in his face," Lee later wrote in a 1945 story for *Outdoors*, "nothing but the pleasure he'd had in playing him." However both Lee and Arnold both caught small grilse shortly afterward.

The action got no better as the rain began to fall in sheets and the railcar came back for the party. They had hot coffee and sandwiches as the car took them back to the base. The two generals were on their way back to Washington an hour later—with a few grilse caught in Newfoundland.

Lee's headquarters in Corner Brook was a small clapboard house near the shore which was paid for by the Tourist Board. After living—at least part of each year—in Newfoundland since 1937, Lee had made many friends. Most of them were male fishermen, but some, like Ella Manuel, were women— some of whom liked to fish while others were business people from Corner Brook. Never fond of small talk, Lee nevertheless could spend hours talking about the things he loved with people who were interested in the same things. He was particularly comfortable in the company of fishing guides and especially those who had spent many years doing it.

Over the years in the wilds doing his own photography and writing and building his own camps he had developed a philosophy.

He was dedicated to the outlook that the best way to live and succeed was to do it yourself. Earning your own way was what he preached to his boys and anyone else who would listen. Free, self-confident and physically well-equipped for any challenge in the wilderness, Lee lived for the outdoors. A successful writer, a good photographer, a superb fly fisherman and skilled big game angler, he was supremely qualified for the role he had chosen for himself. He gradually became a good rifle shot and had the reflexes to be a fine wing-shot with a shotgun.

By the end of the year 1944, with the war winding down rapidly in Europe, Lee was forced to admit he did not want to return to New York. He had tasted the salt air of the Gulf of St. Lawrence every year for almost eight years and considered Newfoundland his second home and favorite spot on the earth to live. He realized his life with Helen had been productive and that she had been a good and faithful wife for 15 years. He loved his two young sons, but knew, if he were forced to return to a life in the vicinity of New York City he would be terribly unhappy. In his own way he loved Helen and the thought that he would be separated from his boys was agonizing, but one he knew he would have to face if he were to pursue the life he wanted.

The alternative would be to have Helen and the boys move to Newfoundland and live either in the small community of Corner Brook or the larger city of St. Johns. He knew in his heart that Helen, a sophisticated, educated woman who was as at home in Paris as New York, would never be happy in Newfoundland. He had spent months agonizing over the problem and knew he would have to face up to it when he returned to Shushan on a permanent basis at the conclusion of the war.

Lee and Ella Manuel had become good friends in the later years he had been based in Corner Brook. Divorced a few years earlier, Ella had two small sons roughly the same age as Lee's. A fine fly fisherman, a professional-level guide and an attractive, dark-haired woman in her thirties, it was almost inevitable that she and Lee would become friends. From a casual guide-client relationship in the early war years, they had begun to spend considerable time together when Lee was in Corner Brook—which was most of the time.

As lovers they discussed what the future might be for the two of them and it looked bleak as long as Lee was married. People did not live together in 1944 as they might today and Lee could only promise that he would work something out when he returned to Shushan that winter. But, with all good intentions, Lee could not force himself to bring up the subject of Newfoundland as his permanent home, or divorce in that long, uncomfortable winter of 1944-45.

By January the U.S. Sixth Army landed on Luzon and a task force of 850 ships sailed into Lingayen Gulf, 100 miles north of Manila and most people began to hope the war would be won in the Pacific, eventually.

The Yalta Conference was held in February and heralded the end of the war in Europe. By March the U.S. First Army crossed the Rhine River—the first army to do so since the days of Napoleon. The Pacific island of Iwo Jima fell on March 16th to the U.S. Marines after 36 days of bloody fighting and the loss of more than 4,000 Marines and 15,000 wounded. With Iwo Jima and Saipan in American hands the main islands of Japan were now within reach of American long-range B-29 heavy bombers.

Lee returned to Corner Brook just after the surrender of Germany and the celebration of Victory Europe (VE-Day) on May 8, 1945. He had agreed to do a documentary movie for the Bowater Paper Company based in Corner Brook, on the complete process of pulp-wood and paper manufacturing—for which he would be paid well. Ella helped him with the movie. A man named Cyril Parsons hosted a radio show in Corner Brook called the "Corner Brook Round Table" which was concerned mainly with environmental issues of the day.

Lee, who spent the spring photographing the woods segment of the operation, prior to photographing the interior operation, appeared frequently on the show—as did Ella, who had a fine radio voice. Ella operated a fishing lodge at Lommond which served as a combination rooming house, bed-and-breakfast for anglers on the way to nearby camps and a base of operations for the temporary camps Lee had begun on the Humber and Lommond Rivers. He had only a few clients—mostly local anglers—but he expected soon to interest a number of U.S. fly fishermen with stories he was writing on his operation in the outdoor magazines. Getting anglers from the base lodge in Lommond to the camps took quite a bit of logistical planning—mostly by boat—and the weather played havoc with such transportation. Lee at times wished he still had the use of military float planes.

The war in the Pacific was finally over—with the dropping of two atomic bombs on Japan in late August—with complete and unconditional surrender. Lee and Ella decided they could work together as a husband-and-wife team—Lee operating salmon and trout fishing camps on a number of Newfoundland rivers he had come to know so well and she running the lodge for his fishermen in Lommond—just north of Corner Brook. After eight years in the lovely land of Newfoundland, Lee was certain of two things: man was doing all he could to ruin nature and all its creatures—certainly the great Atlantic salmon. And he knew something else, the only way to get around a country like Newfoundland was by plane. He had covered nearly the entire country by military plane and knew, if he were ever going to make a living running salmon and trout fishing camps in this part of the world, he was going to have to get a small float plane and learn how to fly it himself.

But first, Lee had to return to Shushan that early fall and straighten out his life with Helen and his two sons.

Lee, his first wife Helen and their two sons, Allan (left) and Barry at their Chappaqua, New York home about 1947.

Taking to the Air

The divorce was painful. Helen realized their marriage had become strained because of Lee's long absences, but did not realize another woman was involved. The dispute was bitter and the boys—though young—knew there was conflict between their parents and grew uneasy whenever there was an argument. But, finally, Helen agreed there was no future for either of them if Lee intended to spend the majority of his time in Newfoundland.

While waiting for the divorce to become final, Helen moved to Rochester, New York—where her parents lived—and took the boys with her. Lee stayed in the Shushan house and continued his writing, concentrating on trying to get as much exposure for his salmon camps as possible in the outdoor magazines. Tap Tapply was a great help running at least a story an issue in *Outdoors* and, as Fishing Editor, Lee was able to discuss Newfoundland salmon fishing a great deal.

With the divorce final, Lee traveled to Newfoundland and he and Ella were married in a quiet ceremony in Corner Brook shortly after the first of the year. In midwinter it was too cold to fish or hunt, so they settled for making plans for the coming spring when they would begin their joint venture of running both a lodge and a string of fishing camps.

In early spring Lee began to fish the Battenkill again and Helen made sure the boys spent as much time with their father as possible—coming down to Shushan on weekends. Since the death of Lee's father a year earlier his mother had been living as a widow in San Diego. She had come east to keep house for him. She was better able to provide meals and care for the boys on week-ends than Lee.

There had long been the belief on the part of many fly fishermen and guides, that when men stepped into deep water or fell from a boat wearing heavy chest waders, they were sure to drown. The belief was that the air trapped inside would rush to the boot section of the waders and an angler would be tipped upside-down. Lee, with his penchant for reasoning things out, thought this nonsense. His engineer mind told him water would simply displace the air if his waders filled with water and he knew things in water weighed less than in air. Also he believed if a drawstring around the waist were fastened tightly one could easily swim with air in waders.

He figured the best way to prove his theory was to dive into a large body

Lee diving off a bridge into the Battenkill River to prove chest waders will not cause one to drown. Allan Wulff photo.

of water from a height. He thought about making his experiment by walking into deep water from the bank, but figured others would say he had let air out of his waders first. So, with his mother and Allan—who was nine then— watching, he dove off a bridge near his home into the Battenkill. As he later wrote in a December 1947 issue of *Outdoors,* the early spring water was pretty close to freezing.

"My dive was no masterpiece," he wrote, "I did go in head first, though my wader-clad feet followed at a sloppy angle. The water was cold. I could feel its strength as it closed around me and swept me along over the dimly sunlit gravel of the pool's deep bed. My momentum, together with the angle of my hands and the curve of my back, swept me around in a neat curve and my head popped up out of the water almost as quickly as you could say 'Arnold Robertson.' The midday sun was shining smack into my eyes with a friendly warmth. My mouth was free to drag in all the pure country air my lungs could hold, and my feet were floating nicely but with no tendency whatever to push my head under."

He was able to swim easily and thought the broad, flat felt-soles of his boots helped that. When he floated on his back he found if he simply sat in the water he would comfortably ride the current. He let all the air out of his waders and let them fill up with water. As he knew, his waders when filled with water weighed only the difference between their weight when dry and the weight of the water they displaced. His waders weighed only six pounds when dry and no matter how much water he let into them they weighed a lot less than six pounds submerged. Having proven his theory, he hoped his magazine story would put to rest the unproved theories held for years by guides that one would drown in waders.

Lee had written a letter to the Piper Aircraft Company suggesting that he do a 30 minute, 16 millimeter color and sound motion picture film about why a light, single-engine, pontoon-equipped float plane would be a boon to fishermen in the north woods, hoping the company might loan him a plane for the duration of the film-making. He figured the use of the plane for at least one season would really help him transport clients to some of his salmon camps as far away as Portland Creek and River Of Ponds. To his amazement and joy, Jake Miller, sales manager of Piper, agreed with his proposal and suggested, instead of paying in money for the project Lee take in exchange a J-3 Piper Cub. Lee was overcome with enthusiasm, but knew he would have to take flying lessons before he received the plane which was scheduled to arrive in early April.

He contacted an instructor, Lew Lavery, who had a flying school close to Schenectady at Round Lake, New York. Lavery worked with the Piper

Company and they delivered the float plane to Round Lake in early April. Lee stood looking at the bright yellow plane tied to a dock on the small lake, bobbing in the bright spring sunshine. She was beautiful. The plane was equipped with Edo floats and sported a 65 h.p. Continental engine. It was a dual-seater with a seat forward and aft. With dual controls a pilot could fly from either seat. It had a main 12-gallon tank and an auxiliary five gallon tank mounted in the wing above the cockpit. Her number was NC 6194H, she had a 36 foot wingspan and was covered with stretched fabric over an aluminum frame. Empty she weighed 725 pounds but with the floats on came to 1,400 pounds. The air speed was about 65 mph—the ground speed depending upon how fast the wind was flowing and from what direction.

Blessed with excellent reflexes and in good physical condition for 42 years of age, Lee took naturally to flying. He quickly learned landing and take-offs and soon was into more difficult maneuvers. He was not fond of power stalls as his stomach reacted to the sudden drops, but he soon learned everything—including spins. Lavery transferred him from the two-wheeled trainer to his J-3 Cub and soon he was making water landings and take-offs with ease. He passed the flight physical easily and in three weeks made his first cross-country flight and soloed. Even Lavery, a veteran flight instructor, was impressed with the speed and ease of Lee's progress. He did not realize how much Lee wanted to be flying over his salmon rivers.

On the morning of June 8th, Lee loaded his gear and bags into the Cub and took off from Round Lake on the first leg of his flight to Newfoundland. It was a beautiful morning and the countryside spread out lush and green below him as he headed for his first refueling stop at Lake Winnepesaukee, New Hampshire. Leaving in late morning he continued on to Waterville, Maine for more gas and then to Eastport, Maine where he cleared customs and stayed overnight.

The following morning he left early—in clear skies—and flew to St. John, New Brunswick where he went through customs again and headed to Sydney, Nova Scotia. Skirting the coast of New Brunswick in early afternoon Lee peered down at fishing boats and small harbors from an altitude of 1,000 feet, thrilling at the feel of the small plane and the way she reacted to the controls. With only 50 hours flying time under his belt—mostly over land—he nevertheless felt confident in his ability to fly. He was getting to the point where he felt a part of the plane.

The long, thin land of Nova Scotia stretched to the horizon on his right and he could make out the east coast where years before he and Helen had camped at Ecum Secum. Late in the afternoon he approached Sydney and flew over the northwest coast where he had caught his first salmon in the

Margaree River. Pilots reading this today may think this flight routine, but one must remember nobody flew tiny, single-engine planes in that part of the world in the 1940s—let alone over great stretches of water. There were no radar stations, few OMNI ranges and weather forecasts were unreliable. Winds were often 50 miles per hour or higher and came up suddenly. There were hardly any emergency landing strips anywhere and few places where a float plane pilot could find anchorage or gas. Even for two people flying together it would have been an awesome experience—let alone one man flying solo.

Lee filled his tanks at Sydney and carried two spare five gallon tanks on the seat beside him from which he could transfer 80 octane aviation gas with a hand pump in case he had to land. Too late to make the long crossing to Newfoundland in the late afternoon, Lee flew the 40 miles or so up to the tip of Nova Scotia and landed the small plane in a cove at Dingwall. It was nearly dark so Lee made himself a small campfire on the shore and cooked a meal. Excited at the thought of the 100 mile flight in the morning, he slept fitfully in his sleeping bag, a rope from the plane's pontoon wrapped around his wrist in case the plane moved from its mooring.

In the early light Lee could see the day would be overcast with a wind blowing from the east. He lifted off from the small cove at first light and set a heading of 60 degrees magnetic. As he climbed he could see whitecaps below him and, for the first time, began to wonder if the flight was a good idea. He had wired Ella from Sydney that he would land at Stephenville Air Base—which had reverted to the Newfoundland government after the war—sometime about midday.

There was an overcast and Lee leveled off at 1,000 feet. The wind buffeted the small plane and Lee tightened his safety belt trying to see some sign of land ahead. In a few minutes he made out the hazy shoreline of St. Paul's Island directly ahead. Spreading the aeronautical chart out on his lap, he knew he was at least on course so far.

Though he was confident that everything was working satisfactorily with the plane, he began to think the 65 h.p. motor was running very rough. It seemed to change pitch every few minutes and the sound of its running varied now and then. He had been told by pilots that every aircraft engine sounded rough over large stretches of water and not to worry about it. A World War I flight instructor, Billy Bruce, had earlier told him to have confidence in the engine. As long as the oil gauge read O.K. Billy had said, don't worry. The motor will run forever.

The southeast wind—though it was causing whitecaps below—was a tailwind and was carrying him along faster than his 65 mph reading on his air speed indicator led him to believe. On he flew in a gray world, surrounded by levels of white and gray clouds on all sides and with only the choppy sea below. Such a flight probably had never been made before in a small, private plane. Only military aircraft made such a crossing. Had Lee been a more cautious man, or less adventuresome, he might have flown up the coast of Quebec—far up to where he could make a short hop over water to Newfoundland—instead of trying to make a 100-mile crossing.

Finally, after an hour and 40 minutes of anxiously looking for signs of shore, Lee spotted the hazy outline of mountains ahead and moments later saw the coastline below. Breathing a huge sigh of relief, he turned left and flew up the coast, south of the Long Range Mountains, until he saw the town of Port aux Basques and the railroad that ran up the coast to Corner Brook and Stephenville—his destination.

Being new to flying distances, Lee had failed to file a flight plan to Stephenville Air Base and did not realize it was against aviation rules to land civilian planes at military fields. Coming into the stretch of water used by military seaplanes, he made a bad landing—bouncing once before settling down—and finally taxied up to the dock. A military policeman came to the dock to ask him what he was doing at a military installation and Lee was taken to the Officers Club for interrogation.

Fortunately for Lee he had been there before, during the war years, and was known to some of the personnel—Warrant Officer Dave Sawyer for one—who vouched for his identity. He was finally cleared with a warning about the correct procedure to land at military bases and released to fly on to his home at Corner Brook. Ella and her two sons, Jonathon and Tony, had driven down from their home to meet Lee at the base. There was a happy reunion and Lee was given permission to leave the Cub temporarily berthed at the base until he could find a permanent spot at which to dock it. Lee had not only become a pilot experienced at open water flying, but he now had the ideal way to get around in the Newfoundland wilderness.

That spring Lee was to set up tent camps on a number of rivers—the best at the Humber, Portland Creek and the River Of Ponds, but weather was still a problem when it came to getting clients in to them. Only one fisherman at a time could be flown in the Cub and many times it was a rough flight.

Ben Wright, the long-time publisher of *Field & Stream* and a fine fly fisherman, recalled one trip he made while public relations director of American Airlines in 1947. American, which had an overseas division and stopped for fuel at Gander, Newfoundland, had been carrying a group of newspapermen from New York on a week-long salmon fishing trip Ben had set up with Lee. The party put up at Ella's lodge at Bonne Bay before Lee would take them into the salmon camps. Unfortunately the weather turned stormy and the previous group of anglers were weathered-in at River Of Ponds until Lee could bring them out and the new group in.

"I had six nervous salmoneers biting their nails at the lodge," Ben recalled. "After two days of booze and gin rummy, I begged Lee's wife to figure out something to keep the lads happy. She cranked up a leaky cod boat, loaded the group aboard and took them out into the bay, of all things, jigging for cod. The group never let me forget that one!" he added.

But the disasters were few and far between and most of his clients had fine fishing—if not an enjoyable time with the mosquitoes and black flies. There were not many effective insect repellents in those days and a good smokey campfire was the best method of keeping them away. Helen had allowed the boys to come to Corner Brook for summer vacation and they got along well with Ella's two sons. Allan, the older and more adventuresome of the two, was interested in the fishing and especially in the Piper Cub. He was with Lee in the small plane as often as he was allowed and pestered Lee about learning to fly it. Barry, more interested in the camp and the other children, stayed closer to home.

Between flying his fishing clients to the various tent camps, Lee had time to explore new rivers from the air. His favorite river that summer was Western Brook which rises in Western Gorge in a long, narrow freshwater lake with sheer cliffs on both sides rising at least 2,500 feet vertically from the lake surface. Looking down from the Cub it was easy to see salmon and big trout lying in the clear water. There were small ponds along the river where Lee could land the cub and fish. From the air he could spot where the salmon were lying in the pools and taxi up to those spots.

It was a 90-mile boat trip from the lodge at Lommond up to the River Of Ponds and then 15 to 20 miles by dory to the fishing camp. It took nearly three days to reach the camp that way, but it was only 90 minutes for Lee to fly guests from the lodge to those same camps. Lee would fly to the upper reaches of the big river and land on ponds near the river's source—catching bright, fresh-run fish just in from the ocean.

Later in the summer he flew the Cub up the Blue Stream where it flowed into the big lake from Rocky Gulch and saw a sight that would be impossible to see from the ground. There were great black patches—from 5 to 8 feet wide and perhaps a hundred feet long—looking like rock outcroppings. They were salmon lying close together in a long line while they waited for the September rains to raise the river and allow them to reach their spawning grounds.

"The fishing was spectacular," he later wrote in *Outdoors*, "and it was all mine because any earthbound angler would have had too long and too tedious a journey to have reached that spot."

And the flying itself was fun. He flew, with Ella aboard, north to St. Anthony and circled the Strait of Belle Isle where the mainland of Labrador lies only nine miles from Newfoundland.

"I flew to go fishing," he wrote, "and I flew for the flying itself." In the December 1947 issue of *Outdoors*, he wrote:

"I flew over the mountains, sunlit and bright. I absorbed the beauty of the blue water—cupped in pale green marsh grass and darker evergreen. I flew through the valleys when they were gray with mist and rain. I learned to fly in the whistling winds that sweep in from the sea, to ride the updrafts and downdrafts as I picked my way across the blue-green map below me. I drew deep pleasure in flying safely over the fluffy headlands, looking down to the swirls and rosettes the wind patterned on the water, thinking as I flew that some of those dark, windswept canyons would be a severe test for a pilot and a plane should he ever have to enter them.

"My plane was like the average man's car. When I wanted to go somewhere I climbed in and flew there," he wrote.

When the summer ended and the boys went back to school, Lee and Ella decided Lee had much to do about his promotion in the States and his contacts with magazines and film companies and that he should spend a couple of months there. He would come back when he had finished his business. Ella could take care of herself, Lee knew.

Leaving Stephenville at noon one day when the birches were yellowing on the mountain slopes, Lee made the 100-miles cross—this time with ease—and landed at Sydney for gas and spent the night at New Glasgow. Just for old times sake, he flew on the next day and landed at Wedgeport—the sight of his tuna fishing days. He took up one of the boat captains with whom he had fished years before and they watched the tuna fleet below in the waters of the great rip.

He spent two days fishing for the big bluefins and caught a 685 pound fish the first day and two fish the second—a 595 pound and 464 pound fish. The next day he took off and flew to Eastport to clear customs. The U.S. agent there told him he had heard that Lee had crashed the previous spring and was killed. So much for rumors, Lee thought. By the time Lee reached Round Lake and taxied up to the small dock, he felt as safe in the Cub as he did in his own car.

The Salmon Camp Years

In the States, Americans were complaining about post-war prices and there was a severe housing shortage. Overseas the Marshall Plan was earning the gratitude of European nations and the chief concern of the U.S. seemed to be Communists in government positions. President Harry Truman issued an executive order banning Communists from holding offices in the administrative branch of the government.

Lee—with the boys back in school in Rochester—took the time to visit editors of the outdoor magazines in New York to keep up his contacts. Not that he wasn't doing well with his writing and photography. Tap Tapply alone had bought dozens of stories from his fishing editor and other editors of what were called the "Big Three" of outdoor magazines, *Field & Stream, Outdoor Life* and *Sports Afield*, were more and more interested in Lee's Newfoundland experiences. *Field & Stream* Editor-in-Chief Hugh Grey bought half a dozen stories on trout and salmon fishing and Bill Rae, Editor of *Outdoor Life* suddenly discovered Lee also. It would only be a year or so before he began placing stories in *Sports Afield*—the third of the best-paying outdoor publications.

During the fall months Lee had to fill a number of speaking engagements at sporting clubs and had managed to schedule a few showings of his new hunting and fishing films. He was becoming well-known. His books were selling steadily and he had high hopes of publishing, in a few years, a definitive book on salmon fishing, which he had been writing whenever he could find time.

Late fall 1947 he was invited to come down to the Florida Keys to try for bonefish on flies. Dave Meyers of Tycoon Tackle wanted Lee to discover what was becoming a very popular fly rod sport. Lee, eager to get in as many hours flying as he could, flew the J-3 Cub down the east coast to Miami where he picked up Dave.

He was soon to find a new and exciting fishing world which he had never expected. Though he had caught bluefin tuna on the big tackle, he was to become fascinated with the flats, knee-deep water in which dwelled some of the finest game fish in the world—tarpon, bonefish, permit and barracuda. Flying over Grassy Key, he saw for the first time the flashing of tailing bonefish schools. Landing in shallow water and wading from where the Cub was tied to mangrove roots, he and Meyers stalked and cast flies at the slim, silvery torpedoes which have so captured the imagination of fly rodders over the years.

Lee was amazed at the speed of hooked fish and later wrote in a 1982 story for *Rod & Reel*: "That first surging run of a healthy bonefish on a shallow flat is something to remember . . . "

Lee thought he was one of the very first to catch bonefish on a fly, but there had been a lot of unsung fly rodders who had caught them years earlier, including professional Islamorada guides Bill Smith and his wife Bonnie. Bill had taken a bonefish on a fly in 1938 and earlier that year Joe Brooks had taken two 8-pound bonefish on a fly while fishing with veteran guide Jimmie Albright at Islamorada.

Nevertheless that trip introduced Lee to a sport he was to follow all his life. He was later to learn well the myriad forms of life on a bonefish flat and grow to love the peace and serenity of fishing amid the stalking shore birds, circling gulls, pelicans and man-o-war birds.

He returned to Corner Brook for the holiday season where he and Ella laid out plans to expand the facilities at both the lodge and the camps. Fierce winds battered the Newfoundland coast off the Gulf of St. Lawrence and much of the country was buried beneath ice and snow, but Lee knew salmon were already beginning to search out the faint taste of their home waters in the huge sea.

He flew the J-3 Cub back to Newfoundland in late May quite confident of being able to handle the long trip with ease. Lee established his first camp at Portland Creek because of the convenience for his visiting anglers. The river was only slightly more than a mile long, but contained some of the biggest salmon in all of Newfoundland. It was relatively easy to reach fish from the tent camp. Lee had used up just about all his money building up the camp, plus paying for land on both sides of the railroad, with a 35 foot right of way. Lee, Ella and the guides had constructed wood frame beds, covered with ever-green boughs, to serve as beds inside the big tents.

Most of his clients flew from the States to the big base at Gander and then took the railroad to Corner Brook. They would stay in Ella's lodge until Lee could fly them into the main base at Portland Creek or to auxiliary camps—such as the one at River Of Ponds. Lee had no trouble getting good guides from Lommond and Portland Creek. Most were good woodsmen and trappers and knew survival well. Almost all of them were lobstermen and cod fisher-men in the winter months and knew everything from carpentry to how to bake excellent bread. They ranged from 70-year-old Arthur Perry, who taught Lee the Portland Hitch, to young men in their 20s. They were independent people and used to long weeks in the wilderness alone. The only word they received from the outside world during the long winter months was from the Gerald A. Doyle newscasts each day on their small radios.

Lee established—with Allan's help—a heavy anchor and buoy arrange-ment to hold the Cub offshore. They were not able to keep her tied ashore because of the 6 to 8 foot daily rise and fall of the tide. Other guides were Herb and Oscar Perry, both excellent fishermen themselves. Herb's wife became the camp cook at Portland Creek and many a salmon fisherman remembered her in later years with great fondness because of her meals.

Lee later flew to George's Bay to pick up his old friend and guide Jack Young to act as chief guide. Jack trained the newer guides and helped modernize the camp over the next several years. They built permanent cabins and even put in sliding glass windows. Lee and Ella began to feel as though the business was going to provide them with a decent income. All four young boys spent the sum-mers with them and though the two Wulff boys had to return to the States for school each fall they eagerly looked forward to the coming spring.

Though the camps were coming along well, Lee had problems with local poachers and there didn't seem much he could do about it. The new govern-ment—Newfoundland had just become a province of Canada in 1948—had no game wardens to spare for the west coast. The general attitude on the part of local people—hardy souls who had grown up taking all they could from the sea and rivers—was that the salmon, trout, cod and lobsters belonged to them. Their total lack of understanding or concern for conservation dismayed Lee, but there was one ray of sunshine on the otherwise bleak horizon that year. A group of concerned salmon anglers in Quebec had banded together to form the Atlantic Salmon Association. They were concerned by the fact that in Newfoundland, as well as in other areas such as Nova Scotia, commercial netting interests were taking 85 percent of the salmon each year. Sport anglers accounted for only 15 percent of the take. Lee, encouraged at the prospect that someone finally was beginning to see the danger to salmon, wrote to the secretary-treasurer, F. Stuart Molson, for more information.

The summer of 1949 went even better for the camps. Lee's public relations campaign in U.S. magazines was beginning to pay off. His bookings began to jump to 10 to 12 anglers a week and the camps were buzzing with activity. Allan learned how to fly the Cub that summer, but had a long way to go before he could fly it alone. Barry, always the more social of the two, made dozens of new friends in the nearby camps and spent more time with his chums at Angus Bennett's general store in Daniel's Harbor Pond. In fact he was so generous to his buddies that he ran up a $100 charge account for candy and sodas—which did not amuse Lee.

Black flies and mosquitoes were always a nuisance to the anglers and guests, but Lee did not suffer much after learning a trick taught him by Arthur Perry. Arthur, who completely ignored black fly bites, told Lee the secret was to let them bite him until he developed an immunity to them. It was difficult, Lee wrote later, but he let the bugs bite him for several days—not slapping at them at all. He said he felt faint and nauseated for several days, but after that the black flies would bite him, leave a red spot—which in a few minutes turned into a black spot—and after that the bites did not bother him. The local people did not seem to be bothered by black flies and Lee assumed they had all developed a natural immunity over the years.

That summer Lee was able to spend more time with his sons—teaching them woodcraft and much about nature. Barry said they would sit beneath a tree as Lee explained the ways of birds, animals and fish. The year before Barry discovered there were no frogs in Newfoundland, so in early spring he kept half a dozen he caught near Shushan and smuggled them in in one of the Cub's pontoons. They were released into the bogs near camp.

The boys discovered Lee had a practical-joke-type sense of humor they had not seen before. He would load the boys into the Cub in the evening and take off toward the west. The sun would be going down over the Gulf of St. Lawrence and Lee would wait until the sun was low on the horizon then drop down just over the surface of the water. Local fishermen and their families would be gathered on the shore—after the day's fishing—and could see almost nothing looking into the setting sun. Lee would come swooping in from the sea and, with a great roar as he changed the propeller pitch, would "buzz" the crowds. It always came as a sudden shock and surprise to them and Lee would roar with laughter as he pulled up into a climbing turn over the town.

Weather forecasts came in each day with the Doyle newscasts, but were never too reliable. The weather for each locality was given, but they were always about the same. Long distance forecasting was not available. Gasoline for the Cub was never a problem—though good aviation gas was scarce. The boat fuel used locally was ACTO gasoline and Naptha was used for ordinary appliances and some generators. Lee used Blue Gas which was almost 80 Octane and had washed ashore during the war after a British Navy ship had been torpedoed by a German submarine in the Strait of Belle Isle. Fortunately it had floated in 50-gallon drums and was available for years after the conflict.

Medical care became available that year when a doctor, Noel Murphy, took up residence at Corner Brook and locals even had a nurse. She was English and the wife of Angus Bennett, who owned the store at Daniel's Harbor Pond. Lee by that time had accumulated a collection of excellent guides—some of them characters. There was the giant—Edgar House, a 6 foot, 3 inch man who weighed 320 pounds. An antagonistic guest, a former boxer, once threatened to punch him in the nose for dropping his bag on a cabin floor.

"Now, Sir," Edgar said, "that would be a two-handed job."

And there was Isaac Biggins who after watching an inept angler fish for a day with poor results told Lee, "That man won't live long enough to catch a salmon."

Lee had completed the 16 mm sound and color film for Piper during the winter and the company was very pleased with the results. Allan had helped Lee with the photography and had become quite good at it himself.

But not everything ran smoothly. There were clashes between the guides and clients. Most guides did not read or write and some of the more educated fly fishermen found it annoying to deal with them. Lee was constantly moderating disputes. There was local resentment about a foreigner making money off Newfoundland and many local anglers thought Lee was "taking fish away from the public with his private camps." Lee was discriminated against, he thought, when the government charged him duty on everything he brought into the camps—stoves, tractors, trucks, glass and tools—while the locals could import everything for free.

The biggest irritation Lee suffered was the poaching. Locals thought it their right to take as many of "their" salmon as they wished. Lee finally got a game warden, Fred Guinchard, assigned to the area, but—though he was honest and worked hard—he didn't make much progress against poachers.

One teen-age boy, related to one of Lee's guides, foul-hooked 17 salmon in one of Lee's pools but nobody thought it much of a crime. Lee, furious, flew to St. Johns and brought back a judge who fined the boy and his father $100.

Not only did the locals cut every one of the camp's birch trees down that winter for revenge, but the boy was appointed warden of the area the next year. He did nothing to stop the poaching and never came near Lee's camps.

Among Lee's clients that summer were two old friends and pilots from the Shushan area—FAA Inspector Al Nogard and Okey Butcher—who sold animal scents. Both were excellent fly fishermen and Okey an expert fly-tier. They caught lots of salmon and Okey won $10 from a skeptical guide who swore a salmon would never take one of Okey's large bucktail flies. They had made the trip up in an Aeronca Chief.

(Left to right) Allan, Lee and Barry in Lee's salmon camp at Corner Brook, Newfoundland in 1950.

By the end of the season Lee figured the guides had never made as much money in their lives and most of his clients had gone home satisfied with the fishing. He flew the boys back to school in early September and went to work on his book, *The Atlantic Salmon*, which A.S. Barnes Co. of New York had agreed to publish.

Harry S. Truman was re-elected President in an upset that fall defeating New York's Governor Thomas E. Dewey. Books that year included, *The Naked and The Dead* by Norman Mailer and Dwight D. Eisenhower's *Crusade in Europe*. The first Polaroid Land Cameras went on sale.

Lee made his tour of illustrated lectures and was writing nearly full time by the time he was ready to return to the camps. He flew both boys back and they were ready to enjoy their third summer at Portland Creek. Everything went well until late August when an early season hurricane moved up from Nova Scotia. Lee and the crew tied down everything they could except the yellow Piper Cub which was moored just off the beach.

They were preparing to fasten her down with long ropes and stakes when the radio announced that the hurricane was veering off to sea and would by-pass Newfoundland. After dinner they went to bed, only to awaken in the middle of the night with gale winds tearing up the camp. By the time they reached the Cub it was upside down in the saltwater—her pontoons sticking up from the sea. She was a total wreck and Lee was devastated.

He called his friend Al Nogard and Al found Lee an inexpensive, second hand J-3 Cub with wheels, but before that could be fitted with the wrecked Cub's pontoons, he flew over an Aeronca Sedan—a 4-place, single-engine plane that had a big cabin and a 125 h.p. Continental engine. The plane had a wheel instead of a stick for control and not only did it have landing lights but an electric starter, too, Lee would no longer have to climb out on the pontoons to spin the prop to start the plane.

The bigger wing surface gave Lee better lift, but a slower—40 mph—take-off speed. He was now able to carry three fishermen and himself to the camps instead of the previous one. He was happy with the new plane, but it had a few kinks he would discover to his sorrow. Flying one Sunday morning with his old friend, salmon fly fisherman Neil Marvin and his new wife, Connie, the Aeronca suddenly quit flying after taking off from the water at the River Of Ponds.

Lee almost crashed into a line of trees, but remembered in time that a little gas is always left in the lines when a motor quits. He pushed the primer and barely got enough lift from the engine to make a safe landing. Gas had to be carried in the next day on the back of a guide. On later inspection they found that the cap to a wing tank had been left off and that all the gas had been siphoned out of his neoprene tanks when they collapsed empty inside the wings.

Not a month later Lee was about to take-off near a saltwater breakwater in fairly high wind carrying two anglers, Keith Kennert and Bud Norris, when he went to turn into the wind, because of the Sedan's peculiar design, Lee sunk a pontoon, a wing tip caught a wave and the plane flipped upside down. Everyone got out safely but the plane had to be towed to shore. Lee thought the plane too, would be a total loss, but Al Nogard sent an excellent mechanic, Gene Geunther, over and they righted the plane. Gene took the engine apart and carefully assembled the parts. She worked beautifully and Al flew the plane back to the States where it was later sold.

Al flew the second J-3 Cub to Portland Creek where they put the old pontoons on her. The little plane was painted bright red and she was immediately named "Rudolph" for the red-nosed reindeer. Though it flew well, Lee never had the confidence he did with his beloved yellow Cub. Perhaps because of the angle of prop pitch, she did not get off as quickly and her speed was not quite as fast.

One night at the end of the season sitting on the porch of a cabin at Portland Creek, Lee and Ella decided their marriage wasn't working and that they should go their own ways, remaining friends. Lee never explained to anyone what the reason was, but later said she wanted to become more involved with running her own Inn. They talked about the boys and the camps and what they might do with their own lives. Lee later said it reminded him of the Cole Porter song:

"If we thought a bit, at the start of it . . . "

But he also said later a friend of his told him:

"If you knew one-tenth as much about women as you do fish, you'd have a happy life."

Lee sent the boys home to school by ground transportation and flew the red Cub alone to the States. Because he didn't have full confidence in the plane, he skipped the long over-water crossing and flew down the lengthy coast of Quebec to the U.S. The trip took him 8 days instead of the usual three.

Hope for the Salmon

The summer of 1952 was the best season so far and the camps were humming with activity. Jack Young organized the best carpenters among the guides and they installed hot showers in some of the cabins and even a refrigerator in the main kitchen. Using a new tractor Lee lengthened the runway to 3,000 feet and they could now handle planes up to the size of a DC-3—the old "Goony Bird" of World War II days.

Barry, almost 13, was now trusted enough to drive a white camp pickup truck and was promoted to full-time camp helper. Allan, now 16, was so adept at flying that Lee purchased a used J-3 Cub and allowed Allan to help carry gear and supplies. Allan couldn't wait until he could get his license at age 17.

With the 3,000 foot runway they were now able to accommodate planes in the twin-engine category and more and more private planes were being flown in. Companies hearing about the marvelous salmon fishing were using corporate planes to fly in company fly fishermen. Lee, however, was increasingly concerned with the damage to the salmon population. Of the 2,000 salmon rivers in Newfoundland, almost none had fishing compared to a few years earlier. He complained to the officials in St. Johns, but got nowhere with the bureaucrats who were far more concerned with the commercial return of salmon than angling uses.

In September Lee flew the Piper to Montreal for the September 15th conference of the newly-formed Atlantic Salmon Association. He had been corresponding with Stuart Molson, the secretary-treasurer, and realized the group was thoroughly aware of the problem confronting the salmon. At the meeting he met Stewart Bates, deputy minister of fisheries at Ottowa, and was delighted to find someone in the Canadian government who shared his concern for the salmon.

He attended the meetings and found out—due to pressure from the ASA—the government for the first time had increased sea patrols for the purpose of inspecting salmon nets. He read a report, prepared by W. J. Menzies, on "The Present Position Of The Atlantic Salmon Fisheries of Canada" and was impressed at the scientific approach to the problem. Later he met Percy Nobbs, Editor of the *Atlantic Salmon Journal,* who had just put out the second issue of the organization's house organ. Nobbs was delighted that a man who knew so much about salmon fishing and had the writing background Lee did, would consent to writing for the publication. Lee promised to contribute to upcoming issues.

Flying the Piper back to Shushan, Lee for the very first time realized he could channel his talents in one direction to aid his beloved salmon. Unfortunately, there was no such organization in the States to which he could belong. There had been some talk about re-introducing salmon into the Connecticut River, no longer as polluted as it had been, and a few Maine rivers were being considered for salmon restoration projects—the Dennys, the Narraguagus and the Sheepscot.

Somewhat to his surprise during the winter of 1952-53, Lee found he was becoming a celebrity in trout and salmon circles. Much of that was due to his writing and lecturing, but his camps had become internationally-known for the best salmon fishing around.

He was invited to give a series of talks at the prestigious Anglers Club in New York City in February 1953. At the first one, on February 5th, he told a standing-room-only crowd of anglers that he had caught salmon on reel and line without using a rod—the line held in his hand. That got their attention.

"The strength of the leader and the skill of the angler," he told them, "govern the play of the fish, not the rod. A heavy weight can be cast with a light rod providing the timing is perfect," he said—adding that he used a 2-ounce, 6 1/2 foot rod.

Against all prevailing tradition, he told them he does not stop his rod at 12 o'clock on the back cast, but brings it all the way back to the horizontal. He emphasized that perfect timing is essential. By this time the room was dead quiet.

On fighting salmon, he cautioned, "Slack will not lose a fish except, occasionally, toward the end of the fight when the hook hole becomes worn . . . " He urged them to use psychology on trout or salmon. "Fish think," he said, "if you can convince him that he hasn't a chance, he will give up a lot sooner."

Lee told them he marked his fly line with half-inch rings of black paint at 40, 50 and 60 foot so that when he moved a fish or it swung at the fly and missed, he could gauge the exact length of the cast and, after resting the fish, cast to the same spot again. He also told them that he preferred single-hook flies to double-hooked ones but said he always carried a few smaller double-hooked ones because they have a different silhouette from a single of the same pattern.

"I don't worry much about pattern," Lee said, causing a near-stroke for the many guests in the audience who had spent a fortune on flies, "it is mostly a matter of presentation."

In discussing dry-fly fishing, Lee emphasized the principle of using different *types* rather than *patterns* of dry flies to give a variety of appeals, and the importance of using types of flies which the fish are not used to.

He classified salmon dry-fly types as standard flies, spiders, bivisibles, skaters, Wulffs, the Jennings stonefly type and what he called the beetle type. With the variety of fly types he also uses variety of presentation, casting alternately on the nose and 6 feet ahead of a fish that has shown some interest, varying this with one or two casts 40 feet ahead.

"If I miss a fish I put the fly right back over him once or twice and if he does not respond, I rest him and fish for another fish. But if they are all in a lump together," he said, "it pays sometimes to pound them steadily."

As to why salmon take, Lee said that the way they take a fly shows they are not feeding, there could not be food enough in the stream to support such huge fish, anyway. Part of it is a remembered conditioned reflex, he thought, but most of it was simply the joy of living, the expression of vigor and prowess and the strengthening sex stimulation in a powerful fish cooped up in narrow quarters.

"I have never found a stream," he said and was quoted in a 1953 issue of the *Angler's Club Bulletin*, "in which the dry fly will not work, and I have taken fish on it almost as soon as they entered the river."

For the "purists" in the audience, he had some advice.

"In salmon fishing," he said, "you are not dealing with salmon but with a salmon, the one foolish fish out of perhaps a dozen which shows interest in your fly. You are dealing with an individual. There are no rules of dry fly fishing that cannot be violated; there is no one way."

Mac Francis, an old friend of Lee's, and a club member, said he was treated

Lee, a bluefin tuna and his second float plane—a Super Cub—in 1955.

to a standing ovation and invited back to speak on February 11, 1953. Lee did two more talks that month and became a regular member.

The year 1953 was the last year Lee and the boys were satisfied with the way things were going, and even by the end of that season Lee was disgusted with the damage being inflicted on the salmon and trout. He had established a camp far up north on the Castor's River, but the poachers had ruined the fishing. One of his guides stole a valuable knife from the baggage of a client—causing Lee to fire the man—but what really soured him on the summer was the wholesale foul-hooking of both trout and salmon at the river.

On August 2nd, Lee decided to let Allan make his required cross-country flight. With his student's pilot license, Allan was allowed to fly solo, but was not allowed to carry passengers until he got his regular license when he was 17. Lee chose a flight from Portland Creek to Hawke River, Labrador—a round-trip of 500 miles. He flew the Pacer and Allan flew the silver and blue J-3 Cub.

They left at 6 a.m. and the weather was fair—some scattered clouds. Lee was forced to make periodic circles to keep the Cub in sight as his speed was far greater than that of the little plane. He could not slow down to the Cub's speed without heating up. They stopped at Pinware Lake to make a cache of gasoline for later use and went on. The wind picked up considerably but both planes slid into the cove at Hawke's Bay with no trouble. The flight back was also uneventful and Allan landed the Cub in 8 hours with a total now of 36 hours of solo time. Lee was very proud of him.

Allan was quite the celebrity in his home town of Rochester by the end of the summer. The Rochester *Times Union* in a September 1st story, ran a long story of his flying career. There was a large photo accompanying the story of his mother Helen, his brother Barry, a neighbor friend, Roger Hoadley, and himself sitting at the controls of the silver and blue Cub. He had just flown the Cub back from Newfoundland solo and the newspaper, rightly, considered it unusual enough for a major feature piece. The story said Lee and Barry had made the flight alongside Allan in the Pacer.

Allan, who attended East High School in Rochester, would be 17 in February. Barry was 13 at the time of the story.

It was difficult, but Lee had decided, without talking about it to anyone, that he would sell the camps. He knew they were becoming well-known and figured the time was ripe to get a good price for the operation. He could see the handwriting on the wall and knew the salmon were in trouble in Newfoundland. He didn't want to be a part of seeing the sport of salmon angling die in his adopted land. He had his eye on some exploration further north, in Labrador, and thought perhaps the future—at least for a time—of salmon fishing, might lie there. He put out some feelers through business friends who told him they would let him know if anything came up. Frank Frazee, a partner in helping him finance the camps—and an old friend— agreed they should try for a buyer.

Lee was surprised when he was contacted that winter by Great Lakes Carbon Company which agreed to pay him his asking price if he agreed to stay on as manager at a salary he could not turn down. He figured he could work a year or so at the job and with the money he had made on the sale of the camps, plus his salary, he would have enough for a nest egg. He had recently been introduced to a woman, Kay Gillette, by Frazee, and was seeing quite a bit of her whenever he could get back to Shushan. Kay, a striking, auburn-haired beauty, was living in Wingstead, Connecticut and Lee was quite smitten with her that year.

The summer of 1954 saw considerably more improvements to the camps and by August they were handling as many as 30 anglers a week. They employed several more pilots—some were corporate pilots of Great Lakes Carbon—and even Allan, with a pilot's license, was hired. By the end of the season, Lee was ready to move on, but agreed to serve as manager one more year until the owners were satisfied the camps would run well without him.

Jack Randolph, Outdoor Editor of the New York Times and Lee and Lee's plane in 1958.

In the summer of 1955, Lee signed a contract with the Newfoundland Tourist Bureau to make a color and sound film on bow hunting for moose and caribou. Instead of using the Pacer—which was too fast to land on the rivers and ponds Lee wanted to explore—Lee made another deal with the Piper Company and they traded him a new Piper Super Cub to use for the job. It was yellow—like his old J-3 Cub—but was a far more powerful plane. It had a 150 h.p. Lycoming engine, two 18-gallon wing tanks and would cruise at 95 mph while equipped with floats. It had flaps which allowed Lee to land in a much shorter distance and take-off flaps that got him off the water quickly. With an auxiliary tank in the baggage compartment Lee had a 700 mile range to play with now.

So at the end of his summer at the camps Lee was free to explore Labrador—at the same time making his hunting film. Lee, unmarried since his 1949 divorce from Ella, had decided the single life was not for him. He and Kay were married quietly and Lee hardly told anyone about it except for a few close friends like Neil Marvin, Okey Butcher and Frank Frazee. Allan and Barry were attending Kent's Hill, a prep school in Maine, and were not due to graduate until 1957. Of course Lee told his mother, Lilly, who was back living in San Diego and she was pleased.

Reading his September issue of the *Atlantic Salmon Journal,* Lee was startled to see that almost all of Canada had experienced a poor salmon season. At the same time he was relieved to see members of the Atlantic Salmon Association realized the salmon were in trouble and planned to do something about it.

"Probably at no period," said an editorial in that issue of the *Journal*, "of the Atlantic salmon fisheries have the threats of impending crisis set off so many alarm bells. To many it represents a preview of what happens when a rich and traditional resource reaches the verge of final surrender."

Lee had been in constant correspondence with the salmon association, reporting at great length the conditions on Newfoundland rivers. The association was extremely grateful to have Lee on the scene in Newfoundland as they were never sure of getting factual reports of the angling situation from officials in St. Johns. Lee's reports that year to the association were no more cheerful than reports from other provinces of Canada. He promised to survey conditions in Labrador and report back to the association.

That winter Lee decided that he could make hunting and fishing films on a full-time basis. With the money he had made from the sale of the camps and two year's worth of salary, he had enough money to support himself for a couple of years if he were frugal in his spending. He had learned a great deal about photography—both still and motion pictures—and was not worried about his ability in those fields. He was selling magazine pieces on a regular basis and had sent out any number of queries on new stories on Labrador. All the editors he queried were enthusiastic about his upcoming plans for Labrador coverage.

Lee knew he could count on one film a year for Newfoundland and he had been talking to some people at CBS who thought there was the possibility of using some of Lee's films for an upcoming sportsman's program they had in mind.

His first year of flying the Labrador bush—1956—was a tough one. Labrador was far more remote than Newfoundland and the combination of uncertain weather and great distances caused Lee to ponder the wisdom of his choice. However, he found some marvelous new rivers, ponds and lakes and discovered not only great salmon fishing but unbelievable trout fishing— huge brook trout in many lakes. There were even some lakes and ponds with an abundance of northern pike which Lee could take on big streamers.

He realized he might be able to do the same thing for the military people stationed in that remote land as he had done for the military in Newfoundland during the war—provide them hunting and fishing recreation on a contract basis. He made two good films that fall and was making plans for more the coming year when Newfoundland's Tourist Board had a budget problem. It meant no films for 1957. Lee would have to depend upon his military connections.

Both Allan and Barry graduated from Kent's Hill in 1957 and both decided to get their military obligations out of the way before college. Allen ended up being assigned to Panama for a 3-year hitch and Barry ended up as a radar specialist in Pittsburgh for the same period of time. Lee had been pushing hard on his book and it finally came out in 1958—an excellent job. *The Atlantic Salmon,* published by A.S. Barnes Co., was the definitive book on the subject. In a large format and 222 pages, it was well illustrated by Lee's black and white photographs and good line drawings. It was destined to go into three printings by the late 1960s and was well-received everywhere. Kay had been a great help to Lee and the book the last several years and he dedicated it to her.

The *Atlantic Salmon Journal* published the first story from Lee in their December, 1959 issue, "Common Blunders Of The Salmon Angler" in which Lee summed up all the things not to do in fly fishing for salmon. The new editor, Robson Black, a salmon angler himself, was delighted with the piece and urged Lee to submit more. Lee's salmon book was also well-reviewed by the *Journal*.

Lee's flight to Labrador—really a part of Newfoundland, but considerably larger and farther north than the main island on which Lee had been living and working since 1937—was a rough one. Battered by ferocious winds he was constantly forced to land in some remote pond or river to await the falling of the winds. Much more remote and rugged a terrain than the island, snow was present in many spots as late as July each year and great outcroppings of rock protruded everywhere.

Goose Bay Air Force Base was a sprawling military installation on a gravel plain at the mouth of the Churchill River which flowed into Groswater Bay. Stationed there were 10,000 U.S. troops and 2,000 Canadian soldiers and air-men. The base was a huge radar point on the great network of radar stations that protected the U.S. and Canada from the north. On October 4,1957 the Russians had launched Sputnik, the world's first earth satellite and the U.S. was startled to learn of the Russian's progress in space technology. As a result of the scientific leap, tensions had grown in the Cold War.

Lee now had a radio in the Super Cub and was able to contact Goose Bay before he landed. The land of bogs and outcroppings spread out beneath him from an altitude of 2,500 feet and icebergs could be seen dotting the Sea of Labrador offshore. Lee quickly made friends with the base commander and officers assigned to recreation. Outside of the frequent entertainers flown in by the USO, there was little for the personnel to do in their off-duty time. There was no fishing close to the base and to find a spot, Lee discovered, would mean a 30 mile or more flight from the base. The Newfoundland gov-ernment did not allow hunting in Labrador outside of the citizens who depended upon wildlife for subsistence. So it was up to Lee to establish camps on the various rivers and find a way to get the military personnel there.

The Air Force had only one camp set up for recreational fishing at what Lee called "No-Name Lake." Lee flew in several of the recreational officers and found there were great numbers of huge brook trout. They made plans to set up permanent recreational camps. Word spread through the military "rumor mill" and it was not long before a general officer flew in a party of officer cronies and caught 250 of the big trout and carted them down to Washington, D.C. Lee complained to Chief of Staff General Thomas White who issued an order that there would be no more of that. Lee had made a life-long friend in "Tommy" White.

Lee explored further and found the Minipi Valley where there were brook trout galore in the 5-6 pound category. He convinced the military to set up camps and enforce a 2-fish per day limit.

The Canadian forces had a camp established above the falls on the Eagle River where the fishing was excellent. Lee found there was good fishing for salmon on the Sandhill River, where a small camp could be established. But, like Newfoundland, he found the same problem—netters. The rivers empty-ing into the Sea of Labrador were strewn with nets during the salmon runs each year. There were even ships lying offshore with nets—highly illegal—but the place was so remote nobody seemed to care about enforcement.

A boat, the S.S. *Blue Peter*, hung offshore and salmon could be iced-down there for shipment. At the mouth of the Eagle River there were, embedded in cement, huge iron rods to which one could fasten nets for in-coming salmon. Lee found, and reported to the Atlantic Salmon Association, that most of the nets were of the small mesh type. Big salmon could only push themselves through far enough to get their gills hung up and get caught. The small salmon were able to push through and as a result most of these rivers produced only small salmon.

For the seasons of 1956 to 1958 Lee had been employed by the Newfoundland government the same way he had been in World War II—working with the military for recreational fishing. He came to know Tommy White well and he and the fly fishing general explored many of the remote northern rivers together, such as the huge Maccovic in northern Labrador. He was writing stories on Labrador for all the outdoor publications and had taken the time here to make some excellent sound and color films on the country. Three of the best were "The Way It Was—Angling In Newfoundland," "Three Trout To Dream About—Minipi Discovery" and "Soliloquy To Salmon." He showed these to U.S. sporting clubs and they were warmly received.

Lean and fit from months outdoors and tanned by the sun and winds, Lee looked every bit the outdoorsman he was. His hair—always left militarily short—was now beginning to turn gray and it gave him a distinguished look. At 54 he was still able to walk a salmon river—breasting the strong currents in waders—and he could still run on the tundra when necessary carrying heavy camera equipment.

In the spring of 1959 the Newfoundland government—still his best employer—commissioned Lee to do a study of trout and salmon in Labrador. They wanted to use it for tourism. Lee was happy to do so since the Atlantic Salmon Association also wanted to know as much as possible about the Labrador rivers and the condition of the salmon there.

He was writing on a regular basis now for the *Atlantic Salmon Journal* and was highly regarded by the officers of that organization. Lee was flattered when, in late 1959 Robson Black, editor of the *Journal* told him in some con-fidence he was being considered for a position on the Board of Directors of the huge salmon association. Reader replies in the Letters-to-the-Editor col-umn were running high on Lee's regular stories, the editor said, and it was becoming generally known among salmon anglers that few people had more experience with, and knowledge of, Atlantic salmon than Lee. By now Lee was convinced his mission in life, besides his writing and photography, was to save the Atlantic salmon as a game fish. He knew a way to do this would come to him.

That year he was fascinated, as an engineer, with the concept of the Borland Fish-Lift—a unique fish ladder that would allow salmon to safely by-pass hydroelectric dams and reach their spawning grounds. The lift had been designed by a Scotsman, J.H.T Borland of Kilmarnock, Scotland and 24 of them had been successfully installed on rivers in Scotland, Ireland and Wales.

By late 1960 Lee had completed his exhaustive study of Labrador's trout and salmon rivers. He turned it in with numerous recommendations—among them that Newfoundland set aside sanctuaries for salmon and trout, such as at the Minipi Valley—so that future generations might see such great fish. The government took the suggestions under advisement.

"Dear Lee," wrote P. J. Murray, Deputy Minister of Resources, "I have been through your report and may say that I think it will be very useful to us. As a matter of fact we are now preparing a submission to Government, on the basis of it, looking for a decision to establish a definite policy toward Labrador sport fishing . . ."

The letter went on to ask for more information on such things as Lee's recommendation for special licenses for particular areas. Lee completed that and billed the government $3,000 for the study—a considerable sum for those days. Lee had decided his future was in producing outdoor films. Perhaps, with luck, some of his films would result in educating people on how to conserve the salmon. In 1960 his marvelous film on the trout at Minipi had been purchased by CBS and became the first outdoor film on the "CBS Sports Spectacular," to be shown on network television. As the year 1961 arrived, Lee was too busy to fly his beloved bush anymore and decided making outdoor films was now to be his life's work. As though to crown his resolve, he was made a director of the Atlantic Salmon Association—a post he had only dreamed of holding.

Barry, after giving up hope of becoming a big league baseball player, enrolled in the State University of New York and began his studies to become a biologist. Allan, not sure what he wanted to be yet, enrolled in the University of Colorado at Boulder, then transferred to Berkeley in California a year later. Lee, as he had promised both sons, continued to pay for their basic college education. He had told them years before that he would pay for their four years. After receiving their BA's if they wanted to go on with graduate work, it would be up to them to do it on their own.

Television Years

Lee, who fished for salmon with a tiny 6 foot, 1-3/4 ounce bamboo fly rod from 1952, constantly wrote about the way he fished. He had been given a 7 foot, 2-1/4 ounce bakelite-impregnated fly rod designed for him by Wes Jordan of Orvis in Manchester, Vermont in May of 1946.

But before that he had used a 9 foot, two-piece bamboo fly rod.

"The nine foot, two-piece, five strip impregnated rod," he once wrote, "was made for me by Union Hardware, for whom I was doing rod and other consulting work at the time. The rod was made in 1938 or 1939. The strips were made at Union and sent to my friend Fred Longacre of Yonkers who invented the impregnating (bakelite) process which was later taken over . . . by Orvis. Then the strips, were sent back to Union who finished the rod for me. I used it mostly for bass-bugging, although I caught salmon on it before I went to lighter rods."

Everyone who knew Lee well watched him do demonstrations and catch fish with the tiny rod for years, but there were a lot of doubters—particularly those who fished the big rivers of Scotland and Canada with the long, 15 foot, two-handed Spey rods of the time. The 6 foot rod Lee used was also a one-piece rod which made it even more inconceivable to the British.

Salmon anglers in both Canada and Europe received the *Atlantic Salmon Journal* regularly and all had been enjoying a spirited debate between Lee and

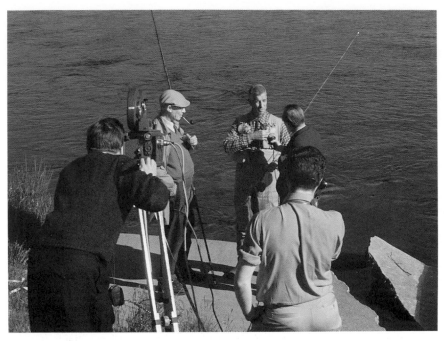

*Interview during Jock Scott/Lee Wulff challenge match (long rod vs. short rod),
River Dee, 1962 (Lee won).*

Britain's most famous fly fishing writer, Jock Scott—the pen name for Donald
Rudd. Rudd was no devotee of Lee's short rods and used a 16 1/2 foot
Greenheart two-handed rod to make his long roll casts across the famous Dee
River in Scotland.

Lee had been pounding away at his theory that it was line speed, pro-
pelled by a short fly rod, that made it easy to reach salmon and that it was
skill and arm control that brought the fish in quickly. Lee was also an advo-
cate of the dry fly for salmon and most British had long ago given up on the
dry fly after LaBranche and Hewitt had failed to take salmon on them. For the
most part all used wet flies for salmon.

After debating each other for months—to the delight of anglers on both
sides of the Atlantic—a challenge was issued by Jock Scott. Lee was to bring his
tiny rod and dry flies to England and a match would be arranged on the River
Dee in the Spring of 1962.

Lee got there a week early so he could explore the river. By the time the
match took place, he thought he knew it well enough to catch a salmon on
his #8 White Wulff. It was a tough competition—the weather being typical,

rain and wind—but he managed to catch one small salmon. Jock Scott caught none and Lee was declared the winner.

The loser took it as a sportsman. In a letter to Editorial Assistant Winnifred Wright of the *Atlantic Salmon Journal*, Donald Rudd wrote:

"To me the most interesting aspect was the fact that both Lee Wulff and Gerald Curtis caught fish on a dry fly. Now we know that Dee fish will take a dry fly. To my mind this is the great event of the meeting, as it opens up a new field to the British dry fly man. He can now go after salmon with some confidence."

But he fudged a bit on whether the short or the long rod was best for salmon.

"There is, of course," he wrote, "no one best rod for both dry fly and wet fly (on) any or every river, just as there is no one universal tool for dismantling an automobile engine. So I like to remember Lee Wulff as the man of the dry fly—not the man of the tiny rod."

Back in Shushan things were not going so well, as incredible as it seemed to Lee, a divorce was imminent. Though they fought a great deal, Lee had chalked it up to two giant egos, but apparently it was more than that. Lee was totally consumed by his career—fishing, writing, lecturing and now, making films almost full time. If he was not in Newfoundland or Labrador making films he was in Venezuela or Nicaragua, or the Florida Keys, or the Bahamas making films. Kay felt left out—not too surprisingly. It was beginning to look as though Lee's advice from that old friend in Newfoundland in 1949—"If you knew one-tenth as much about women as you do fish . . . " was coming back to haunt him.

The divorce was not pretty. Lee was angry and Kay fought back as people who feel they are hurt and neglected are able to do. It boiled down to her lawyer giving her advice about property settlement and Lee hung the phone up on Kay several times before the divorce decree was final in the fall of 1962. The case was heard by the court of New Hampshire since Lee and Kay had moved to Hinsdale from Shushan, New York a few years earlier.

CBS had run a number of Lee's Newfoundland and Labrador films on their outdoor sports programs, but Lee was now negotiating with them on a whole new series of hunting and fishing films to appear in the spring on the "CBS Sports Spectacular." The deal involved a good deal of money and the last thing Lee needed at that time was personal problems.

As if the divorce were not enough, a woman named Valerie Lewallen, a good friend of Lee's mother in San Diego, wrote Lee a long, helpful letter telling Lee she thought it time to place Lilly in a nursing home. Lee had been the sole contributor to his mother's welfare for nearly 30 years since his father's death. Neither Audrey nor Lillian—with whom Lee seldom communicated—had ever contributed anything to their mother's financial needs. She had been living in a small apartment and had a few friends. Miss Lewallen was one of them, but was in the Foreign Service and was being transferred. She was worried that Lilly would suffer after she left. She told Lee of a good, inexpensive nursing home and recommended he consider placing her there. Lee, grateful to find out about his mother's condition, wrote back asking her to give him more details and planned to follow her advice—knowing his sisters would be on the scene.

A disagreement with Allan over college tuition did nothing to help Lee's peace of mind. When Allan asked Lee to pay for his advanced studies, Lee reminded him that he had told both him and Barry he would pay only the tuition for the basic four-year college term. As a result Allan did not communicate with his father for at least 10 years.

One of the few bright moments of that early spring was when Lee received a letter from his friend, the new president of the International Game Fish Association, Bill Carpenter, that Lee had been elected Representative for Newfoundland.

In February he attended the 14th annual meeting of the salmon association in Montreal. He was encouraged by a talk by Dr. A. L. Pritchard, director of conservation and management of the Canadian Department of Fisheries, who said a new regional committee, composed of government fisheries people and representatives of the Board of Directors of the ASA, had been formed to study the salmon situation. During the session Lee showed two films—one on Norway and the other about his experiences on the Dee River with Jock Scott.

In March Lee's good friend Bill Pearsall, account supervisor of Oristano Associates, a public relations firm in Manhattan, sent Lee the announcement that Lee's "CBS Sports Spectacular" would begin March 31st at 2:30 to 4:00 p.m. each Sunday. Lee was a co-producer along with John Pokorshy, executive producer of the weekly series. All the sequences had been filmed by Lee. The script for the show was written by Craig Gilber. The first segments would be concerned with films Lee had done in the north: "Fly North For Brook Trout," "Hunting In Newfoundland," "Fishing In Newfoundland," "Beautiful Bonne Bay," "Double On Bluefins" and "Recipe For Moose."

Lee had already flown down to Central and South America with several cronies—including Tommy White—and did a film on tarpon in the big rivers that flow into the Caribbean. He was the guest of General Somoza and left a pair of spinning outfits with the general and his son when they left. He later got some excellent footage of a 129 pound tarpon being caught by Dick Wolff off Florida's Little Torch Key on light tackle. The guide was Stu Apte who had just taken leave as a jet pilot with a commercial airline to take up flats guiding as a living. Dick was with Garcia Tackle at the time and Lee was acting as a consultant for Garcia—in addition to everything else.

Lee and his approximately 130 pound fly-caught tarpon taken on a 10-weight fly rod.

He had been thinking constantly about designing the perfect saltwater reel for both fresh and saltwater and had Garcia interested in the prototype. Working with his long-time friend, reel-maker Stan Bogden, Lee wrote him in March:

"Dear Stan:

It was good to talk to you the other day. Here's a sketch of where I think the pressure block for the drag should be placed on the reel . . . It needs more spool width to get enough line on the reel. 1/4 inch more width would be enough . . . I count on using a reel like the 3-3/8th inch Hardy St. George. I'm so used to that weight I don't notice any imbalance and, of course, have compensated for it by the position of my hand grip."

With his engineering background, Lee was adept at designing anything and was forever improving the design of fishing tackle and flies. Though he had been experimenting with different forms of plastic flies since the early 1950s, his flies had never caught on—though Lee kept after the concept the rest of his life. In 1951 he and a partner had started Form-A-Lure marketing plastic-bodied flies as the thing of the future. Using a system of injection-

The reel Lee designed. Joan Wulff photo.

molding, Lee built the molds into which he injected plastic and set in hooks—figuring that just because tiers used feathers and thread for centuries didn't mean ready-made plastic-bodied flies wouldn't work just as well, if not better. The bodies varied on the hooks with the type of flies needed. Though they did not sell well from the shop at Shushan, Lee believed they were the fly of the future.

Now that the CBS series was launched Lee knew he would be busy full-time with new films. He launched a new series—with a number of saltwater themes—for the upcoming seasons. Nineteen sixty-four and 1965 were filled with things to do. Campaigning on the promise of the Great Society, Lyndon Johnson was elected President by an overwhelming vote. There was racial violence in a number of southern cities and foreign relations reflected continuing tensions with Cuba and Berlin. Greater military and economic assistance to Vietnam on the part of the United States signaled upcoming trouble in that area.

Lee wrote an excellent piece on releasing salmon for the *Atlantic Salmon Journal* which caused considerable discussion. Most salmon caught were kept for food, traditionally. The cost of salmon angling—both in the U.S., Canada and Europe—over the centuries had led to keeping the fish as prizes for the table. Lee had begun to emphasize his life-long theme of catch-and-release.

Lee attended the 16th Annual Conference of the Atlantic Salmon Association in Montreal where he heard his long-time friend Wilfred Carter talk about the changes in policy of the Quebec Government regarding the opening of salmon waters. "Wilf" as he is affectionately known throughout salmon circles, began as a fisheries biologist and at that time was director of the Gaspe area of the Wildlife Service of the Department of Tourism.

Lee also showed a film of his taking a 24 pound salmon on the tiny 1 3/4 ounce rod in 23 minutes which caught everyone's attention. T.B. "Happy" Frazier, president of the ASA, reported an increase in the take of salmon by anglers over 1963—a cheerful report, but Lee was not convinced the salmon was by any means out of danger.

Lee was unanimously re-elected to the Board of Directors and immediately left for the Florida Keys where he was scheduled to make several films for CBS—one on tarpon fishing with a fly and another on bonefish.

The year 1965 was almost a duplicate of the previous one, but Lee was now becoming so adept at film-making it was becoming almost second nature. Lee heard nothing from Allan, but Barry was engaged to Ella May Thomson—a very nice girl, Lee told friends—and was planning on marriage in the spring. Lee went to the annual meeting of ASA again, but this time it was held in New York City as a joint meeting of the Theodore Gordon Flyfishers and ASA. Nearly

600 anglers attended the huge meeting and Lee's friend, Arnold Gingrich, publisher of *Esquire* magazine—and a fine fly fisherman—was chairman of the afternoon sessions. The highlight of the conference was the address by the director of the Greenland Department of Fisheries, who reported on the sudden increase in the commercial take of Atlantic salmon in his country. Lee and the rest were startled at the fact that these salmon were taken from the wintering stock of salmon that each year returned to Canadian rivers.

That spring Lee met with some other saltwater fly rodders and helped found the Salt Water Flyrodders of America at Cape May Courthouse, New Jersey. With Lee was a collection of the pioneer saltwater fly fishermen of the country, among them Joe Brooks, Bernard "Lefty" Kreh, Charlie Waterman, Mark Sosin, Frank Woolner, Stu Apte, Hal Lyman, Harold Gibbs, Gene Anderegg, Leon Chandler, Dick Wolf and Kay Brodney. Elwood "Cap" Colvin was elected the first president of the new organization and Lou Rodia secretary-treasurer.

This was Lee's year for new organizations. Along with anglers like Gene Anderegg, he had been working at some length to form a national organization of fly fishermen only. That summer he went to Eugene, Oregon for the first organizational meeting of the Federation of Fly Fishermen. Lee was a founding member and quite sure the federation would grow and last.

Lee had met Joan Salvato Cummings at a New York Sportsman's Show years before, but during the summer of 1966 Lee was asked to do an ABC sportsman's show on giant tuna fishing and his co-star on the film was scheduled to be singer Kay Star who became ill and had to cancel the trip. A world's fly casting champion and a fine fly fisherman, Joan joined Lee in Newfoundland and they became acquainted while making the film. She caught a 572-pound bluefin tuna with Lee—which impressed him greatly. Both had been unhappily married and they fell in love during the course of the trip.

Lee and Joan would make a bass fishing film together in Florida for ABC. They discovered they liked the same things and soon they were close friends, Lee had begun to think seriously about proposing marriage.

Also in the marriage department, Barry and Ella May were married that year, Lee could not attend, but was pleased at the thought he might become a grandfather one day.

He was seriously hooked on saltwater fly fishing by this time and doing as much of it as he could—in addition to making his films. He had taken a 130 pound tarpon on a fly and had caught a Pacific sailfish on a long rod. The next step—he promised himself—would be to try for a marlin. Only one had been caught on a fly and he thought he might be able to top that in weight. He was soon to try.

Day of the Marlin

It was the 6th of May, 1967 and the Pacific was oily smooth 15 miles off the tiny Ecuadorian fishing port of Salinas. Woody Sexton, Florida guide and fly fishing expert, steered the small, 15 foot wooden boat—driven by a 33 h.p. outboard motor—westward as the huge swells undulated beneath the small boat and the larger crafts holding the ABC TV crews.

Lee had convinced Producer/Director Lorne Hassen catching a marlin on a fly would make a marvelous segment for his highly-rated "American Sportsman" show. Lee realized it would be a great show, but was also astute enough to know a week off Ecuador might not be enough to accomplish the feat. Only one marlin had ever been caught on a fly and that one—a 145 pound striped marlin—had been taken off Rancho Buena Vista on the East Cape of Baja two years earlier by Dr. Webster Robinson. "Doc" Robinson, with his wife Helen, had been one of the first to catch sailfish on a flyrod— off Florida a half dozen years earlier. It had been submitted and declared a world record—filling all the requirements of the Salt Water Flyrodders of America, the agency of record-keeping for saltwater fly anglers. Lee had been a founding member of the organization in 1966.

Lee knew Robinson had used a 2/1 ratio fly reel and had added a 6-inch fighting butt to his fly rod—which was legal according to SWFROA rules. But Lee figured if he used a single-action reel and did not use a fighting butt, he could claim to be the first fly fisherman to catch a marlin "on true fly-fishing tackle"—a somewhat moot point. However it had succeeded in convincing show host Curt Gowdy it would be a first and that was all that was needed.

"To take one of these tough, durable marlin on true fly fishing tackle, I realized," Lee wrote later, "would be comparable to scaling Everest, an angling feat not yet achieved by any man."

Lee had chosen a tough 9 foot, 10-weight fiberglass Garcia fly rod weighing a heavy 5 ounces. It sold, at the time, for about $12. His reel was a Farlow "Python"—single action, with a strong click to keep the line from overrunning. It too was inexpensive—about $30. He used 90-feet of 10-weight-forward fly line with 300 yards of braided nylon squidding line as backing. He used about a foot of 80-pound shock leader and his tippet was 12-pound mono. He had tied up a 4/0 double-hooked streamer fly made up of long white, red and yellow rooster feathers.

That first day, the two boats had left the small fishing town an hour and a half after sunrise and an hour and a half later were spotting striped marlin dorsal fins and tails ahead of them on the calm surface. Lee felt his heart speed up as he watched the black fins cutting the water. He knew he had to cast the fly at the cruising fish as the rules forbade trolling a fly. And it was also necessary that the boat be in neutral when the fly was cast. Sexton knew that and had been carefully coached—not that it was any great task to slip the outboard out of gear for a moment.

Lee balanced himself in the bow—hatless as usual—while Sexton eased

Lee and guide Woody Sexton with Lee's world record 148 pound striped marlin caught on a fly in May, 1967 off Salinas, Ecuador.

up to the first marlin. The fish was cruising slowly just beneath the surface, but the wake from the slowly-moving boat reached it before Lee could get within casting distance and the big fish sank out of sight. Sexton, squinting out from beneath his tan Florida Keys guide cap, turned the boat and headed for the marlin again as its tail showed black against the pewter-tinted surface. This time Lee—quickly using a double-haul—landed the big fly a dozen feet ahead of the marlin. The fish showed not the slightest interest in the fly as Lee stripped it in foot-long movements through the water.

"Damn!" Sexton said as he let out his breath.

Spotting a second marlin, they decided to try that one. Cameramen aboard the TV boat were using long lenses.

"With ABC's American Sportsman crew all set to film the attempt," Lee wrote, "failure would be very distasteful."

The marlin came up to the boat as it rested quietly on the smooth water. It was headed directly toward the boat and Lee cast the fly when the fish was about 60 feet away. The fish turned and looked at the moving fly then followed it until it saw the boat—then slid down out of sight.

The next two fish showed no interest in the fly, though Lee landed the fly close to both. Lee thought the 80-pound shock leader was making them uneasy, but Sexton thought it was the presence of the boat.

The hours passed and a slight breeze came up making it more difficult to see the dorsal fins and tails on the surface. The only way they could get the flies close to the cruising fish was to move parallel to the marlin at the same speed then cast the fly just ahead of the fish. The marlin got a quick glimpse of the fly as it was pulled away and three of them followed it close to the boat before sinking out of sight. By the time they decided to leave for Salinas at 3:30 p.m. Lee figured they had spotted at least 70 marlin. He was discouraged—realizing they had only six more days to catch one. If he'd only had a strike from one, he knew he could hook a fish. He sat in the bow of the small boat staring morosely at the rugged shape of St. Helena Point looming in the distance. For five days they kept up the futile pursuit.

A breeze came up early the morning of the sixth day—making it difficult to spot marlin fins for the first three hours. At 11:00 a.m. the breeze slackened and suddenly, as if by magic, there were marlin fins everywhere. They moved in on fish after fish without being able to present the fly properly to any of them. Finally Lee decided to speed up close to the fish then slip the motor into neutral and coast.

The fourth fish was quite a ways below the boat and Lee had to strain to get the bulky fly close to it. The marlin came up from beneath it, suddenly slashed at it with its bill, turned back and engulfed the fly. It was just a few

123

minutes past noon. Lee set the hook solidly, but did not put much pressure on the fish.

At first the fish moved slowly, apparently not realizing it was in any danger. It swam slowly away from the boat as Lee fed it line not putting much pressure on the reel spool. He wanted to avoid as long as he could the sudden, thrashing jumps he knew were coming.

Little by little Lee put more pressure on the reel. A school of pilot whales slowly came up behind them on the same course. Sexton kept the small boat pointed at the swimming fish. As the whales came close to the two boats, the marlin swerved off from them and Lee had to increase the pressure. The big marlin suddenly seemed to realize it was in danger and made the first towering leap for which striped marlin are so famous.

The click of the reel began to scream as the fish tore off line and Lee, holding the rod high above his head, could only hope the leader and backing would not break. The marlin jumped at least a dozen times as it headed off toward the horizon—taking hundreds of yards of backing. Sexton headed the boat in the direction of the leaping fish.

The fish stopped jumping and dove for the depths. Lee was almost out of backing. It was difficult for Lee to see in what direction the fish was moving because the line was slanted almost straight down. Finally both men noticed a slight angle to the line and Sexton moved the boat in that direction. Lee was slowly gaining line when suddenly the marlin began leaping almost 200 yards off to their left. Knowing the fish had brought at least part of the line up, Lee realized he could put more pressure on the fish in order to straighten out the belly of the line.

Lee was 62-years-old that year and though in good condition his right arm began to feel the strain of fighting the big fish. There was no rod butt extension to shove into his stomach in order to absorb the pressure. He held the fiberglass rod as close to his body as he could resting his elbow against the side of his chest. The battle settled down to a long, silent fight between Lee and the fish swimming deep below them.

After two hours both began to tire. Though the marlin jumped now and then, its jumps were not as high nor were they made as often. Perspiration ran down Lee's face and his long-sleeved shirt was plastered against his body from moisture. The marlin began to swim tiredly away from the boat just beneath the surface. Lee could feel the steady beat of its tail against the butt leader and the end of the fly line.

When they had closed the distance between the boat and the fish to about 30 feet, a pair of striped marlin suddenly appeared and began to swim parallel to the hooked fish, about 30 feet to each side. Sexton kept the outboard in slow idle and the fish and boat moved together. The TV boat was now within 50 yards—the boat captain careful not to get too close to the struggle.

The temperature was in the 90s and there was little in the way of a breeze to help cool them. They skirted a school of mackerel and Lee saw the dorsal fin of a solitary shark off in the distance. He silently prayed it did not come near the hooked marlin. Both men could see the swimming fish and occasionally Lee could see the fly in its mouth.

Several times the marlin heaved itself halfway out of the water and shook its head and bill wildly trying to rid itself of the fly. After the third time it thrashed out of the water, they moved the boat up closer and Lee saw—to his horror—that the leader was wrapped around the fish's bill and the fly was dangling free beside the head. He felt like giving up at that moment. He knew it was only a matter of time until the marlin jumped and fell back—causing slack in the line and freeing the fly.

The camera boat now moved up close to give the cameramen close-up footage and the marlin, aware of both boats, stayed down about 20 feet deep. Lee kept up as much pressure on the fish he thought possible with the tackle, knowing he could not afford slack. The fish suddenly came to a stop and began to slide backward into the water, a move Lee was afraid would let the fly slip loose. But the marlin surged upward and Lee saw that the fly had caught in the mouth again and seemed to be in solidly.

The fly stayed in place as the tired marlin began to come in. When Sexton grabbed the long-handled gaff and began to close in Lee held the rod high and kept as much pressure on as possible. The fish was beginning to dive again when Sexton reached out and sank the gaff into it close to the tail. As water flew in all directions, Lee slid a glove on and tried to reach the bill, but the fish's head was too far away from him.

When the marlin swung around, Lee dropped the rod and grasped the fish by the dorsal fin, then grabbed the bill with his gloved left hand. Still thrashing, the big fish was lifted over the side by the two men landing with a slithering thud on the bottom of the boat. As the shouts and cheers from the people on the camera boat reached them, Sexton quickly dispatched the marlin with solid blows to the forehead with a stout wooden club.

The two men embraced and pounded each other on the back as they stood in the rocking boat. The captain of the camera boat suddenly began blowing the boat's horn, over and over, and the crew waved wildly.

Lee suddenly sat down on a wooden seat. He was desperately tired and soaked with sweat, but it was a sweet, sweet feeling of accomplishment. He reached out and slapped the slippery, wet side of the marlin, secretly thanking the gods of angling for the gift.

A New Life

In 1967 Lee and Joan were married in a small, intimate ceremony. Joan had been married and divorced and had two small boys—Douglas and Stuart. They made their home in New Hampshire as the town of Keene was close to good hunting, trout and bass fishing and also within driving distance of New York City.

Lee had high hopes for a reel he had been designing at this time and talked about it later in a letter to Ray Pryzgoda who had been with Garcia Corporation at that time.

"I designed the 'Ultimate' reel in late 1966 and on behalf of Norm Thompson asked Stan Bogdan to make one up. This was to be used on my record marlin trip to Ecuador the following spring. Later he made another prototype of the salmon size. Stan Bogdan worked out the click arrangement but the idea of the elimination of the frame was mine. This permitted the use of the entire outer edge of the spool as a brake by finger pressure and was a step further than the small push-plate operating on the outer spool which I had set up in a reel I had designed previously and which Bogdan had made up (which I have here).

"Peter Alport of Norm Thompson Outfitters with whom I was working at the time, told me he paid Stan Bogdan over $600 for his work on the reel model.

"In 1967 Farlow and Company of London had 100 replicas of the salmon size made up in England and they were sold as the 'Lee Wulff Ultimate' reel by Norm Thompson Outfitters through their store or mail order . . . or from Farlow in England."

Outfitter Thompson used Lee's name on Farlow Bamboo Impregnated rods, a Cortland fly line, vests, flies and the Ultimate reel.

Lee later tried to interest Garcia in the reel, but they turned it down. Today it is on the market as the Orvis CFO. The design was sold to them by Bogdan. Both Lee and Joan were to work for Garcia Corporation for a six year period—1969-1975—as a team.

While Lee was discovering saltwater fly fishing and making some impressive inroads, not everyone was impressed with his accomplishments. He was considered in some circles—mostly the south Florida area of experienced flats fly rodders—of being a "new kid on the block."

"At the time," wrote Tom Paugh, today the retired Editor-In-Chief of *Sports Afield*, "I was living in Miami, Florida (as saltwater editor of *Sports Afield*) and there I had heard grumbling among some of the saltwater fishing elite that while Lee was undoubtedly a fine freshwater and even bluefin tuna angler, he had a good bit to learn about catching certain other superstar fish, such as tarpon, marlin, permit and bonefish on a fly."

A lot of that was professional jealousy. No one can do anything in the professional fishing field without a certain level of the industry finding fault. There is that segment of outdoorsmen that—if they cannot accomplish a feat themselves—will take pleasure in knocking the success of others. It is usually accomplished by starting a rumor, which quickly spreads. Lee was in the vulnerable position of having his accomplishments portrayed on national television.

Lee's 148 pound striped marlin was entered as a world record in the Salt Water Flyrodders of America and the Metropolitan Miami Fishing Tournament. The episode of Lee catching the marlin also ran on ABC's "American Sportsman" narrated by sportscaster Curt Gowdy—in prime time nationally. Naturally there were those who were jealous and there were others who began to spread rumors the catch was faked for television.

A Miami attorney, perhaps spurred on by an honest regard for the sport of fishing, reported he heard that Lee had fastened a balao to his fly and actually caught the marlin on bait not a fly. E.S. "Ed" Corlett wrote to Lefty Kreh, at that time an official of the Miami Metropolitan Tournament, that he, his wife and Judge and Mrs. William Mehrtens had been at a dinner party where a citizen of Ecuador, a Mr. Lucho Flores, said he had witnessed Lee putting a balao on the hook and catching the marlin. Since the entire episode had been photographed by ABC and Lee had been accompanied by Woody Sexton the whole time, the claim seemed frivolous, but Kreh, in his capacity with the SWFROA, took it upon himself to investigate the claim.

On November 28, 1968 Lefty wrote Flores in Quayquil, Ecuador enclosing Corlett's letter and asking for substantiation.

"I am enclosing a copy of a letter written to me by an old friend, Ed Corlett. The letter explains that you saw Mr. Wulff catch a world record marlin

on a fly rod. Mr. Wulff, according to the story you told Ed Corlett, caught the fish using bait on his fly rod.

"This is a deliberate violation of the rules for which he claimed the record. As an advisor of the Salt Water Flyrodders of America (the organization which keeps the world records) I am investigating the situation.

"Would you be kind enough to send me a notarized statement that indicates that Mr. Wulff was observed by you to catch one or more marlin during the film for ABC, and that none of these were caught on a fly, but that bait was used? . . ."

Lefty, while representing the SWFROA, was also asking for such information because of his position in the Miami Met Tournament—in which Ed Corlett was interested. Why the fish was entered in a Florida tournament when it was caught in Ecuador no one seems to remember.

There is no record of an answer from Flores and no such notarized statement ever turned up. Subsequently a man named Donald J.S. Merten, wrote Lefty saying he personally had seen Lee catch the marlin on a fly and that Flores had been mistaken. Lefty wrote and thanked Merten and sent a carbon copy to Corlett.

Corlett wrote to Merten on December 10, 1968 explaining his part in the controversy and ending with: "I for one have no doubt that your letter of December 5th is completely accurate and since this fish was entered in fly casting competition, I am pleased for the sake of the sport that it was accomplished in the manner you described."

Lee, in the meantime, had written to his old friend Fred Schrier, a member of the board of SWFROA.

"Word reaches me that my marlin catch is being investigated. This is something I welcome. No one realizes more than I that records are often phonied by applicants and no one goes to greater lengths to be honorable. Woody Sexton, who more than anyone else on the trip could verify this catch, was chosen because of his complete integrity. There may be better marlin guides or better boatmen but no better fly fisherman-guide and no one more honorable. Woody was at my right hand every moment. I suggest your committee contact him. If you need more names I can give them. Inasmuch as this is a matter of importance to me from both the private and public standpoints I would appreciate a report when your investigation has been concluded. Your committee has instituted this and if there are any whisperings or otherwise harmful rumors I am sure you recognize your responsibility to make certain they are all scotched, completely scotched.

Sincerely,
Lee"

Lee needn't have worried, according to Mark Sosin. Sosin was then head of the SWFROA and would have been the one to conduct any investigation. Sosin said as late as 1993 that he had talked to Woody Sexton and Woody said Lee had as many as 1,500 shots at striped marlin in the two weeks they fished and "blew them all except that one." He never said a word about Lee doing anything illegal or unethical.

"I wrote the rules of the Salt Water Flyrodders of America," Sosin said. "Officially I can tell you, nobody ever filed a protest against that fish."

The furor gradually died down and nothing ever came of the charges by Flores.

It is easy to see how the public might suspect that there are shortcuts taken in the filming of television outdoor programs. With the cost of cameramen, writers and directors, crew time is expensive and one has to "improvise" now and then for economy's sake.

Tom Paugh, for example, tells of participating in the shooting of one of Lee's striped bass films in Virginia.

"The very loose story line of the TV segment," he wrote "called for Lee and me to catch a channel bass in the surf, and for the first few days we fished hard, cameras rolling, without result. In addition to the camera crew of four, our entourage included Claude Rogers, a Virginia gentleman and local fishing legend, who headed up his state's saltwater fishing tournament, and Zack Taylor, *Sports Afield's* boating editor.

"Channel bass, redfish and red drum are one and the same species. The important thing to know is that while redfish are eagerly sought in southern Florida and along the Gulf Coast, respectable ones there run only about 10 pounds. Whereas in the Northeast, the coast of Virginia for example, 50-pound channel bass are not uncommon, with a few monsters reaching over 70 and even 80 pounds.

"I think eventually both Lee and I knew we weren't going to catch a channel bass in the surf in time to get it on film, though I don't believe we actually said so. Claude Rogers knew for sure, for, on the sixth day he took off alone in his boat. When he returned later we watched him as he came into view with the engine throttled way down. He had two heavyweight, and quite lively, channel bass in tow.

"Now I had a bit of a problem because as saltwater editor of *Sports Afield*, I had a rule that I had never broken that I would not pose for a photograph with a fish I had not personally caught. Here, the upcoming scenario was becoming clear; Lee and I would have to "catch" Claude's fish with the cameras rolling.

"Not being experienced in the ways of television production," he continued,

Lee and Tom Paugh, then saltwater editor of Sports Afield, making a movie on red channel bass fishing for ABC's "American Sportsman".

"I at first refused on moral grounds, and in fact was seriously considering walking out. Cooler heads prevailed, however, as both Zack and Claude convinced me to continue. After all, there was a lot on the line here for certain individuals, especially Lee. He was the one responsible for bringing back enough raw film out of which a one-third segment for the hour-long TV show could be created. Since he was already well into his budget with the hiring of the camera crew and other expenses, to fail to produce a show would have cost him a nice bundle ($25,000, if my memory serves).

"So Lee and I "battled" our channel bass in the surf, landed them, weighed them (Lee's was 46 pounds, mine was 47) and congratulated ourselves before the cameras while Claude looked on. Afterwards Zack Taylor and I walked one of the still-alive fish back and forth in the water until it revived enough to swim off on its own."

"Claude knew I felt guilty about faking it with the fish so immediately after the filming had been completed, he offered to take me to his secret hotspot where I really did catch a 63-pound channel bass. I felt somewhat cleansed.

"None of these niceties seemed to concern Lee in the least. I can only assume he had caught so many significant fish in his life that pretending with this one was no big deal for him. After all, he had enough problems to concern himself with, and as producer, the film was the all-important thing. To his, and everyone else's, credit this bit of film turned out to be a small gem— a very compelling piece of work that was favorably received when it eventually aired in the spring of 1973. Lee's final words on the show were, 'Let's do this once a year'. "And, of course, Lee never had any intention of entering the channel bass for world records.

But while Lee was learning about saltwater game fish, his real love and concern was the Atlantic salmon. The ASA reported that the sudden increase in the use of drift-nets off New Brunswick and Newfoundland had resulted in alarming catches of salmon. "Happy" Frazier, now manager of the association, reported that combined drift-net catches in the Bay of Fundy, Miramichi and off Port aux Basques, Newfoundland, had jumped from 35,000 fish annually in 1963 to an alarming 115,000 fish in 1967.

What worried Lee and the others on the board of the ASA, was that the Canadian drift-nets were not the only threat to the salmon. A new drift-net fishery had developed on the high seas in international waters.

"We shall be hearing more and more about drift netting," wrote Frazer, "and its serious effects upon salmon stocks from now on and therefore it is well to understand what the operation consists of and how the cream of our salmon crop is harvested before it reaches our shores."

It was the first sign of impending disaster to the high seas salmon fishery and Lee was again grateful that there were organizations watching out for just such developments.

But while Lee was doing considerable writing in the outdoor magazines, he was not able to get editors to devote much space to the problems of salmon. They were far too interested in the where-to-go and how-to stories so popular in the outdoor magazines.

"Lee was a frequent contributor," said Zack Taylor, an associate editor of *Sports Afield* at the time. "But he always wrote about Atlantic salmon and always in the most pessimistic terms. He was right. We were decimating our salmon stocks."

Nineteen sixty-seven was a big year for Lee. In addition to the striped marlin he fought a 597 pound bluefin tuna to a standstill and a world record on 50 pound line at Conception Bay in an incredible 13 hours and 25 minutes.

Later in the summer of 1967 Lee and Joan found time to fly to Jackson, Wyoming where they attended the first meeting of the newly-formed Federation of Fly Fishermen—an organization Lee had long helped to organize. As a founding member he was delighted that it was finally underway and had a feeling it was going to expand and thrive.

While there they got in some fine trout fishing on the Snake River. That was the year Jack Dennis, today a successful fly shop owner, lecturer and outfitter in Jackson, first met Lee. Jack was only 17, but already a successful trout fishing guide.

"I could hardly talk when introduced to him," he later wrote, "He was bigger than life. He had been my hero for those formative years. He had a smile that was genuine. He chose his words carefully and thought carefully before he did things. This was a man who knew the secrets of the outdoors."

Lee's 148 pound striped marlin was declared a world record on 12 pound tippet by the Salt Water Flyrodders of America and in October his friend, Joe Linduska, associate director of the U.S. Fish and Wildlife Service wrote him.

"Suffering cats!" he wrote, "Yesterday I picked up a copy of *Outdoors Unlimited* (the bulletin of the Outdoor Writers of America) and saw where you had been selected Outdoorsman of the Year by Winchester-Western. Today's mail brings a copy of *Trout Unlimited* in which I note that Lee Wulff, along with Congressman John Saylor, were recipients of the Trout Conservation Awards from that organization. I can't imagine a more deserving recipient for both these honors. Congratulations to you."

Jim Rikhoff, the able and popular public relations director of Winchester, had nominated his friend, Lee, and 5,000 outdoor writers and conservationists had cast their votes for their choice of the award. It was quite an honor and nearly as important to Lee, a good wing-shot, was the presentation at a banquet in August of an engraved Winchester 101 over-and-under 20-gauge shotgun. The award, Rikhoff, said was as much for Lee's work in wildlife conservation as his communication skills.

Making films still took up most of Lee's time. Joan went on a few locations, but not all. As if he didn't have enough to do with the ABC series, Lee was doing films for individual corporations, like Winchester and Garcia, and in June proposed an outdoor series of 15-minute films which Marvin Josephson Associates, Inc. wanted to propose to Coca-Cola as a possible sponsor.

Fred Schrier wanted Lee and Joan to come down to New Jersey to address the annual dinner and banquet of the Salt Water Flyrodders, but that week was already filled. He and Joan were in another bluefin tuna film that Lee was making and Lee was scheduled in early October to do a film on woodcock shooting in Maine for Winchester.

Lee didn't get in much salmon fishing that spring except for a very successful trip to the big river Moise in Quebec and another trip to the Sandhill River in Labrador where a bunch of fly fishermen—headed by Lieutenant General Randy Holzapple—were organizing a salmon club on that great river. Lee was already a member and some new ones were suggested for election that summer—among them Jerry Jacobs and society band leader Peter Duchin of New York City. The initiation fee for the club was to be $2,000—plus yearly dues of $100.

Life was good. Lee wrote his old friend Tap in October.

"It's too bad your auto conked out for the Rochester Show (at which Lee spoke) as I had hoped to get a chance to catch up. I've been busy right on through until now, just getting back from a week in Oregon for a film for Winchester (on pheasants). Oregon because that is where the ringnecks were originally introduced.

"I enjoy my work . . . to a point where I'd do it for nothing if I weren't able to get paid for it . . . but I don't want to be away from Joan and the place here any more than I have to. Joan can come with me occasionally but, because of the kids she's tied to the ranch most of the time . . . all is well and we are a happy group.

"I'm going to knock off for a few days and go deer hunting. Other than that I have stacks of mail . . . half a dozen stories to do and four films to edit. Enough to keep me busier than I need to be until spring. Life is good, however and these are the happiest years of my life. I'm very glad to have lived so long."

The salmon runs in 1968 were fairly good, but on almost all the rivers—in Quebec as well as Newfoundland and Aticosti Island—all were late.

"The question in my mind," wrote Happy Frazier that year, "is why are the salmon runs late and why are they considerably reduced over 1967?"

Lee thought he knew. The catches of salmon which had spent two years in the sea were down appreciably in 1968—both in Canada and the British Isles—indicating that the reduction was inevitable because of the increasing inroads made upon the salmon stocks by the Greenland shore fishery, the high seas drift-netting and the Canadian drift-netting near shore.

On a hunch, Dick Buck of New Hampshire, a devoted salmon conservationist, approached Lee with a plan to document the Greenland netters. While Lee agreed the film should be made, he could not do it himself, but did find two capable photographers for Buck. Salmon conservationist Joe Cullman contributed $15,000 to the project and some excellent photos of Greenlanders netting salmon on the high seas were obtained.

Frazier summed the problem up well in the 1968 issue of the *Atlantic Salmon Journal:*

"I repeat to the Canadians and the Americans what I told the British people in April: How many decades of blood, sweat and tears have been expended on these islands to preserve salmon? Can you gentlemen see this resource willfully destroyed by man? God placed the salmon in our countries long before man came. Surely he did not send us here to destroy His handiwork. What will our netters turn to for a living? What will the gillies, guardians and bailiffs do? What will the hotels and lodges and their help do for a living? How many out of the tens of thousands of salmon anglers will become unbearable to their wives and humanity when we can fish no longer?"

The only dark spot on Lee's horizon that year of 1968 was the death of his mother, Lilly. Lee had been devoted to her his entire life and was desolate for several weeks following the funeral in San Diego.

The "American Sportsman" was going very well. In addition to sequences that year of Texas Governor John Connally hunting elephants in Africa, the excellent sequence Lee had shot on the San Juan River in Nicaragua with Curt Gowdy and golfer Jack Nicklaus was shown. The producer that year was Lorne Hassen.

Some marvelous segments followed that group: Bing Crosby and Phil Harris hunting for sand grouse in Africa, and a fine sequence of actor Van Heflin fishing for blue marlin. Louisiana's Grits Gresham did some hunting and co-starred in an excellent film on falconry with master falconer Hal Webster. Curt Gowdy did a wonderful film on teaching his children how to fly fish on the North Platte River near Laramie, Wyoming—the same river on which he learned to fly fish with the help of his father.

New Friends

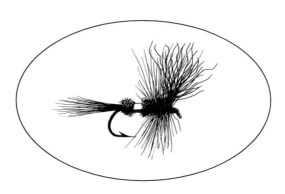

The country was in an uproar over Vietnam all of 1968—with the Tet Offensive, the decision by Lyndon Johnson not to run for re-election and the furor over the Democratic National Convention in Chicago. The killing of both Martin Luther King, Jr. and Robert F. Kennedy had done nothing to ease tensions in the nation.

As the country moved into 1969 with Richard Nixon as President and the Peace Talks on Vietnam making slight progress in Paris, Lee was busy making films and doing what he could about the salmon problem. Lee was never much interested in politics—whether on a local or international level. He had little interest in or regard for politicians, perhaps because of his unpleasant contacts with those bureaucrats in Newfoundland. But his own views on politics sprang from his love and knowledge of nature. He believed in the survival of the fittest and reasoned nations could work out their problems along the same lines. Conservative by nature, he believed everyone should make his own way in life—asking and receiving no help or charity if one could help it. He knew in nature that only the strongest and best survived to pass on the strongest genes to succeeding generations and saw no reason why these same immutable laws should not work with the human race. He had little use for the welfare system in the United States and believed there was work for everyone if they simply wanted to work. He regarded as nonsense the liberal view that the poor were deprived and that society was to blame.

Lee and Edward Janes, at that time eastern editor for *Outdoor Life*, got together and Janes agreed to edit a collection of Lee's fishing stories into a book, *Fishing With Lee Wulff*. It was handled by veteran editor Angus Cameron of Knopf—himself a fine fly fisherman and salmon angler—and was tentatively scheduled for publication in 1972.

Lee attended the 19th Annual Conference of the Atlantic Salmon Association held at the Biltmore Hotel in New York on February 20, 1968. It was a huge turnout probably because of the high seas fishery problem that was damaging the salmon population. Lee was re-elected to the board of directors and joined other delegates to hear Peter Liddell, founder of the Atlantic Salmon Research Trust, and chairman of the Fisheries Committee of the Association of River Boards of the United Kingdom, speak on the deep seas salmon fishery and international efforts to ban this dangerous practice.

The delegates were told that the netting fishery in the Davis Strait and along the west coast of Greenland increased by at least 75 percent—from 95,000 to 165,000 fish. Everyone there knew something had to be done, and done soon, before salmon stocks fell to a level where there would be no return.

A new organization to aid the salmon was started that year and Lee was involved, as he was in all matters that concerned the salmon. It was a U.S. group and the Atlantic Salmon Association worked closely with it to see that it gained tax-exempt status. The two men most closely associated with the group were Francis Goelet and Charles Engelhard along with Joe Cullman, Dudley Mills and John Olin.

The foundation's first executive director was Wilf Carter, who was appointed on October 1, 1969. The IASF operating headquarters was in Gaspe, Quebec, but the organization was hoping to find a location more central to both Canadian and U.S. salmon activities. It began looking toward moving to St. Andrews, New Brunswick where it eventually located in 1971.

Lee was snowed under with work on both films and his writing. He was lecturing everywhere and attending one convention after another. Joan—when she could find sitters for the two boys—accompanied him. He was the featured speaker at the annual Trout Unlimited convention, and traveled to Sun Valley, Idaho for the annual conclave of the Federation of Fly Fishermen.

On the overseas scene, he and Joan went to Paris to visit with Charles Ritz, owner of the famous Ritz Hotel there. Charlie, as he was known by his angling friends, was a prolific fly fisherman and designer of fly rods.

Again on the salmon front, Lee was active in efforts to get high seas netting stopped and followed both ASA and IASF progress as both organizations sent representatives to the 1969 meeting in Warsaw of the International

Commission for the Northwest Atlantic Fisheries (ICNAF), where a resolution to ban high seas netting for a period of ten years was proposed. The resolution was adopted by a majority of 11 votes—Denmark and West Germany dissenting. It was, however, necessary to have the government of every member country ratify a resolution before it could be implemented, meaning both Denmark and West Germany would continue netting on the high seas in 1970.

Lee and Joan spent three pleasant days in New Jersey as speakers and delegates to the annual convention of the Salt Water Flyrodders of America where Lee had the chance to meet George Cornish—a veteran saltwater fly fisherman and marvelous taxidermist from the Florida Keys.

Though he was still doing the occasional TV film for ABC's "American Sportsman"—that year a ruffed grouse hunt—he was finding it more and more difficult to work with some of the network crews. ABC was bringing in more new and younger film editors and writers who didn't always agree with Lee's methods. (He had a run-in with his long-time producer, Lorne Hassen, about a Norway salmon and sea trout film in March of that year that was unpleasant at best.)

One of the highlights of the summer was the making of a TV film for the outdoor recreation market of a family traveling up the west coast of Newfoundland in a Winnebago motor home. Joan and her two small boys joined Lee and they had a wonderful few weeks traveling all the way from Port aux Basques up to Lanse-a-Meadow.

It was a nostalgic journey for Lee and the family had a chance to see the camps at Portland Creek on August 10, 1969. Though they missed the lobster season there was plenty of home-made Newfoundland bread and Lee shot photos of Douglas catching brook trout at Western Gorge. The only real salmon fishing trip of that year was one to the Moisie River where the fishing was not too good due to the small run of big salmon.

Hoping to tie in with a large corporation and get a steady income rather than depending upon freelance writing and film-making, Lee came up with a proposal to Winchester-Western to do films on a regular basis. Though he was making enough films a year to keep him in a reasonable amount of money, travel, expenses, an apartment in New York—which he kept full-time—and the house in Keene, New Hampshire were a considerable drain. He was not making much on outdoor book royalties. As every outdoor writer knows, an outdoor book seldom sells more than the first edition or a second and third printing. One hopes for as big an advance as one can get from a publisher—knowing that will be the largest segment of pay that will come along. Some publishers of outdoor books are also famous for quickly remaindering books that do not sell well on the first printing.

Lee with a 600 pound bluefin tuna caught from a 17-foot Boston Whaler, skippered by Larry Cronin, in the summer of 1970 in Notre Dame Bay, Newfoundland.

Lee's proposal to Winchester was that he receive an annual fee of $15,000 for doing one film—not to exceed 30 minutes in length. The company would have the option of having Lee do other films at $8,000 each for another half-hour film. For a 5-year agreement Winchester would give Lee an additional $20,000 a year as a consultant and to do public appearances on behalf of the company. He cited his films for ABC and Garcia and pointed out that he had already won three "Teddy" awards for his outdoor films. He stated he would not work for competing companies and reserved the right to do the writing on his own and continue to work for the government of Newfoundland in the summer months. The proposal was taken under advisement, but nothing ever came of it.

As the winter and spring of 1970-71 approached, Lee became obsessed with the idea of taking a bluefin tuna from a tiny boat—just to prove it could be done. Though the ABC "American Sportsman" show that spring ran a segment of Lee and Joan fishing for bluefins from a regular-sized boat in Newfoundland, Lee wanted to make a more spectacular film.

Joan had caught and landed a 572 1/2 pound tuna in 1967 and it was replayed that spring. The fact that she landed the big fish in one hour and 22 minutes provided viewers with considerable excitement.

But Lee wanted to use a small boat. He proposed the film to Garcia for tackle, Boston Whaler for a boat and Fisher-Pierce for a motor. Lee contacted both Dick Fisher, president of Fisher-Pierce and Chet Palmer, their director of advertising, and got a 17-foot Boston Whaler and a 55 h.p. Bearcat engine assigned to the project. He also got a boat skipper, Larry Cronin, assigned by the company.

Lee's old chum, "Robbie" Robinson, vice president of sales for Garcia, came up with an additional $5,000 for promotional money—plus the use of big-game fishing tackle and Garcia lures (built into the script, of course).

Lee, Joan and the TV crew—Jack Hegarty and Doug Sinclair—arrived at Cottrell's Cove, Newfoundland that summer. They were followed by Larry Cronin in a 4-wheel drive vehicle and a boat trailer with the Whaler. Lee knew from his earlier days that the Notre Dame Bay area was the best for bluefins.

The first day they went out into New Bay to catch mackerel for bait. Passing a 60-foot-high iceberg, they looked for circling gulls. Catching the mackerel, Lee rigged about six of them to form a "daisy chain" for trolling. The rest of the day they looked for tuna, but saw schools only in the distance.

For the next two days they looked for tuna schools—even heading out to the open sea in the small boat. But it was not until the morning of the fourth day that Lee had a strike. Joan was in the photo boat using a small 35-mm camera. They were trolling past a rock ledge when a tuna came out from under a flock of gulls and hit the trolled mackerel.

Lee was using 80-pound braided Dacron line, but rather than fight the big fish from the stern of the boat, he had mounted a fighting chair in the bow. The big fiberglass rod bent double and Lee was able to brace his feet on the small forward casting platform of the Whaler.

At the end of an hour the boat was spinning slowly as the fish bored for the depths. Finally Lee was able to bring the fish up under the boat and Larry swung the outboard motor up so the line would not become fouled in the lower unit. When Lee managed to get the fish on the surface, both men gaffed the big tuna amid a shower of spray. The cameras were grinding as they slid the head of the tuna up on the bait board and headed back toward the dock.

The tuna weighed 625 pounds and Lee gave the fish to the people of Cottrell's Cove.

But just to prove he could not only do it again, but in deeper water, they went out again near the mouth of the bay. The weather was terrible—wind and rain—and the next tuna that hit was totally different. When it took the bait it headed directly out into the open Atlantic. The two men fought the big fish in high seas and wind, taking water over the bow as Lee leaned into the fish.

For an hour and a half they battled the big tuna until Lee finally got the double line into the guides. But at that time the fog settled in and they couldn't see the shore. The photo boat stayed close to them, however, and it was another hour before Lee could get the fish up again. When the fish was just beneath the stern Lee gave Larry a knife and he cut the mono—releasing the tuna.

If the film did nothing else it proved tuna could be taken from a tiny motorboat and provided the average TV viewer with an exciting show. Of course all this had been known for some time by seasoned tuna anglers. Big game anglers, such as Michael Lerner, fishing with seasoned guides like Tommy Gifford, had been taking huge bluefin tuna since 1935 from open dories powered by nothing but oars. I remember reading Gifford's marvelous book, *Anglers and Muscleheads* (E.P. Dutton, 1960) in which Gifford and Lerner had taken three bluefin tuna on the same day at Wedgeport, Nova Scotia in September 1935, and a woman—Mrs. Gordon Gibbs—had set a world record at Soldier's Rip way back in 1938 with a 575 pound tuna. Also I could still remember the record 831 pound bluefin Mrs. George Bass had landed off Bimini in 1950 on 45 pound test line.

I was still managing editor of *Field & Stream* when Lee's story ran in that magazine and I remember not being very impressed with all the talk about his catch from a Whaler. I had grown up on Narragansett Bay in Rhode Island and had caught bluefin tuna in both Prince Edward Island and Cat Cay by 1970.

The Editor-In-Chief at that time was Clare Conley, who bought Lee's story, but Conley was from Idaho and knew next to nothing about the sea. I suppose I considered it somewhat of a gimmick story.

The following year Lee accepted a position on the New Hampshire Game & Fish Commission which gave him some clout in the regulation of game and fish laws in his state. He was to become a controversial commissioner, but then nearly everything Lee did was controversial. He had strong opinions on almost everything.

That year Lee began writing a regular column for *Sports Afield* magazine which had a circulation of about 1 million readers. The extra money came in handy and it increased Lee's audience. And in that year Lee was to make a number of interesting TV films—one a fascinating show on deer hunting in which he featured a pure white albino whitetail buck. Another was a bass fishing film in Florida in which Lee fished with *Sports Afield's* great fishing editor, Homer Circle and featured Garcia tackle prominently. Homer remembered the trip.

"Lee asked if I would loan him an extra bait-casting rod, one he called 'fairly forgiving of an inept caster.' He said he seldom used anything but a fly rod. I gave him my lightweight rig and a few bass lures. It was a bit windy and on Lee's first cast he had a back-lash and a "bird's nest."

"'Uncle Homer' Lee said, "that's the last time today you'll see me doing this," as he picked the mess out."

He and Joan made a trip to Ecuador where Lee made a TV film for the "American Sportsman,"—again featuring Garcia tackle—this trip was for marlin. Co-sponsors were National Distillers and Garcia. They caught several striped marlin and dorado (dolphin-fish) on conventional tackle.

On another trip to Acapulco, Mexico both Lee and Joan stayed at Tres Vidas and had some interesting surf fishing, including some snook in the surf at the mouth of a river. At that time transportation to a number of fishing spots was becoming a great deal easier due to a new program instigated by Braniff Airways. E. L. "Buck" Rogers had convinced the airlines that they would get considerable exposure in the outdoor magazines if they sponsored free jaunts for outdoor writers. The experiment was short-lived.

I was Editor-In-Chief of *Field & Stream* in the summer of 1972 when I received a phone call from Lee asking if I would like to be his guest on a salmon fishing trip to Iceland. I had shot trap and skeet with Lee at the frequent Winchester-Western shoots, put on by public relations director Jim Rikhoff in Connecticut. We also had been attending regular Wednesday lunches at the Wings Club in Manhattan. The Midtown Club—as we called ourselves—was made up of Arnold Gingrich, Lee, myself, artist John Groth and a few other fishermen.

I was flattered to be asked though I had been in the magazine business long enough to know Lee wanted something from our big publication. Though a life-long fly fisherman, I had only fished for salmon in Quebec and New Brunswick. Iceland would be an exciting experience.

We flew over on Icelandic Airlines in early August and I was struck first by the unusual odor of Iceland—carried on a wind across the miles of rolling green hills. There are almost no trees in this strange land of volcanic activity. Lee was involved with a number of press interviews, arranged by Asgeir Ingolfsson, president of the Reykjavik salmon fishing club. After a day or so of Lee giving casting demonstrations and attending a cocktail party we moved to the famous farmhouse lodge on the Grimsa River—designed by American architect and salmon fishing expert, Ernie Schwiebert.

A group of Icelandic salmon fishermen and guides (with Lee Wulff and author Jack Samson side-by-side—4th and 5th from left.) Jack Samson photo.

The fishing was marvelous on the Grimsa, the Nordura and the clear, almost-unpronounceable Haffjardera. The salmon, for the most part, were fairly small—from 10 to 15 pounds on the average—but the weather was clear and sunny and the rivers beautiful as they ran down to the sea.

I had brought a 9 foot Abercrombie & Fitch fiberglass salmon fly rod which I had used on the huge George River in Quebec with success, but Lee would have none of it. He quickly replaced my big rod with a 2-piece, 7 foot split bamboo rod and a small Garcia fly reel he had helped to design. As it turned out, it was plenty big enough for those Icelandic rivers.

I was fishing several hundred feet below Lee on the Grimsa one day and having only fair luck in hooking salmon. Lee, above me, had been hooking and releasing one salmon after another. He reeled in his fly and came down the bank to where I was wading. I had been casting a double-hooked Blue Charm—a favorite on Iceland's rivers.

"You might have better luck," Lee said, wading out to join me, "if you tried a different fly." He reached into a side pocket of his bulky fishing vest and produced a handful of yellow and black feathers. Quickly taking out a hook and some thread he whipped together a fly with huge, gnarled fingers and handed it to me. It looked as though it had been tied at home in a vise.

"Here," he said softly, "try this. I call it the Lady Joan. It works well on these rivers."

He waded out of the river and I began to cast again. In the next 30 minutes I hooked three salmon.

It was a fine trip. Both Lee and Joan were great hosts and so were the Icelandic anglers and guides. The closest I came to disaster was when one river host, Tor Tors, saw me wading the Nordura one cold and rainy afternoon and came down to ask if I was cold. I was freezing.

"Here," he said, handing me a bottle of clear Aquavit. I took one swallow and nearly choked on the burning liquid.

"Good," said Tor, nodding. "That was for one leg. Now take a swallow for the other."

At Kennedy Airport on the return trip, Lee handed me an autographed copy of his new, *Fishing With Lee Wulff*, just off the press. The introduction was by the late, great fly fisherman Arnold Gingrich. It was a fitting end to the trip.

Lee and Joan were moving to an old house near Keene—built in 1815— and the move took weeks. The move was a terrible chore, but the house was close to some good woodcock and pheasant cover and the deer hunting was excellent.

That summer and fall Lee became deeply involved with efforts to re-stock some north American rivers with salmon—beginning with New England. Richard Buck of Dublin, New Hampshire was elected as a director of IASF. At a special meeting of the directors, held in New York on January 12, 1970, a special committee was appointed "to investigate and implement the best procedure for disseminating to the general public the result of the Foundation's non-partisan analysis, study and research on the plight of the Atlantic salmon . . . and the committee be given the power to expend the sum of $15,000 in furtherance of its purpose."

The committee was to be called the Committee for the Atlantic Salmon Emergency (CASE). Both Dick Buck and Lee were appointed to the committee. Others appointed were: Reverend Robert A. Bryan, Wilf Carter, Sydney Howe, Dr. Robert Hutton, Arthur Landry, Elisha Lee and David Scoll.

At its board meeting May 4, 1970 the directors approved the following resolution:

"Resolved that the corporation extend to the members of the CASE committee its sincere thanks and congratulations for the fine job which the committee has done in placing the facts of the Atlantic salmon crisis before the public; and that the function of such committee having been completed, the committee be and is hereby terminated."

Subsequently Dick Buck re-activated the CASE committee as an entity separate from IASF. Later still, CASE evolved into Restoration of Atlantic Salmon in America (RASA), which still exists today.

Joseph F. Cullman III, chairman of the board of Phillip Morris, and then president of IASF, asked Lee to head up the IASF committee to look into the restoration of salmon in New England. In December Lee attended an organizational meeting of this committee at Chicopee Falls, Massachusetts for the purpose of discussing the possible restoration of salmon to the Connecticut River. Wilf Carter reported the $6,000 from the IASF treasury might be available to study fish ladders and other ways of bypassing dams on the big river.

Lee and Wilf made a pitch together for support and funding for the salmon at the semi-annual convention of Game Conservation International in San Antonio, Texas. Though a conservation group concerned mainly with big game animals in North America and Africa, Game Coin's president, Harry Tennison, was an ardent salmon fisherman and encouraged the representation on the program that year.

Lee's, *Fishing With Lee Wulff* did not sell well and Angus Cameron planned to remainder the book in early spring of 1974—much to Lee's distress. He had thought the book would make him some money, but strangely the public did not buy it.

More Responsibilities

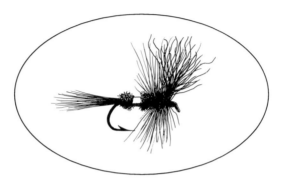

Lee was elected vice president of the Atlantic Salmon Association the year he turned 70—a fitting tribute to his many years of devotion to the cause of saving the salmon.

Some progress had been made in the high seas fishery problem and the Greenland high seas fishery was finally phased out—with their coastal catch restricted to 1,190 metric tons. Meanwhile the U.S. was approaching some sort of normality with the end of the Vietnam War—even though the evacuation of Saigon was agonizing to watch. President Gerald Ford's clemency program for Vietnam era military resisters was extended to March 1st. For their part in the Watergate cover-up that resulted in the forced resignation of President Richard Nixon, former White House aids John Ehrlichman, H. R. Halderman and former Attorney General John Mitchell were each sentenced to 30 months in prison.

Lee was elected to the board of directors of the Outdoor Writers of America and attended their annual convention at Quebec City. He had been nominated by an old friend, fly fishing great Enos Bradner of Seattle, Washington.

He had also been elected as a member of the Rod & Gun Editors Association of Metropolitan New York—a group of writers with whom he enjoyed meeting each year.

He took his annual physical at the Keene Clinic and Dr. Teng Go found him fit—with just a slight elevation in his cholesterol.

Lee had been corresponding for some time with ultra-conservative William Loeb, publisher of the Manchester, New Hampshire *Union Leader*. Bill Loeb was an ardent salmon fisherman and depended upon Lee for the latest information on the salmon situation. Loeb that season was vitally interested in the New Hampshire debate raging over whether it was sensible to stock west coast coho salmon in New England rivers. Lee, by that time chairman of the New Hampshire Game Commission, was strongly against it, feeling the stocking program was not only too expensive, but the coho would compete with the Atlantic salmon.

Lee and Joan had a wonderful week on the moisieRiver. Writing to Bill Loeb, Lee wrote:

"The Moisie was wonderful. It is not easy because the fishermen at the club below have worked the fish over quite hard but the big fish do come through and in normal time at least a few are available. I handicap myself a little by fishing with #16 flies (single hook) to see how big a fish I can get on these midget hooks. I took four this year on #16s and the largest was 26 pounds (I still hope for a 30 pounder.) My largest previously was 27 pounds and I've taken ten over twenty pounds and many smaller fish on 16s there."

Lee had another fine trip to the Delay River with Gene Hill—who later wrote:

"We had a wonderful time together and I learned a lot about Lee and salmon fishing. One of the lessons was when I had waded out far too deep, standing close to Lee, and I told him if I hooked a fish I couldn't move an inch.

"You don't have to," he said, "and at that moment a salmon rolled and Lee cast and hooked it and immediately let out a couple of yards of slack line so the fish wouldn't feel any hook pressure; the fish moved right back into the lie where he'd been hooked and Lee strolled over and landed it—two or three minutes at the most. He went on to say that most fishermen make the fish panic and turn a simple situation into a complicated one. I later tried the same thing and nine out of ten times it works."

Lee's old 1930s crony Dan Bailey—now owner of the famous fly shop that bears his name in Livingston, Montana—invited Lee and Joan out to fish the Smith that summer and they had excellent fishing. They also had a chance to fish the Firehole River with another of Lee's old friends, Bud Lilly.

"We fished the Firehole in early August," Bud remembers, "in the same party was Arnold Gingrich. August is a very difficult period on the Firehole due to water temperatures approaching 80 degrees. Despite that Lee was able to hook several trout on grasshoppers that he was then developing with plastic bodies. Joan did as well. Arnold was busy unhooking his fly from the grass on the back cast. He was fond of very short rods."

As the winter of 1976 approached there was some progress to report on measures to save the salmon. At the Atlantic Salmon Association meeting in Montreal in March, Lee heard Executive Director Ken Reardon report to the members that 1975 did see the final phasing out of high seas fishing for salmon under the ICNAF agreement. Also the Canadian government had finally moved on salmon poachers and fines now were in the range of $500 to $1000 and punishment was in the form of jail terms—in many cases years, not months.

Dick Buck, writing in the *Atlantic Salmon Journal*, reported:

"It is now generally agreed that nations will extend their fisheries jurisdictions within the next few years—either by acting unilaterally or under a treaty arising out of the Law of the Sea Conference. Final approval under LOS could be as far away as five years, so there is increasing support in the U.S. for interim legislation to protect our fisheries from overexploitation and exhaustion by distant ocean fleets of foreign nations.

"The House of Representatives has voted to approve H.R. 200, the Studds-Magnuson 200-mile Fish Conservation Zone Bill. The 208 to 101 vote was a triumph for the broadly bi-partisan coalition in support of the bill. The Senate Commerce Committee has unanimously passed its bill, S.961, and once the full senate has passed the measure, it will go to a joint House-Senate Conference Committee to iron out the differences between the two versions. Thus, there is now a strong possibility that this legislation will be on the President's desk this winter."

Lee, brusk as usual, got off on one of his pet peeves that spring while speaking to the Canadian Fly Fishing Forum in Toronto. Long at odds with fisheries biologists over the management of salmon and trout, he blamed fisheries biologists in general for the deterioration of the sport.

He said the results in Newfoundland had been disastrous for Atlantic salmon and brook trout. He said there were fewer salmon and that they were much smaller in size than in previous years.

"Equally as disturbing for Wulff," reported the *Globe and Mail*, "is the continued exploitation of Labrador's brook trout rivers.

"'It has been the same old story time after time,' Lee was quoted as saying . . . "An operator sets up a fishing lodge. His guests concentrate on fishing the inlets and outlets of the river system. That's where the fish all concentrate. In a few years time the fishery collapses and the operator tries to find a buyer for his lodge. You really can't blame the fishermen traveling to the lodge. They assume that the regulations have been set according to some logical management plan. They are actually set for political reasons. Biology doesn't enter into the picture and biologists know it.'"

He added that he had been arguing this problem since 1940, "but not a single Canadian biologist has ever given me his support."

Naturally the reaction on the part of the Canadian fisheries biologists was somewhat strident. Wilf Carter, his longtime associate on the Atlantic Salmon Association and International Atlantic Salmon Foundation and life-long fisheries biologist took the charges calmly.

He said he and Lee had been friends and co-workers for years, but that Lee had always disagreed with the scientific approach to salmon management.

However, the majority of salmon and trout fly fishermen tended to support Lee. They needed a hero and he certainly fit the mold. U.S. conservation advocates considered him a leader in the field and early that year Lee received a letter from Gary Everhardt, Director of the U.S. Department of the Interior, asking if Lee would consider serving on an advisory panel to make recommendations concerning trout fishing on the National Park System. Lee was flattered and accepted.

That summer Lee went up to Caraquet—on the northern coast of New Brunswick—to fish for bluefin tuna. Fishing out of a small boat owned by Captain Victor Lanteigne, Lee fought and landed an 895 pound bluefin in rough seas in 2 hours and 15 minutes. The fish was submitted as a possible IGFA world record and was later certified as one by IGFA president Elwood K. Harry. It was not so much that the fish weighed 895 pounds and was caught on 80-pound line, what was unusual was that Lee was 71 years old at the time.

He attended a meeting of the Bonneville Chapter of the American Fisheries Society in Salt Lake City in early February. Lee and Joan had long discussed the idea of opening a fly-casting school, but realized Keene was too far from large centers of population for such a venture. They both finally realized a place close to New York would be the best solution and settled on a large parcel of land at Lew Beach, New York on Lee's long-favored Beaverkill River. Most of the river in that area was privately owned and their land held the rights to a long stretch of river.

Although both Lee and Joan had given fly casting lessons many times, neither had any experience in running a school. Lee asked some of his friends for advice and Koke Winter of Denver had some observations.

"In the Denver area alone there are already several fly fishing schools announced for this year. Hank Roberts Sport Shop (Norm Leighty) is doing one this weekend for the meager price of $100 and this with Doug Swisher. Doug gets $75 of each hundred. At 13 presently signed up, this means a gross take for Doug of $975. But of the other $2,515 goes to the lodge where it is being done, and $10 to Norm, which only just pays for his advertising. Ken Walters (The Flyfisher—an Orvis shop) will be doing a school in a few weeks for $50—which includes two protracted evening sessions and then an all-day session on a river. Fenwick does three schools near here at Winter Park, the last weekend in May. They get $120 for the schools.

"I suspect there are a myriad of others. With all their extensive operation (and expensive logistics), I happen to know that Fenwick just breaks even on its schools, some years losing money. I truly worry about the price you suggest in the neighborhood of $250, but I worry about a price any less on the grounds of profitability . . . but it would have to be done in places where there are enough people to pay the freight."

Lee on an Iceland salmon river in 1972. Jack Samson photo.

Lee thought the New York area might be the spot. It was only a few miles from the prestigious Beaverkill Trout Club and Lee inquired about joining. Samuel Croll, Jr. answered his query.

"I do not believe you would have any problem in joining the Beaverkill Trout Club," he wrote, "although there may be a time factor involved. We do have a waiting list and, since I am not on the membership committee, I do not know how many candidates are on the waiting list. I would, of course, be glad to be your sponsor and Van Parr, who has met you, indicated to me today that he would be glad to second you." Lee, however, never joined the club.

Lee and Joan, at the invitation of Gardner Grant, attended the Eastern Conclave of the Federation of Fly Fishermen at Roscoe, New York, June 11th and 12th and got in some good trout fishing on Gardner's private water on the Beaverkill.

Both Lee and Joan went west again to fish the trout streams of the Rocky Mountains—a yearly ritual. Lee's old friend, Charlie Meyers, outdoor editor of the Denver *Post*, wrote them, hoping they would come to the FFF conclave in Jackson, Wyoming in August.

"Don't let the streams dry up or the trout die off before we get there," Lee wrote back. "I'll hold this letter until we know where we'll be in Denver and we can hope to have lunch or something."

Charlie today remembers those trips vividly.

"Over the years I fished with Lee many times, the typical mountain stream expeditions that generally produced solid, but unspectacular results. However, a number of things struck me as extraordinary. Foremost was that Lee seldom played the chalk. If others were fishing dry flies, he would try streamers. If the hatch was for No. 20 Hendricksons, he'd tie on a No. 12 Royal Wulff. Apart form his life-long maverick nature, the motivation was an innate curiosity that commanded him to find out more about what stimulated trout. He knew he could catch fish with the Hendricksons and certainly was secure in his reputation. The most compelling thing was the experimentation."

In the later years of his life, Lee became more concerned with the challenge of fly fishing. He had caught thousands of salmon and trout and the mere catching of them no longer interested him. It was more fun to try and catch them on something different and perhaps in a different way. And as his time to fish grew shorter, he began to value the tiny gems of the sport.

Bob Jacklin, owner of Jacklin's Fly Shop in West Yellowstone and another old friend of Lee's, put it another way:

"Another memory I have of Lee Wulff was one day when Joan and Lee were fishing with me on the Gallatin River near Big Sky, Montana. Lee and

Joan had fished this area with me several times, the river was low and clear. Lee always enjoyed the upper portion of the ranch waters. The pool was about 50 yards long and had a gentle flow. A large pine had fallen into the river and caused a deep cut at the tailout of the pool. I will always remember Lee Wulff releasing a 7 inch wild rainbow trout. I thought to myself, as I snapped the photograph, here is Lee Wulff—who has caught world record game fish on a fly, Atlantic salmon and sailfish carefully releasing a small rainbow trout . . . fooling a fish on an artificial fly was the essence of sport fishing to Lee."

The same was becoming true in his salmon fishing. In a 1976 issue of *The Anglers' Club Bulletin* Lee wrote of his forming the Sixteen-Twenty Club—a group of salmon anglers who had caught a salmon of at least 20 pounds on a #16 fly.

"The setting was the Ouapatec Camp on the Moisie and our small group of light tackle salmon anglers was happily talking over the exciting points of the fine fishing day. Somehow in the conversation I made a statement that perhaps the key to our great respect for the Atlantic salmon was that, on the average, he took the smallest sized hook in relation to its weight of any game fish. I mentioned that I'd taken an eighteen pounder on a sparse 16 spider when I couldn't coax him to take any other fly and had even bigger fish rise to that fly.

"How big a fish could be caught on a #16 single trout hook? I felt there was no specific limit . . . and that if there were it certainly would be well over thirty pounds. On the spur of the moment we set up a club, the 'Sixteen-Twenty' Club, with the qualification for membership being the taking of a salmon of more than twenty pounds on a sixteen fly.

"We toasted the idea with a libation and I later settled at the table to celebrate by tying a fly that I thought would be most suitable . . . I crammed three long badger saddles on the shank of the hook, the tails of which I used to make up the tail of the fly. In the front I added a bucktail "snout" to give it much more certain floatation . . . I named it the Prefontaine, in honor of my host (Alain Prefontaine)."

The next day, at dusk Alain hooked a salmon on the #16-sized fly and as the rest of the club members went along, fought the fish in the darkness until it was finally netted by a guide. Everyone trudged along as they took the fish up to the lodge and weighed it—20 1/2 pounds. The club had its first member and its first president.

In the next few days Lee caught two salmon on the last day of the trip—both twins at 24 pounds each.

The years went by and the members used #16 flies regularly. Lucian Rolland once caught a 19 1/2 pound salmon—just missing the mark. Five years later Lucian caught a 22 pound salmon to become the third member of the club, but up until 1976 there were only three members who could wear the 16-20 lapel pin.

On the salmon front—as 1977 came to a close—Lee and others were involved in efforts to re-stock New England rivers with salmon and the International Atlantic Salmon Foundation, under the leadership of Wilf Carter and Joe Cullman, offered $250 for the first Atlantic salmon caught in salt or brackish water off the Massachusetts coast by a commercial fisherman. The fish, if alive, would go to a hatchery of the Massachusetts Marine Fisheries. That way fresh eggs could be used to raise fry to stock rivers.

Joseph Cullman, a wealthy New York businessman and chairman of the board of Philip Morris, Co., Inc., is an ardent outdoorsman and early became interested in the problem of the Atlantic salmon. His concern was due in large part because he owned a lodge—Runnymede—on the banks of the Restigouche River in New Brunswick. Joe devoted a lot of his time—and a good deal of his money—to saving the salmon. He was president of the International Atlantic Salmon Foundation—an organization that was compiling and providing the scientific information necessary for understanding the salmon and its problems.

As the year moved into 1978 Lee and Joan were confronted with the considerable chore of moving all their belongings from New Hampshire to their new home on the Beaverkill at Lew Beach, New York.

The year 1977 had been good to Lee. He had been elected chairman of the board of the Atlantic Salmon Association—the organization he had been so delighted to write a few stories for nearly a quarter of a century earlier.

The School

The move from New Hampshire to the Beaverkill was a nightmare for both Lee and Joan. They were finding out how much junk one can accumulate in a lifetime. The problem was that improvements on the Beaverkill property were taking forever to complete and they had sold the New Hampshire house.

In January, while still trying to get organized, Lee wrote:

"Right now we're jittery because we've sold our house here and still haven't a place to move in the Beaverkill area. We have to be out of here on April 3rd and hope we can move directly to a new spot but finding a suitable place isn't easy and we may have to buy land and build on it . . . renting until we can move in . . . and storing our furniture and all my movie and other equipment . . . which would be rough."

Lee charged $400 a night, plus expenses, to do shows for groups. The expenses included transportation by car, or plane, and lodging in a hotel or motel. Many times Joan would go with him—at times to give casting demonstrations or to show films. It was a good income, but it kept them busy.

Barry and Ella May had moved to Connecticut and Lee had at least a chance now and then to see them and his grandchildren—Sabrina, now 8 years old and her younger sister, Tasha, 5.

Allan, who had married a lawyer, Ginger McGuffie, finally at Ginger's insistence contacted his father. It was a good meeting between Lee and Allan, and at least they had flying to talk about.

In the first part of the year, Lee had a running battle with Julian Yoseloff, president of A.S. Barnes—the company which had originally published his classic, *The Atlantic Salmon*. The company had never declared his book out of print, was still holding several hundred copies in reserve and would not grant Lee reprint rights. Nick Lyons, Lee's old friend, wanted to reprint the book, but was unable to until Barnes took some action. Lee was later forced to hire Attorney Myron Friedman to contact Yoseloff in effect demanding that Barnes either reprint the book or give Lee rights to do a new edition. Lee finally got the reprint rights in 1978.

Lee attended the annual meeting of the Atlantic Salmon Association at the Ritz Carlton Hotel in Montreal March 9th as chairman of the board of ASA. Delegates heard ASA President David Lank report on achievements of the past year. Lank promised the organization would continue to press for a shorter commercial netting season for Newfoundland and the abolition of coastal netting.

Dick Buck, president of the Restoration of Atlantic Salmon in America (RASA) was named an honorary director and Lee personally presented the fourth annual T. B. "Happy" Frazier Award to Joe Cullman, president of the International Atlantic Salmon Foundation since 1972. The award was presented annually by the ASA in appreciation for an outstanding contribution to Atlantic salmon conservation over a period of time.

In the April issue of the *Atlantic Salmon Journal*—for which Lee had written regularly—Lee wrote an article entitled "Sanctuary For Salmon." Lee wrote that he saw nothing wrong in allowing spinning tackle in the taking of Atlantic salmon provided such tackle was restricted to using top surface, single-hook spinning lures. The article brought a fire storm of reader mail—most violently opposed to spinning tackle being used for any form of Atlantic salmon angling. Lee, as usual, stuck to his guns saying the only sanctuary for salmon in rivers was the deep pools and all lures, flies included, should be restricted to the surface.

By the end of March, Lee and Joan had things about ready to go from the New Hampshire house. They had been given an extension there and expected to move into the Beaverkill property on May 4th. Lee couldn't afford the price wanted for the entire 600-acre Doubleday estate, but as he wrote his old friend, Dr. Ralph Maxwell, in March:

"We have a lot of things to do . . . get a mortgage . . . plan for school . . . Though Stuart may stay here with friends to finish his term. The negotiations on the place down there were long and tedious. We couldn't afford the whole

155

estate . . . so a group got together and bought it and they agree to sell us the part we want.

"We have nearly a hundred boxes of fishing tackle packed and have just started on film and equipment . . . the Green Machine and all the other mowers or rototillers, etc., will be a problem . . . as will the boat and canoe."

The national media was full of Nicaragua and President Jimmy Carter's announcement that economic aid to Lee's old fishing buddy, dictator Anastazio Somoza, was being reduced in an effort to convince him to deal with the revolutionary Sandinista movement.

Lee's longtime fishing friend Arnold Gingrich died and Lee received a letter on Federation of Fly Fishermen stationary from President Gardner Grant asking for a donation for a Gingrich memorial. The contribution, due by July 7th, would be placed in the Arnold Gingrich Memorial Fund which was to finance one or more Memorial Life Memberships to be announced at the FFF Conclave at West Yellowstone in August.

Lee and the Midtown Club members attended a testimonial luncheon to fellow member fly fisherman and illustrator John Groth at the Overseas Press Club in Manhattan. Lee showed a segment he and John had done for the "American Sportsman" series about art, war and trout. John was having a major retrospective show at the Rhoda Sande Gallery that month.

Lee and Joan were also invited by Jim Rikoff to Gene Hill's 50th birthday party. It was hosted by Club "21" owner and salmon fly fisherman Pete Kriendler, May 17, 1978.

Lee and Joan Wulff open their fly fishing school at Lew Beach, New York in 1979.

"The bad news is," Rikoff's note read, "you had better start taking your health pills now and, perhaps, obtain a note from your doctor before joining us." Rikoff was, and probably still is, the head organizer of a rowdy group of outdoorsman called "The Winchester Irregulars."

Lee and Joan managed only two salmon fishing trips that spring—one to the Tobique, which was a wash-out, and the other to the Grand Cascapedia which turned out to be a marvelous trip.

"They had low water," Lee wrote to Nick Lyons, "and poor fishing, but for us the fish responded. Joan caught two—the largest 18 pounds and I four—the largest 25 pounds . . . I took two on #16s and our fishing amazed everyone."

In a wonderful surprise, salmon began returning to the waters of the Connecticut River that spring topping off efforts by Lee and others to re-introduce the species to the once-great salmon river. A total of 73 salmon returned to the river as of June 20th fulfilling hopes of the RASA, of which Lee was a vice president. Sixty three were taken alive and moved to a hatchery for the taking of eggs and roe for later stockings.

Lee and his longtime friend, Wilf Carter were at odds over the disposition of buildings and property of the International Atlantic Salmon Foundation at St. Andrews, but it was only a disagreement among old friends. Lee was truly touched by a note from Wilf that ended:

"I know, more than most people, how much you give to the cause of conservation, and to the IASF in particular in other ways. Few people on this continent have been more devoted to a cause they believe in and which they defend with such honesty and eloquence both in your written and spoken word.

With all best wishes to you and Joan for 1978.

Yours sincerely, Wilf"

That year saw the first discussions and efforts to combine several salmon organizations. Wilf wrote Lee saying he had talked with Joe Cullman in New York about trying to bring together the Atlantic Salmon Association and the International Atlantic Salmon Foundation under one umbrella organization. He said Cullman told him he did not think it was a good idea—that it would be hard to do and the benefits, if it were done, would not be that great. Lee wrote back, saying he agreed with Cullman—at least for the time being.

In early November John Merwin, an editor of *Fly Fisherman* magazine and writer from Vermont, wrote Lee asking whether he could contribute stories to a new magazine he was just starting: *Rod & Reel*. Lee queried *Sports Afield*'s editor Tom Paugh, who quite rightly told Lee he couldn't go along with Lee writing a column for a competing outdoor magazine—however small. Merwin, a friend of Lee's, in turn gave Lee a sales pitch about being able to write anything he wanted as an Editor-at-Large and offered him a good salary. Lee, flattered and glad to have a podium that was not controlled by the Hearst Corporation—owners of *Sports Afield*—quit the bigger magazine and went with Merwin.

As January, 1979 arrived Lee knew he would be faced with a busy spring at the new school and didn't plan many trips. As he wrote a Canadian friend, Fred Webb who ran an outfitting operation in New Brunswick, the school was coming along:

"Our school is going to keep us very busy this spring and summer. We'll have to be on hand every moment and I don't think we'll get much rest.

"The salmon situation seems pretty much up in the air. The Indians sure have raised hell and everyone wants to compromise . . . which I am sure they will take as a sign of weakness. I think they should be the same as any other Canadian as far as sport fishing goes."

Lee was talking about the current battle between the Canadian Indian tribes and the government in which the Indians wanted free rein to catch as many salmon as they wanted on their own reservations. The federal government had issued a "Discussion Paper" which proposed that the tribes have authority to manage their own fishing—commercial and sport. The ASA was worried that such authority would give Indians at the mouths of rivers the right to manage the fish that would go all the way upstream.

Lee had begun writing a regular column for the *Atlantic Salmon Journal* and for the first issue of that year wrote about "Sex In Salmon Fly

Lee and Joan crossing the Grand Cascapedia. Lucien Rolland photo.

Selection"—discussing the fact that certain flies can be fished for male and female salmon. Lee wrote that in fishing for large salmon, he had found the Stonefly to be his best pattern. He attributed this to the fact that perhaps the stonefly was more, or better, imprinted on a parr when it was small than any other insect.

Lee and Joan attended the annual conference of the Atlantic Salmon Association—again at the Ritz Carlton Hotel in Montreal—on March 29, 1979. There was good news in that the salmon might at last get high seas protection, according to a report from RASA.

A proposal that the salmon might get protection on their way to and from their winter Greenland feeding areas, was proposed at a meeting on February 21st by Larry Snead of the U.S. Department of State. He said the U.S. was planning to initiate multilateral discussions and negotiations to establish a new international commission, with the objectives of conserving, managing and retaining Atlantic salmon stocks in the North Atlantic. Countries to be affected by such a treaty would include all those nations producing Atlantic salmon and those wishing to fish for Atlantic salmon. The ASA would officially endorse the Canadian delegation to go to Washington concerning the proposed treaty.

Another important suggestion made at the annual meeting was that the ASA and IASF should join together with other groups to deal with the problems arising from the Indians' Native Food Fisheries.

The ASA was the recipient of the U.S. American Motors Conservation Award, presented by Ed Zern, associate editor of *Field & Stream*. Zern, a humor writer for the big magazine, was also an ardent salmon fly fisherman.

Lee's column in the ASA magazine that month was about the physical differences between salmon of different rivers. It had long been known that salmon of different rivers had strikingly different shapes—like the differences between salmon of the Newfoundland's East and Torrent Rivers. The East River and the North River were long, tortuous rivers difficult for salmon to travel. The flows, on the other hand, of the Torrent and Eagle Rivers were slow and leisurely. The latter rivers produced long and slender salmon while the first rivers were well-known for muscular, short and heavy salmon.

Dick Buck, a highly controversial figure in salmon circles and president of RASA, antagonized a number of people with his comment in *Trout and Salmon* on a Dr. Derek Mills article "The Atlantic Salmon Symposium."

His criticism raised the ire of Joe Cullman, president of the IASF, who wrote him and questioned whether he should remain on the IASF board of directors. He carboned Lee, Wilf Carter, Bill Brewster, Francis Goelet and Marshall Field.

Buck later resigned from I.A.S.F.

Both Lee and Joan participated in the annual Izaak Walton Fly Fisherman's Clubs Fly Fishing Forum March 31st and April 1, 1979 in Toronto—for the usual fee.

The school was getting its first students and it was a busy spring and summer. Lee wrote his longtime friend, Tap, in July:

"The school has been our life for this spring and summer. We just barely have time to keep up with some letters and a little writing. Joan is a consultant for Uni-Royal of women's waders and things.

"The place here is beautiful and it is a pleasure to be here. However, we're still not unpacked from our move well over a year ago as the house isn't finished . . . but we're getting close.

"We're going to Iceland for salmon fishing for a week the first of August and will take off for tuna sometime in September. And I have to go out to Yellowstone to talk at the Wild Trout Symposium in late September and Joan will come along and we'll fish the trout streams out there for a week, I think.

"We haven't had any time to fish although the river is right out in front . . . It's low now, anyway, these days."

Lee instructing a class in fly tying.

Elwood Harry, president of the International Game Fish Association in Ft. Lauderdale, asked Lee—among others—on July 5th for input on updating the IGFA rules and regulations.

"E.K." sent several pages of the present rules and regulations and asked Lee for suggestions, particularly on the newly acquired IGFA program of saltwater fly fishing.

On the minimum length of the class tippet—12 inches—Lee wrote that the "12" is o.k., but 18" would be better."

On the maximum length of the shocker leader—12 inches—Lee wrote "The shock leader length should not be more than the present 12"—with the possible exception of billfish where a 3 foot shock leader might be allowed."

On the maximum length of fly rods, Lee suggested a 6 foot minimum and a 9 1/2 foot maximum. He suggested two hooks should be allowed if they were in tandem "and separated by at least a shank's length."

On the question of a flying gaff for saltwater fly fishing, Lee suggested the "same flying gaff rules as now in effect for other saltwater tackle."

Lee's ankles were not getting any better—perhaps caused by years of sports and wading stream beds. As he wrote Dr. Ralph Maxwell after returning from Iceland in late August:

"My ankles are worse, but I still get around O.K. However on the last half day in Iceland I stayed at the lodge instead of plodding a mile and a half over knobby ground to a place where there were only a couple of tired salmon that had already seen thousands of flies."

Lee hunted deer every year since he could remember at Sandgate, Vermont, and at his old New Hampshire home in Surry, and now was thinking about hunting near his new home.

That fall he was invited up to the Adirondacks for deer hunting but opted for his old favorite Sandgate, on opening day.

"There's a chance Doug and Stuart may join us to open the season," he wrote Ralph, "Stuart is on the football team and a second string end. . . We'll be staying here though taking an occasional day in New York and are under pressure for a three or four day trip to Texas to talk to a graphite rod company about consulting work. It's time we settled down and got back to normal. Joan is worrying about programs for next year's schools and we have some bookkeeping and finishing up on that score too. I'm behind on writing and will have the Nova Scotia film to edit . . . We'll be seeing you soon . . . may come up ahead of the Vermont opening . . . sharpen your eye for dead shooting."

At the end of the year Joan joined the staff of *Outdoor Life*, writing a regular column on casting tips each month.

"I now refer to myself," Lee wrote Ralph, "as the husband of the writer."

International Problems

While the United States, Canada and an international committee worked on some sort of settlement to the high seas commercial salmon fishery, Lee had some theories of his own which he expressed as an editorial in the spring issue of the *Atlantic Salmon Journal:*

"The essential ingredients in safeguarding a natural resource," he wrote, "that benefits the public, is an involved citizenry. Until now too few salmon anglers have joined in a determined effort to protect them. They have donated time and money, but have left the government to protect the fish because it is their 'duty' to do so. It will take more.

"I believe one of the best ways to achieve a good protection is for groups or clubs to 'adopt' a salmon river and work diligently for its protection. The river and the great, exciting salmon that enter into it from the sea are too valuable to lose, for they give us pleasure, dreams and memories. By banding together we can save them. If you do not now belong to a club dedicated to the river or rivers you fish it is time to join one."

He advised readers who joined such a club they must report all game violations. After that—if prosecution of violators fails—he urged that the members get the press on their side and publicize the problems of the river. He also recommended that each club get a lawyer member or a legal team to wage the war against salmon poaching.

Not only was Lee advocating action on the part of salmon anglers, but Canadian writers were doing the same. George Gruenfeld, a newspaper columnist and one of the best salmon anglers in the nation, was ranting against the government's apparent inability to solve the Indian fishing problem.

"While important breeding runs of Atlantic salmon are being wiped out," he wrote, also in the *Atlantic Salmon Journal* of October 1980, "three government departments—two Federal and one provincial—are determined to uphold the concept of traditional native rights, no matter how grotesquely these rights are abused. While resentment against native nets brews on the river banks, the Department of Indian and Northern Affairs and the Department of Fisheries and Oceans claim to be working toward a solution without showing us results . . .

"Controversy over the Indian subsistence fishery started as a native assertion of their right to fish, but has flared into a political confrontation in which the victim is the Atlantic salmon. It no longer matters that, at current rates, salmon will disappear from rivers such as the Restigouche within a few short years. Now there's a principle at stake."

There were controversies within the salmon associations themselves. Dick Buck resigned from the board of the IASF after being dressed down by Joe Cullman and Lee agreed with Joe's stand.

"I think the Dick Buck thing has worked out as it should," he wrote Cullman on January 30, 1980. "I'll stay on with RASA and may be of some value if cooperation or communication is needed between the two organizations. RASA seems to be growing a bit and there were about ten at the recent director's meeting instead of the usual 3 or 4. IASF's growth in the ten years has been very good, especially recently. I believe we are going into a period of greatly increased public interest in Atlantic salmon and that the organizations and their work will become much more important than in the past.

"I'll have a story in *Outdoor Life* on the salmon prospects in the issue after next and I think it, too, will help crystallize interest by the public."

Lee nominated Gardner Grant—a wealthy White Plains, New York realtor and investment broker—to the board of directors of the IASF. Grant, a fly fisherman and formerly active in any number of conservation organizations in the U.S., was passed on by both Wilf Carter and Joe Cullman.

The year was starting out as a copy of the one before. Looking forward to the spring and summer, Lee wrote his old friend, Ted Trueblood, an associate editor of *Field & Stream*, in Idaho, on February 20, 1980.

"Thanks for your letter. It is great to know that you've eliminated the cancer bug. All your friends celebrate with you. Great!

"The school goes well. Happy people last season and this year the bookings are going quite well. Last year we tried a fairly long season and schedule of six days and four nights a week which was far too heavy. This year we've shortened it a day and will only run 2 1/2 months.

"Just passed my seventy-fifth birthday and I still don't have sense enough to loaf. Have books to write and can't get at them because of the articles I do . . . and the school . . . and a film on salmon I'm finishing up for Nova Scotia . . .

"However we're both well and this life seems to be good for us. We're enjoying the Catskills which I thought were too tame when I headed off for the bush and the wild places in the thirties. We've settled in easily and have a lot of friends here.

"We're going to try and get a lot of fishing in this summer as soon as we finish the school in late July. We hope to get west for a week or two . . . and somewhere for salmon . . . and some good plug casting . . . "

Both Lee and Joan did a show for the Trout Unlimited Chapter at Valley Forge, Pennsylvania on March 14th before an audience estimated by them at about 700 people.

The salmon movie Lee had just finished editing was one done the summer before for Nova Scotia—with lots of jumping grilse, but no salmon caught. Now the government wanted a tuna movie done there and Lee hoped to do it from another small boat using Joan and two local women anglers who could crew and gaff big fish. He contacted Bill Munro of Mako boats and made arrangements to get a 22-foot, center-console Mako to use in the film. There again, Lee wanted a swivel chair mounted in the bow.

The nations concerned with the Atlantic salmon high seas fishery fought all the way through 1980 and what it boiled down to was that some sovereign nations—particularly Canada—were clinging to the principle that no recommendations could be made by any governing body regarding management of salmon stocks within Canadian maritime waters, except with respect to Canadian interception of stocks of U.S. origin.

On the other side of the negotiations, according to fisheries experts, were the U.S. and the European Economic Community (EEC) which negotiated for salmon-producing and salmon fishing nations such as the United Kingdom, France, Ireland and Denmark.

Negotiations on a treaty were progressing slowly and the next meeting was scheduled for August 1981 in Geneva.

In Canada George Gruenfeld's prediction was coming all too true. All during early 1981 the Canadian press was filled with what they termed the "salmon war." The war first grabbed the headlines in early June when Quebec game wardens, accompanied by a contingent of provincial police, went to the MicMac Indian Reservation near the mouth of the Restigouche and confiscated the

Indian nets. All this was because no progress was being made in the negotiations between the Indians and the government.

The government was trying to restrict the Indians to three days of netting a week, the Indians were demanding six days but were willing to settle for six half-days. All this was fooling no one because the Indians wanted to put their nets in at the mouth of the river at night, when the salmon normally moved upriver.

Then the Indians on the Escoumins River in Quebec set nets across the main river channel after local citizens had been hard at work for several years in trying to bring the salmon back to the river. The resulting battle hit the national press and more hard feelings were stirred up.

And while the Canadian public was focused on the Indian salmon problem, no one noticed that Canadian newspapers were carrying very little news of negotiations that were being held in Geneva on the high seas fishery. The reason, it turned out, was that Canada did not participate in those negotiations.

Michael Huband, chairman of the Atlantic Salmon Journal Committee, took note of the situation in an editorial that fall:

"While less spectacular within Canada than the developments in the Indian fishery," he wrote, "the need to reach agreement on the North Atlantic harvest is far more important in the overall scheme of things. In addition to the allotment of 1,270 metric tons for the Greenland fishery (recently raised from 1,190 tons) the Faroese plan unilaterally to take 1,220 metric tons in 1981-82 (an increase from 50 tons in the 1970s). This translates into 2.6 million pounds or (at an average of 9 pounds per fish) some 600,000 salmon, compared with the 75,000 pounds, or 8,000 fish at stake in the Restigouche salmon war.

"Of course," he continued, "the numbers of salmon harvested anywhere in the North Atlantic have an impact on Canadian stocks. For example, as a result of the burgeoning fishery in the Faroe Islands, which greatly reduces the numbers of European-bred salmon reaching Greenland, more Canadian salmon are captured as part of the Greenland allotment. This means, in effect, that thousands of dollars spent by North American anglers, government and industry, which go toward protecting the salmon and enhancing spawning areas and the salmon's access thereto, are literally being chucked into the sea, to be scooped out by the Greenlanders and the Faroese.

"Without an international salmon treaty," he concluded, "Canadian efforts—to control poaching, the Indian fishery and commercial netting—are like trying to refill a bathtub with cups of water while the drain is left open . . ."

Lee and Joan traveled to Portland, Maine to do a program and show for the Sebago Chapter of Trout Unlimited and Tom Pero, president of TU, wrote and asked if they could do a show that spring for the Boston chapter. The Wulffs raised the price for shows to $500 plus expenses so these TU shows were not only fun to do, but profitable.

Both Lee and Joan had been approached by Elsie Darbee about establishing the Catskill Fly Fishing Center and Museum at Roscoe, New York. The Catskill region had long been regarded as the birthplace of fly fishing in America. Historical fly fishermen like Theodore Gordon, Edward R. Hewitt and George LaBranche had made the area famous. In addition, legendary fly rod makers Hiram Leonard, Jim Payne, Gillum and Garrison used the rivers of the region to test their rods. Fly tiers Harry and Elsie Darbee and Walt and Winifred Dette also had made the area well-known.

Each year thousands of fly fishermen visited the famous rivers of the Catskills—the Beaverkill, the Neversink, the Esopus, the Willowemoc and the Delaware. The idea proposed by the late Elsie Darbee was to establish a headquarters for the collection and museum display of trout fishing artifacts, literature and art.

Among the original incorporates of the Center were Lee and Joan, Elsie and Harry Darbee, Walt Dette, George Renner, Art and Kris Lee, Carolyn and Ken Hobbs, Joe Horak, Alan Fried, Farley Manning and Kim Sprague.

It was established that summer and fall by a completely volunteer group and sported a board of directors of 40 people. A site of 31 acres had been chosen and a tentative offer had already been made to the Van Aken family. The project took a great deal of time for Lee and Joan—who considered it their responsibility to contribute generously.

Though he had fished for bonefish in the Florida Keys and in the Bahamas off and on over the years, Lee began to understand the great pleasure of the tropical flats in these later years. It may have had something to do with his advancing age—76—but the beauty of the tropics and the warmth of the equatorial sun began to absorb him. He fished at Deep Water Cay in the Bahamas and saw big permit though he did not hook one there.

He finally discovered Boca Paila—several hundred miles south of Cancun on the Yucatan Penninsula—and really began to appreciate the beauty of that region. With a Mayan guide poling slowly across the shallow flats, he and Joan learned to enjoy the silence of the vast flats broken only by the harsh croaks of wading shore birds and the chattering laughter of parrots.

After years of fly fishing for salmon and trout, Lee realized that bonefish were a tremendous challenge on a fly. He learned to judge size and was better able to see the silvery fish against the white coral marl of the bottom. He began to develop his own bonefish flies and wrote about these streaking game fish of the flats more and more in the outdoor magazines.

He came to appreciate the solitude of the vast mangrove-studded flats and learned more each year about the ecology of the shallow water—the rays, barracuda, turtle grass, boxfish, conchs, lobsters, snapper and the myriad legions of baitfish schools.

He stalked the ghostly and elusive permit in the deeper waters of the Bahamas and the warm shallows of Ascension Bay off Yucatan—peering into the clear water for the tell-tale, black tiny dorsal fins and the sickle-shaped tails of these impressive and spooky game fish. Though he caught permit up to 14 pounds at Boca Paila, he never pretended to be an expert at this unique sport as did such polished permit fly anglers as Del Brown and a few others.

He also kept up his quest for billfish on a fly and caught some more Pacific sailfish at a number of lodges and resorts in Costa Rica and Panama.

That summer Lee and Joan fished the Gallatin River and Henry's Fork near Yellowstone Park, continued work on the tuna film for Nova Scotia and Lee went back to Labrador for a week. The only good salmon trip that year was one to the Mirimachi River in the Maritime Provinces.

Lee had been thinking for a long time about coming out with his own design of fly lines. After considerable experimenting with types and materials, he finally applied for a patent on a weight-forward fly line he was to name the "Triangle Taper" fly line.

The theory behind it was, as Lee put it:

"The best line for making a roll cast is a line that tapers constantly from a large diameter and heavy weight to a fine diameter and minimum weight near the fly. In roll casting such a line the heavier line near the rod is constantly passing its energy on to the lighter line as the roll moves forward. This is much more efficient than roll-casting level line or level line sections where the line in the roll must lift and push forward line of equal weight. Such full-length, single-taper lines were made years ago especially for roll casting, but have not been made for half a century since overhead casting with forward taper and double-tapered lines has become extremely popular.

"My invention is to have a roll casting line in the front half (approximately) of the line and then use this long roll casting segment as a forward taper or "head" to make long overhead casts with. This forward tapering belly can be used by normal casting to make casts of approximately the same distance as those made by forward tapers or double tapers now available . . .

"This line will roll cast better and with more delicacy . . . than any other type of fly line," he concluded. "In overhead casting it will permit the most delicate presentation of the fly because of the long front single-taper which keeps the heavy, more-visible section of the line farthest from the fish. It will permit "shooting" the forward single-tapered section for long distances in overhead casting while still delivering the fly with greater delicacy than presently available fly lines."

He wrote Howard West of Scientific Anglers/3M asking for some samples to be made up:

"We've run some tests and would like to have some of the new Triangle Taper lines made up. They should be standard floating lines. What color options can we choose from? We'd like the line to start at the fly end with your minimum diameter (we'd hope .030" or under) and taper in a constant increase in diameter to .055 in forty feet, then drop back in about four feet to normal shooting line of .033 diameter for the rest of the 90 feet."

Lee ordered these samples made up and asked for the cost of a minimum order. He and Joan planned to package the lines themselves. Initial reaction to the new lines, on the part of outdoor magazine and industry testers, was very good.

As the year came to a close Lee still had the plight of the salmon very much on his mind—particularly the Canadian government practice of making some rivers "grilse rivers."

"We have not yet put our hearts and souls into the fight to save the salmon; most of us seem to be waiting for someone else to do the job," he wrote in the *Atlantic Salmon Journal.*

"How careless we have been . . . and how indifferent . . . is certainly shown by the action—or rather the lack of it—of anglers when commercial netting was reinstated in 1981 in New Brunswick and the quota for the Miramichi Basin was set at 12,000 salmon and 3,000 grilse. Regret was expressed publicly at the resumption of commercial netting, but little anger about the salmon/grilse ratio was evident in the press or in the various bulletins I receive from the conservation organizations. Protests on this point were neither coordinated enough, nor loud enough, to reflect the extent of injury done to the sports fishing industry. Yet this kind of thing we cannot take lying down if we ever hope to have good Atlantic salmon management.

"Conservation organizations call for the harvesting of more grilse and allowing more large salmon to reach the spawning redds. On the Margaree, the government of Nova Scotia actually limits the early angling take to grilse only and mandates that all large salmon be returned to the river, unharmed, to go on to spawn. At the same time the federal government is reversing that process in the Miramichi, which will make that great river even more of a grilse river than it is now.

"We all applaud Nova Scotia's forward-looking conservation measure. I'm amazed and shocked that the conservationists did not protest more vigorously when the Miramichi was moved towards more grilse at the expense of the bigger fish. The alarm should have been spread for a great public outcry against the move. The quota should have been reversed to 3,000 salmon and 12,000 grilse, or even better, no allotment for large salmon at all.

"Salmon anglers—and the huge industry they represent—must be prepared to fight every inch of the way. What happens to Atlantic salmon anywhere affects all of us. Until we stand up for our beliefs with effort and dollars, we will continue to lose the battle . . ."

Lee tying on a fly at the fishing school. Glenn Lau photo.

The Dwindling Salmon

Lee's longtime friend, Ted Trueblood, veteran associate editor of *Field & Stream* died and Lee got a letter from Tap Tapply on January 9th:

"Christmas got by me somehow, and that's when I usually try to re-establish communication with certain old friends. But to coin an old expression, better late than never.

"I won't be hearing from two old friends this year-end: cancer took Ted Trueblood and Ollie Rodman, among others who were not so closely associated with field sports. You and I shouldn't be considered just old, Lee; we're survivors.

"You must be, what 77 or 78? I'll be 73 my next birthday, an occasion I definitely will not celebrate. Muriel is 66 and looks years younger, and the last picture I saw of Joan she could be your daughter. Hell, granddaughter! I suppose having young wives is good for us. And if one young wife is so goddamn healthy, maybe we each should have two."

As if to counter the bad news, an event took place January 15th that Lee had been waiting for for years: The presidents of the International Atlantic Salmon Federation and the Atlantic Salmon Association signed a historic agreement that created the Atlantic Salmon Federation (ASF). IASF changed its identity to ASF (U.S.) and ASA became ASF (Canada). Both groups retained separate corporate legal status and directors, but staff and resources functioned under a single authority. A management board was established (to set policy) with representation from both ASF Canada and ASF U.S.

The annual meeting of the ASA at Le Chateau Champlain Hotel in Montreal March 4th was a celebration. Lee summed it up in a talk: "I really feel good about this meeting," he said, "We now have brought together the two senior salmon conservation groups in North America into a Federation with the active support of many affiliate organizations. I think we are on course and moving."

Everyone felt good about the new Federation. It was a happy convention. Recipient of the "Happy" Frazier award that year was Stuart Molson—a founding member of the ASA and a director since its inception.

Lee—because of his early involvement in both organizations—played a leadership roll in each. He remained chairman of the board of the Atlantic Salmon Association; a vice president of the IASF and became a director of the new Management Committee of the Atlantic Salmon Federation.

Grizzly Midge fly. Jack Samson photo.

The Management Committee was composed of six directors from ASA and six from IASF. The new chairman was Lucien Rolland, president of ASA. Joe Cullman, president of IASF, became the first vice-chairman and Wilf Carter was the first Executive Director. Carter commented upon the new organization:

"The Atlantic Salmon Federation structure," he said, "will provide an opportunity for participation by all local and national salmon conservation groups, and we intend to move rapidly to invite their support. We hope to achieve this through the formation of regional councils, uniting salmon groups in each region, which will then become affiliated with the Federation. We intend to build the Federation into the most powerful voice for Atlantic salmon in North America and, through overseas links, to strengthen the bonds of conservation on both sides of the Atlantic."

Lee had long hoped for the regional plan and had made many a suggestion himself to that end. As soon as the Montreal Convention was over he made plans for a trip to Newfoundland, New Brunswick and Nova Scotia. The trip—with the help of friends like Joe Cullman—was financed by the ASA, Benson & Hedges and 7-Up. Lee took Joan with him and the purpose of the trip was to raise funds for affiliate clubs and allow them to fund their pet conservation projects, plus getting them interested in joining up with the Federation.

Both Lee and Joan became familiar to more than 2,000 salmon anglers in the Maritime Provinces and Newfoundland as a result of the seven-stop tour in the Atlantic provinces in mid-February.

Included in their program was Lee on film, fly casting demonstrations by Joan and talks by Lee on salmon conservation which stressed the need to revise fishing codes that tended to destroy larger salmon.

Stops on the tour included Corner Brook, Newfoundland on February 17th where attendance at the meeting was at least 400 people. St. Johns, February 20th to a meeting of 300 salmon anglers; Halifax, Nova Scotia February 23 with an attendance of more than 500 people; Saint John, February 24, attendance 300; Fredericton, New Brunswick, February 25, attendance 300, Moncton, February 26th and Edmundston, February 27th.

The tour was both a social and financial success. Many people remembered Lee from years past and considered him a friend of their country and a champion of the salmon. Ray Simmons, outdoor editor of the St. Johns, Newfoundland *Evening Telegram* probably spoke for the majority of Canadian anglers when he wrote on February 20th:

"Lee Wulff, an American sportsman who has killed more Atlantic salmon in his lifetime perhaps than any other angler alive today, returned to

Newfoundland this week to plead once more for a reprieve for this threatened species.

"Accompanied by his wife and business partner, Joan Salvato, a world champion fly caster in her own right, the aging Wulff (I make him over 70) is now on a swing through Atlantic Canada involving enough public appearances, speeches and presentations to hospitalize a less rugged individual.

"Characterized variously throughout his outstanding career as a "swashbuckling mercenary," "far sighted conservationist," "would-be salmon exploiter" and "outdoorsman of the century," Lee Wulff stands alone as the man who has done the most to promote the delights of hunting and fishing in this province . . ."

"Although he did not confine himself exclusively to the Newfoundland scene, it was here, perhaps, that he was most appreciated and yet most criticized. Nobody ever challenged his skill with a fly rod and few bettered him with rifle or bow, but in a small province where communications were poor and politics the principal pastime, it was inevitable perhaps that Wulff and his ideas had opponents as well as supporters . . ."

"Most of the criticism I've heard about Wulff I've put down to pure jealousy or simple misunderstanding. He was given a job to do (by the Newfoundland Tourist Board) and he did it—very well, very professionally and all by himself. For a while he operated salmon and trout fishing camps on River Of Ponds and Western Brook. He employed local guides, cooks and helpers. They made more in one season than their commercial contemporaries who often dumped their salmon catches as fertilizer on vegetable gardens. Wulff sought to perpetuate the fabulous salmon and brook trout angling by having the commercial fishery curtailed. At the same time he sought some protection for fishing lodge operators. You can imagine what the local politicians did with that combination—he was characterized as a 'greedy operator' trying to keep 'poor fishermen from making a living' while he 'cleaned up' catering to 'rich American anglers.' His suggestion that some leasing would help perpetuate the species for all concerned fell on deaf ears. Eventually he gave up his camps, but fishing guides have pointed out the old sites to me and still proclaim that 'Lee Wulff fished here'."

"I don't know what the fishing would be like on River Of Ponds and Portland Creek today if the government had listened to Lee Wulff, but I know that where he used to catch salmon—really big fish, according to the local people—I catch only grilse today . . ."

In Canada in 1982 there were approximately 80,000 salmon anglers— 90 percent or 72,000 of them Canadian citizens. There were about 7,000 commercial salmon fishing licenses, 90 percent of them in Newfoundland.

Since 1972 the average annual salmon catch in Canada was 4 1/2 million pounds. Of that total, on average, 80 percent was taken by commercial fishermen. Which meant that eight percent of the fishermen in Newfoundland had been allowed, under long-existing regulations, to harvest 80 percent of the salmon catch. No wonder salmon fly fishermen could identify with Lee Wulff.

It was going to be a tough fight, but Lee had no intention of letting up on the commercial people.

"Perhaps his greatest contribution," wrote Bill Brewster, Lee's longtime friend and fellow director of the Federation Management Committee, "was to eventually persuade the Board that political clout was needed to achieve meaningful reduction in commercial fishing . . . "

"The membership of the Federation for years consisted of well-heeled American and Canadians who had little political influence and were reluctant to oppose the commercial fishermen. Based mostly on Lee's urging, the ASF added provincial councils—reflecting the views of grass roots anglers and included council presidents on the Management Board.

"Lee was also an early promoter of the important fact that angling was far better for the Canadian economy than commercial fishing. The combination of the two concepts did produce an effective political force which has significantly reduced loss of larger salmon through buy-outs of commercial licenses and elimination of netting in council areas.

"There are many other examples of Lee's advice being followed," Brewster added, "but there are two areas where it has not. For a long time Lee argued that the Atlantic salmon should simply be declared a game fish, which would automatically preclude its commercial capture and sale. Other developments have had almost the same bottom-line affect however. Lee was also very unhappy that ASF's considerable research work was being applied too much to aquacultural salmon and not enough to wild salmon to benefit angling. Lee did not, unfortunately, provide enough specific suggestions as to what projects should be undertaken."

His longtime associate Wilf Carter had the same observations:

"In the first part of my career I worked as a government biologist; Lee did not have much faith in bureaucrats consequently it took some time to convince him that our goals were the same, even though they often seemed easier to attain to Lee than they actually were, given the bureaucratic maze in which I had to operate.

"Later, when I left government to become the first Executive Director of the International Atlantic Salmon Foundation and Lee came on the Board we didn't, at first, work easily together. As he was throughout his life, Lee was enormously impatient; he wanted things done today, if necessary in a confrontational way because that would get public attention for our salmon conservation cause . . . Perhaps we had our most challenging period during the lengthy process of getting rid of commercial fishing nets, that Lee correctly viewed as the principle architects of world-wide salmon decimation. Lee thought that a simple declaration by ASF, proclaiming Atlantic salmon as a game fish would do the trick—while I believed that a slower process, involving strong support for the developing aquaculture industry and massive lobbying of government would get us to the same goal with less confrontation and political obstruction. Today," Wilf wrote in 1993, "I think that both Lee and I were right."

Lee and European salmon fly fishing great, Arthur Oglesby, who was visiting the Wulffs at Lew Beach—circa 1983.

Around the world in 1982 the commercial raising of Atlantic salmon was developing as a giant industry—one that conceivably could support and feed the salmon-consuming world. But to Lee these fish were not the salmon he loved—the sleek wild, creatures of his youth.

There were the usual number of shows to do that spring for both Lee and Joan—the New York State Trout Forum at Oneonta, New York on March 28th, and the Southwest Council of the Federation of Fly Fishers in Los Angeles on April 3-4.

A meeting of the Executive Board of the Catskill Fly Fishing Center was held in Roscoe, New York April 27th which both Lee and Joan attended. Things were progressing well and it looked as though the center would open on schedule in 1983.

They both were invited to the annual fishing trip on the Restigouche and the Upsalquitch Rivers by their close friend Joe Cullman. It was one of the highlights of their year—fishing the big Restigouche and the smaller, clearer river at Two Brooks. The Upsalquitch is a gin-clear stream that runs between the steep walls of a beautiful valley. A tributary of the Restigouche, it was Lee's favorite salmon stream—at least as far as scenery is concerned.

They fished out west in the late summer and returned in time to attend the Annual Fall Sportfest put on each year by the Traffic Club of New York. Joan did her casting exhibitions and Lee his motion pictures.

On October 2nd Lee and Joan received a letter from Arthur Oglesby, the premiere salmon fly fisherman of England and European Editor of *Field & Stream*. Arthur had caught more than 2,000 salmon and was regarded as one of the true experts of the sport.

"I do hope that you will seriously consider coming over to Scotland next May and fishing the Spey with me. It is a serious invitation. You would be my guests in the Seafield Lodge Hotel in Grantown on Spey and you would be able to fish the Castle Grant water of the Spey during your chosen week— also as my guests."

The invitation would carry both of them through the long cold winter coming up.

...e and Joan at Golfito, Costa Rica in the ...ring of 1990. Bill Munro photo.

...e big dry fly Lee used to catch a sailfish ...Quepos, Costa Rica in his 86th year. ...k Samson photo.

Trout ponds on the Lew Beach property. Jack Samson photo.

Lee fighting a bluefin tuna off Newfoundland in 1970. Bill Munro photo.

End of the day. Jim Repine photo.

Catskill Fly Fishing Center and Museum.
Jack Samson photo.

Right: Lee releasing a trout. Joan Wulff photo.

Below: More Alaska fishing.
Jim Repine photo.

Lee and Joan. Art Carter photo.

The Recognition Years

As the year 1983 dawned, President Ronald Reagan's administration was having a difficult year in foreign relations. The Syrian and Israeli forces were being difficult about withdrawing from Lebanon. The government of San Salvador was causing all sort of problems with its civil war.

Lee—far more concerned with his own affairs than those of the Federal government—was finishing up work on a revised edition of *The Atlantic Salmon*, which was being reprinted by Nick Lyons Books.

He and Joan did not think they would be able to make the trip to fish with Arthur Oglesby on the Spey and Lee wrote Arthur on January 3rd:

"Dear Arthur:

I hope you can forgive the long delay in replying to your letter. We have been racing along trying to catch up with things. We went to Nova Scotia in October for a couple of weeks, carrying over into November and I caught a 960 pound tuna which will give us a movie for the Province (which I have to edit next month). We've been working on school schedules and we are staging a direct mail business which is also taking a lot of time. I have hopes of a book on my flying experiences next month, too, but it may not be finished if the film takes up too much of the available time.

We're going to Boca Paila on the Yucatan Peninsula in Mexico for two weeks leaving Saturday . . . bonefish and permit, etc. and are looking forward to a winter break and the southern sunshine . . . "

The Mexico trip was a welcome break in the cold weather and Lee was beginning to feel the cold more and more each winter. Each year he looked forward more to the annual chance to bask in the tropical sun, eat the local food and fly fish for the game fish of the vast flats.

Returning, he wrote Tap on February 1st:

"Not only did Christmas get by me but most everything else seems to. 'The harder I try the behinder I get' sort of thing. However we just came back from three weeks away . . . a combined vacation and seminar set up at Boca Paila in Yucatan, Mexico—where we had fine weather and sunshine and caught a few bonefish and, along with everyone else, avoided Montezuma's Revenge. What more can anyone ask? Then we had three days in New Orleans . . . soaking up Dixieland . . . and two days in Washington visiting Allan in his new house . . . and home to be snowed under with work again. . .

"My 78th birthday will be on the 10th and I'll go down to a preserve shooting meeting with the New York *Rod & Gun* Editors to shoot a pheasant which, while it isn't like hunting grouse with Burton Spiller, may be some fun and a chance to see some old friends . . .

"I'm showing some signs of a tough youth . . . my ankles bother me and I don't run anymore. I had my prostate rotorootered out last June but I'm back to normal and occasionally sleep the night without waking . . . I ache a bit here and there, but I get around.

"My salmon book revision should come off the presses in April if not earlier (whoever heard of a publisher being early?). It was to have come out in October and I sent the manuscript last August.

"I don't know how valuable the films are . . . It may be that the ability to copy them onto (video) tape will give them a longevity cellulose doesn't have and I hope so but it looks as though they may sit in our cellar till the house burns down . . . I too wish I had written more . . . and maybe next year and every year thereafter I'll be able to do a book. I've spent a lot of time saving the salmon and I feel, at last, that I've got the anglers organized and that they can now . . . as fishermen did . . . force some better management.

"Joan runs the school and I help. She does a great job and last year we turned people away. I think all our classes will be full again this year. I'm delighted that she'll have a career she loves to work on and bring in bread as long as she lives.

"I have a John Deere 10-10 bucket loader to do things on our 100 acres here and a Cushman Trackster and a Coot to get around the woods faster than my ankles would carry me. I chain saw the wood for our combination wood-oil furnace but still never get as much exercise as I'd like to.

178

"Yep, we're survivors . . . a few years back I wrote a piece for *Outdoor Life* entitled: "The Wealth Of Age." It will finally see daylight in April or May. We can remember a long way back to where cars didn't have windshield wipers or four-wheel brakes . . . there were no airlines . . . trolley cars and $2 1/2 gold pieces . . . It's been quite a span. I don't know that we could have picked a better span . . . "

Lee went to the Chateau Champlaine in Montreal for the first Atlantic Salmon Federation Annual Dinner on March 3rd. He chaired the two-day proceedings and his opening remark set the tone of the convention:

"Ladies and Gentlemen," he began. "We have a new name."

The ASF Affiliates meeting began with status reports from the five ASF regional councils and a Resolutions Committee was formed to discuss the issues most germane to the objectives of the new Federation. The biggest problem of the day still seemed to be the 85 percent harvest of large, mature salmon by commercial netting interests in Newfoundland.

Lee and Joan giving fly casting demonstrations.

In October the Canadian Department of Fisheries and Oceans had released its long-awaited discussion paper "Management of the Atlantic Salmon in the 1980s." Much of the discussion centering around the new paper was the obvious fact that the government was partial to commercial salmon interests.

"The bias towards the commercial salmon fisheries in the paper is obvious" wrote the always-direct Wilf Carter. "Where is the logic in recognizing the economic importance of salmon taken in a net and ignoring the value of one worth at least four times more (by the government's own admission) when taken by an angler?"

Lee was still writing regularly in the *Atlantic Salmon Journal* and "What Makes an Atlantic Salmon Rise to a Fly?" was a provocative article he wrote for the publication. Many a salmon fly fisherman has wondered why and Lee's explanation was that the salmon spent more time in a river as a parr than it did at sea as a grown-up salmon. Its memory of feeding on tiny surface insects was stronger than its memory of feeding on sea baitfish and when a fly floats by, that stronger memory prevails.

Lee had become enough of a legend by this time that the Anglers Club of New York was scheduling annual dinners at which Lee was either honored or was the featured speaker. The one held that year was a surprise testimonial called "An Evening For Lee—The First Royal Wulff." It was held on March 11th, given by Joe Cullman and Gardner Grant.

Fittingly enough, on the day of the opening of the New York trout season, April 1st, the new Catskill Fly Fishing Center officially opened.

The Roscoe Fire Department siren went off at noon and the formal opening was also signaled by Joan making the first symbolic cast of a Quill Gordon fly designed by Theodore Gordon himself. Notables included Lee, fly tiers Harry and Elsie Darbee, the Dettes and Art Flick—who epitomized the Catskill School of Fly Fishers.

That spring the school went very well. Lee and Joan went to Key West on a Mako-sponsored fishing trip and when the school let out that summer both Lee and Joan went back to fish the Upsalquitch.

More and more Lee was getting into experimentation with both salmon and trout. He had caught so many of both that just one more fish was no longer important to him. He began working on smaller and smaller flies—especially for salmon. Most who fished with him in those days remembered most his restless search for new techniques. So much so, as his old friend, Henry Lyman recalled, that sometimes he forgot his earlier favorite flies.

Lyman was fishing with Lee on a stream in North Carolina one day when he was catching fish and Lee was not.

"Lee was on one bank and I was on the other. I was taking and releasing trout fairly regularly and Lee was taking nothing at all. Finally we reached a bridge spanning the river, Lee crossed over and did not hesitate to ask me what I was using.

"'An inventive angler designed a fly that really works well here,'" I replied. "It's called a White Wulff."

"Lee could hardly believe it. That dry fly would float for only a few seconds in the fast water, but trout would whack it with abandon. Lee crossed over to his side of the river and proceeded to catch two fish to my one."

Wilf Carter remembered a day he and Lee shared on the Matapedia River.

"It was a glorious day and the pool was loaded with fish. Lee insisted on fishing with a tiny skater, probably a #18 or #20, while I was using more conventional dry fly gear.

"In three hours of fishing Lee rose a dozen or more fish, before finally hooking one that jumped furiously, and then was gone. He was obviously enjoying himself greatly. I quickly lost a fish, then rose, hooked and boated a beautiful 12-pound, fresh-run cock salmon. Then I sat and watched Lee fish. His concentration was single-minded; we didn't even speak. Every cast was perfect, the tiny flies dropping gently on the surface then dancing enticingly across the pool. When he did get a rise, Lee's strike was almost imperceptible, just a gentle raising of the rod tip, and if the fish wasn't hooked he would just continue as though nothing had happened and make another perfect cast. It was like watching a famous artist painting delicate brush strokes on canvas—it looked so easy but only a master could do it.

"When he was through fishing, Lee turned to me and said, 'Thanks, Wilf, for being so patient. Patience and tenacity are a wonderful combination. You have one and I have the other.'"

Nelson Bryant, longtime outdoor editor for the New York *Times* and an old friend of Lee's recalls Lee fishing with a #28 dry fly on the Marguerite River.

"That day on the Ste. Marguerite in Quebec was miserable," he wrote, "a sharp, cold rain was falling. Lee and I were fishing the same pool. On my third or fourth cast I hooked and landed a nice little grilse and then stood by watching Lee. He was working his little #28 dry against a ledge on the far side of the pool, and had, if I recall correctly, raised a good fish once.

"The salmon took and surged downstream and Lee had to follow it along the round, slippery rocks on the shore. I knew he had a bad ankle, so I stayed beside him offering him a steadying hand when I thought he needed it. It was a strange and poignant role for me because I knew Lee would have been happier if my help wasn't needed. When he reached a spot along the shore where the pool deepened and widened and he could no longer follow the fish he was running out of backing. I yelled to one of the guides to bring a canoe, and Lee and his guide followed the fish and played it for another 20 minutes. The hook finally pulled out."

Nick Lyons, another old friend and life-long fly fisherman, also fished with Lee and was impressed most by Lee's patience and experimentation.

"It was high summer, blazing hot, and the upper Beaverkill, in front of his house was painfully low—that special lowness that Catskill rivers get, where every rock is visible and the water is as clear and as slow as a small spring creek. I was up from New York and Lee knew that I always wanted to fish, so we walked down to the river from his house and parked ourselves a couple of hundred feet apart, he above me, near the head of a run.

"What struck me as I fished up toward him was the restless experimentation—with different kinds of casts (he seemed to be experimenting with a very high line and a rolling motion that afternoon), frequent changes of flies or fussing with flies. I later learned that he had begun with a dry fly, had clipped it so it became a floating emerger, and then had clipped it more and fished it just below the surface as a nymph. It was a day fated to produce no fish; it was too hot, the water was too clear, there were no fish rising or even showing, but we made a few pleasant hours of it and that quality of using all his time, looking constantly to learn something new, playfully experimenting, all impressed me hugely."

Losing fish was no longer anything Lee worried about. He had both caught and lost so many salmon all that remained now was the challenge. Lee and Joan finally made the trip to fish with Arthur Oglesby on the Spey River in Scotland.

Arthur remembers the days on the great river in 1984:

"It would be nice to record that we caught a lot of fish," he wrote, "but the reality does not permit such a statement. A unique and uncanny weather system came over the Scottish Highlands at that time, bringing sunshine of tropical intensity and a great reluctance, on the part of the salmon, to cooperate in our best-laid schemes.

"Lee did manage to hook a fish which quickly leaped to its freedom; but I was more than content to stay with my cameras and make a record of a happy week. But, most of all we talked about the problems of getting those perverse fish to take our flies and it was interesting to just listen to Lee as he elucidated on some of his philosophy.

"Having caught around 2,000 Atlantic salmon myself, it was good to compare notes with a man who must have caught at least twice that number. Like me, Lee was no longer interested in just another salmon caught. And,

Lee and Joan admire a Royal Wulff dry fly tied by Lee.

although the British tend to use spinning tackle in the colder months of the season (we can fish from mid-January through the end of November in certain rivers), I had long adopted a fly-only rule for myself. But even with his devoted fly-only rule, Lee had started to load the odds against himself many years before. He related how it was important for him to experiment just to see what lengths of improbability a salmon might go in the taking of a fly.

"He showed me some of the flies he had designed and tied merely for experiment. He spoke of how great his ambition was not just to catch a fish on a standard pattern of a fly, but to get one to take a minute offering on a size 28 hook—some achievement! He already records a fish of 24 pounds being taken on a size 16 hook in 1964, but I suspect that the 20 pound-plus fish, on a size 28 hook, eluded him until his dying day.

"Later that week on the Spey, under the same torrid sun, he tried new tactics (to me at least) by skating a fly over a fish we had seen showing regularly. Sadly his tactics did not work, but then I would have regarded it as a near miracle if anything had taken under the prevailing conditions."

Lee and Joan attended the second annual dinner of the Atlantic Salmon Federation at Montreal's Hyatt Regency Hotel on November 2nd. It was a highlight of Lee's career as he was named as the recipient of the "Happy" Frazier Award, which had been awarded to so many famous salmon anglers in the past.

Before an audience of some 400 salmon conservationists, Lee—cradling the coveted award—was introduced by his friend Lucien Rolland. The prestigious award is given each year for outstanding contribution to the conservation of Atlantic salmon over a period of time.

"It is the finest award a salmon fisherman can receive," said Lee to the audience, "I'm glad to have lived long enough to see this group tonight and look forward to salmon fishing in the future.

"When I started to release salmon 50 years ago, I knew that every fish I put back delayed what we have now—a disaster. I knew then, that catch-and-release would be of great value someday.

"We can have better salmon fishing, and nothing will stop us from the tremendous voting power at our disposition. We are on the move."

Lee was right in calling conditions a disaster. The salmon runs of 1983 were down seriously and most people knew it was still a combination of the commercial netters, poaching and the excessive take of salmon by Indians that was the cause. But enough pressure was now being put on the Canadian government by the ASF and others that there were some signs of change.

"We have witnessed in 1983," Wilf Carter told the delegates, "a salmon season most fishermen would just as soon forget." But he went on in more optimistic terms.

"In the short space of two years, ASF has become the unifying voice of salmon anglers throughout eastern North America.

"We are pleased that the Canadian government has finally acknowledged the serious problems in the Atlantic salmon fishery, and pleased, too, that for the first time we have a minister of Fisheries and Oceans who recognizes the importance of the recreational fisher, and is prepared to support major changes to reduce the impact of excessive commercial fishing."

Both Lee and Joan also attended the ASF (U.S.) annual dinner that was held at the Plaza Hotel in New York November 29th and it was almost a repeat of the Canadian version held a week earlier. It had been a busy and productive year. Lee had gathered a number of honors and the school went well. Lee suddenly—as the year came to an end—realized his upcoming birthday would be his 80th.

Mile Marker 80

Though he knew February 10th was his 80th birthday, the response to it surprised Lee.

His friend Neil Marvin presented him with a book containing hundreds of letters from friends and strangers alike and from people he had not heard from or seen in years.

His friend from ABC's "American Sportsman" days, Curt Gowdy wrote:

"Every time I tie a Royal Wulff on one of my favorite Wyoming trout streams, I naturally think of you . . . The week I spent with you filming our brook trout show on the Minipi river in Labrador was one of the best of my life."

"Dear Lee," wrote his friend and humorist Ed Zern, "Unlike some of the young whippersnappers who'll be greeting you on this occasion, I'm not much impressed by those eighty years. Hell, there are alligators and tortoises and parrots who make it to eighty . . .

"For more than half a century you've shown us the way to sounder Atlantic salmon management and a higher level of sport and sportsmanship in all our angling. You've not only added to our enjoyment and understanding and appreciation of the salmon; by taking thought of that splendid resource and by your activism, you've made us think.

"Lee, we're all in your debt, as will be millions of anglers yet unborn, and it has been a tremendous privilege to know you and to be counted among your friends as well as your followers. All of us are looking forward to your 90th."

His longtime friend, reel-maker Stan Bogdan wrote:

"Dear Lee: I just received word that on February 10th you will be celebrating your 80th birthday. Congratulations, and may you still be wading the salmon rivers on your 100th."

"What it really comes down to, Lee," wrote his friend Mac Francis, "is that your intense and constant pursuit of excellence in angling and your willingness to share it with others sets a great example for the rest of us. I am convinced that I can do no better than to lead my life the way you fish. May you live another eighty years."

"Dear Lee," wrote another friend, Ian Mackay, "I am most pleased to have this opportunity to wish you a very happy eightieth birthday. Perhaps you could use this milestone to do a one-ups-man on Ed Hewitt and write a book: "A Trout and Salmon Fisherman For Eighty Years!"

"It is impossible to go fishing in North America without seeing the imagination of Lee Wulff present in our rods, reels, lines and even the clothing on our backs. His axioms for the basis of our sporting principles and regulations, and they will govern the future of angling as much as they have its recent past," wrote his friend Keith Gardner, editor of *Fishing World*.

There were others, hundreds of others, but the one that pleased him, and Joan, the most came as a short note on stationery that bore the Presidential seal.

"Rosalynn and I are pleased to congratulate you on the occasion of your eightieth birthday. We have long admired you as one of the world's foremost anglers, and were pleased and privileged to spend time with you during the Beaverkill dedication last fall.

"It gives us great pleasure to join your many friends in wishing you happiness on this day and throughout the years ahead. Sincerely, Jimmy Carter"

Honors continued to pile up. Lee was made a life member of the Anglers Club of New York and was invited to be the honored speaker at the club's Spring Dinner on March 20th. He was asked to talk about his personal reminiscence, stories and experiences from a lifetime of angling. Lee was pleased and planned to talk of the changes he had witnessed in fly fishing over half a century.

Lee had decided to write a book about his early flying days in the north and planned to entitle the book, *Yellow Bird*—after his old yellow J-3 Piper Cub. It was to be about his flying in Newfoundland in the days when no other private pilots had dared to venture to that unexplored region. He contacted Allan to see if he wouldn't consider helping him with the sections on the early camp days—from the standpoint of a youngster learning flying.

Lee was as active as ever in the battle to protect the salmon. He took issue with one of the recommendations made by the New England Atlantic Salmon Committee regarding hooks.

"I believe very strongly," he wrote Richard Cronin, chairman of the committee, "that double hooks should not be permitted except in very small sizes, if at all. The reason is simple. They are not necessary in the capture of salmon. Any dry fly angler knows that and proved it. However double hooks are necessary for the foul-hooking of salmon, since with single hooks it would be extremely difficult. I know from experience how many salmon are intentionally foul-hooked in places like Newfoundland. Wardens cannot prosecute these fishermen because they are using "legal" tackle. They can only force them to return any fish they *see* being snagged."

Lee's pet project—one he had been considering for years—was to make the Atlantic salmon a game fish. Not many people gave him a great chance of succeeding in this endeavor, but—as usual—that didn't stop him from strongly advocating it. As he wrote in the fall issue of the *Atlantic Salmon Journal*:

"Not long ago I mentioned to a friend that we should be working hard to have the Atlantic salmon designated as a game fish. His reply was, 'We can't do that. What about commercial fishermen, they have rights to be considered.'

"All right, let's consider them. How much did society give the market gunners who sold duck, partridge and venison in my youth when they were stopped? How much to those who were selling trout and other game species? Should we go back to allowing the sale of trout from our streams and game birds from our fields because the commercial "rights" of some of our citizens were denied? Such "rights" are really privileges that are accepted as the due of the people, until the ecological balance—and the management rules— change. In every case, the appointment of a species to the game list comes when that species is threatened and its exploitation for sport is recognized to be of greater benefit to society.

"The early market hunters and fishermen were not compensated when they lost the right to continue to hunt and fish for commercial purposes. But we, today, are prepared to award not only adequate but generous payment for the loss of income. Part-time commercial netters of Atlantic salmon in Newfoundland are being offered a flat $750, or five times the value of the best landings in the past three years, with a maximum payment of $25,000. Full-time operators will be offered large sums in fair recompense for any loss of income.

"A recent Fisheries and Oceans release from the government of Canada stated: 'Recent estimates place the direct economic impact of the Atlantic

187

salmon fishery in the five Atlantic provinces at approximately $50 million per year. Of this amount the recreational fishery accounts for $42.6 million, while the commercial fishery contributes $7.5 million even though the commercial fishery takes in more than 80 percent of the harvest.'

"Anglers can afford to pay for the change. One way would be by an increased cost of the 80,000-odd licenses sold annually. In return, anglers would have a more than 500 percent increase in the fish coming into the rivers—their normal 15 percent plus the 85 percent traditionally taken by commercial fishing—an even greater percentage gain in the large salmon that are now harvested in commercial nets. This would result in fantastic angling compared to the sport fishing we have had in recent years. As the salmon runs regain their strength, the abundance of the biggest and best salmon returning to their natal rivers would make salmon fishing well worth the extra license cost.

"Let's look at the situation. Whether the salmon are caught in commercial nets in the sea or on a fly in the rivers, society can be provided with the same amount of wild salmon to consume. We can harvest the salmon as well in the rivers on flies as in the sea.

"Designation of the Atlantic salmon as a game fish will not deny to the public eating this favored fish. Those who do not have the good fortune to take salmon by angling or don't receive them as gifts from luckier anglers can pursue pen-reared or ranched Atlantic salmon. Raised salmon may well be better for food than wild fish, since they can always be fresh no matter what the time of year, processed under sanitary conditions, and the flavor controlled to a degree by their diets. There may be a need for rules in some areas for a government-controlled sale of angled fish. Universal tagging of all salmon is, of course, essential to efficient salmon management enforcement.

"There is a great joy and recreational benefit from the angling pleasure spread over the thousands of people who fish the rivers, many of whom enjoy themselves even when they do not catch or kill salmon. Insofar as dollars are the name of the game, the economic return to society for each salmon caught by angling in the rivers can be proven to be far greater with regard to guiding jobs and other related industries like motels, suppliers, etc., than the return to commercial netters per pound of fish.

"Any problems that develop in making the Atlantic salmon a game fish will be similar to those we have solved before when deer, grouse and partridge were made game animals, and trout, bass and snook were made game fish. I can think of no over-riding benefit to society for continuing to manage the Atlantic salmon resource as we presently do.

"Salmon anglers have always looked far into the future. We have made major sacrifices to ensure that salmon got through to their spawning redds. The time is right, I believe, to solidify our dreams of securing the Atlantic salmon's future forever for both food and sport for our society. The facts needed for the decision-making are available. This should be the time of decision."

It was—and is—a noble crusade and may some day become a fact. But most expert observers did not underestimate the political clout of the commercial fishing industry—in Canada and around the salmon world. Besides, most of the salmon organizations had come to believe the best way to get rid of the commercial netters was to buy out their lifetime leases—in that way avoiding a political battle.

And the political battles were raging on a number of fronts. The ASF was in the process of suing the MicMac Indians who formed a tribe at the mouth of the mighty Restigouche River in New Brunswick. The Indians, the ASF claimed, had constantly violated their agreements with the Canadian government as to the amount of salmon they were allotted. Also, because many salmon of Canadian and United States origin were being netted on the high seas by Greenland and the Faroe Islanders, the battle for the well-being of North American stocks of salmon was becoming international in scope.

Because of this an organization named the North Atlantic Salmon Conservation Organization was formed to establish proper control over the high seas fishery. In addition to that problem there was also a continued frustration of Newfoundland netters intercepting salmon on the way to other Canadian provinces and the U.S. That problem was somewhat mitigated in 1984 by delaying the start of the Newfoundland fishery and shutting it down altogether in one area.

As Nelson Bryant wrote in the New York *Times* in 1985, one of the major problems for Lee and others in the salmon conservation movement in the United States was that there are, literally, several generations of fishermen in this country to whom the salmon means almost nothing.

"Except for Maine," he wrote, "where a viable rod and reel fishery for salmon exists, the species which once had ascended New England rivers as far south as the Housatonic in Connecticut by the tens of thousands, had been stopped by dams before or shortly after the turn of the century. In recent years, a state, federal and private effort which involves rearing and stocking salmon and building fishways around dams to allow the fish to reach their upstream spawning areas has resulted in some of them returning to various streams, among them the Connecticut and some of its tributaries as well as the Merrimack—which flows through New Hampshire and Massachusetts— and the Pawcatuck in Rhode Island. In 1984, 92 salmon returned to the Connecticut and 20 to the Pawcatuck.

"Realizing the need for broad public support of the salmon restoration program, the Federation in January of 1982 began forming regional councils in this country and Canada. These councils are totally autonomous and the Federation—which has 40,000 members and 50,000 affiliated members— supplies them with technical assistance and occasional financial aid. New Brunswick quickly formed a council, which now has nearly 10,000 affiliated members. Smaller but influential councils exist in Nova Scotia and Newfoundland, and a Quebec council will soon be in existence.

In this country, Theodore Gordon Flyfishers and the Federation of Fly Fishermen formed councils soon after the plan was announced. They were followed by the creation of the Maine Council, which now has 15 member organizations and more than 15,000 affiliated members. Last year, the other New England states formed a council of their own, which now includes 20 organizations and over 10,000 individual members."

All of which meant that the American people—for so long unaware of, and in many cases uninterested in the plight of the Atlantic salmon—were suddenly joining the battle to save this great game fish.

Lee's longtime friend Art Flick became ill and Lee sought to cheer him up.

"Tonight's rain may wash away a lot of the snow that's left here and raise the river a bit. They're in good shape and according to my ear-to-the-river department they're awaiting for one Art Flick to come wading along and do them the honor of letting them look at one of his very artistic flies. Between the East Branch and the Beaverkill there is some argument among the brown trout as to which river you like best. They'll be measuring the hours you spend on each river to determine the winner of the "Flick Favorite" award of 1985 . . .

"I understand this is the year that some of the hybridized nymphs will be hatching out in the new 'how did this one come about' challenge cup. The Two-parts stonefly-one part caddis, is claiming to be the first six-winged ever to hatch out in a trout stream and the mayfly/crawfish combination is going to be the first stream-hatching insect to bring with it as it hatches a grain of sand from the riverbed to drop overland somewhere so that the millions and millions of grains of sand will make the banks higher and the river deeper. The four year water cycle of the Dobson fly/lamprey cross, born viviparously in the belly of a helgramite-bitten lamprey will give it a size attractive to trout over six pounds. The probable winner, according to the grapevine, is the new schmoo fly which flies low over water, low and slow, and when it spots a big trout it does a sort of dance in the air before settling right in that trout's feeding lane. The schmoo fly's dying dance is when it flies off to find a wild strawberry—to suck the juices and then suck a small amount of rich cream from a cow's udder in order to give it that inimitable 'strawberries and cream' that big trout go wild over. So you can see you're going to have a very busy season."

Later he wrote a letter to Tom Pero, editor of *Trout*, in which he talked about his and Joan's doings.

"We've just come back from a couple of months in northern Florida where it was cool. We were holed up without a phone and each of us wrote a book . . . Joan's is on casting and mine on my early bush flying and salmon explorations and camps. I hope it will appeal not only to fishermen and pilots but to the general public. I guess it will take time to find out."

Wilf Carter notified the leadership of ASF that he would like to retire in a few years and Lee and Joe Cullman began a search to try and find someone to take over the job of executive director who would some day step into the vacated president's shoes.

Both Lee and Joan planned to fish a lot for the balance of 1985.

"We'll have a great fishing year this summer if things go well," Lee wrote Pero. "We'll have a week on the Alta in Norway at the end of this month . . . then a week on the Upsalquitch and finally a week on the Grande Cascapedia. Sandwiched in between is the Atlantic Federation Conclave at Corner Brook . . . with a few days fishing in Newfoundland . . . and perhaps a few days on the Miramichi and somewhere else. More salmon fishing than I've had for a long time . . . Oh I forgot, in September we're going to Alaska (Bristol Bay area)."

The trip to the Alta River in Norway was interesting though Lee caught no salmon in spite of trying hard. Joan, to Lee's amusement, caught a 38 pound salmon and one weighing 27 pounds. They only spent three days on the river, but the scenery was spectacular and the river huge. Most of the fishing was from boats and one of the guides annoyed Lee because he wouldn't let Lee stay in one spot and continuously cast to a fish he had risen. Lee wanted Joan to keep her 38 pound fish to be mounted on the wall of their school in Lew Beach. Joan though perhaps just an outline drawn of it might suffice, but Lee was adamant and they had the big fish frozen and carried it to the Gaula River and then back to New York with them to have it mounted.

They fished the Gaula River but it too was very large and with a heavy flow of water at the time they were there they didn't have any luck with the salmon.

Next they traveled to Newfoundland where Joan got a chance to see Lee's old camp at River Of Ponds and they had a chance to fish with Lee's old friend, Arthur Lundrigan. The trip was in conjunction with an ASF-sponsored salmon conclave at Corner Brook—run by the Newfoundland Council. Though Joan enjoyed the visit, Lee was depressed with the fishing. They caught only a few grilse and Lee showed Joan a list of fish and weights he had carved on a door of the main cabin there in the old days.

Lee tied flies as small as #28 without the use of a vise.

a #28 Grizzly midge
tied by Lee Wulff,
in his fingers, without
a vise.

Joan Wulff

They went back to the beautiful Upsalquitch and Lee continued his quest of a big salmon on the #28 dry fly. He had caught a few grilse on the tiny fly—fish of 4-5 pounds—but did not consider them salmon. He was certain he could do it if he just had the right conditions. Nelson Bryant fished with them that week. Lee hooked a salmon on the Upsalquitch and fought it for a while but the leader broke when cut by a rock.

Then they moved down to fish from Cullman's sprawling lodge Runnymead on the Restigouche where Lee was able to fish with his longtime friend and veteran guide Wendell Sharpe with whom he had fished for years.

"He one day asked me 'Wendell would you mind very much if we didn't catch any fish?' I said I didn't see much sense in going out if we weren't going to catch any fish, but then he gave me a funny kind of smile and I knew right then that he had something up his sleeve," Wendell told me.

"He was always trying something new, so I said 'All right, what is it?' So then he handed me something and I looked and it was so small you could hardly see it. So I said 'You sure came up with something this time! What is it?' I asked. 'It's a fly,' he said. 'Well,' I said, 'I hate to tell you, but you forgot to tie the hook on it.'

"The fishing was good. We would use a Skater to find the fish because the salmon would usually come to the Skater then we would put on the #28 fly and hook the fish. But our problem was to hold the fish. It was frustrating, for the hook would break.

"At first it seemed that everything we did was wrong. We talked it over and over—trying to figure out a way of holding a salmon on the #28 fly. It had to be good teamwork as there was no way one man could land the fish alone. And to make matters worse every time we returned to camp they would say

'Have you two gone mad—trying to catch a salmon on a fly you can hardly see?' That made us just that much more determined to do it.

"As time went on we hooked several grilse and six or seven salmon—which got off—but we were gaining experience.

"On the sixth day we were fishing a pool we call Wheeler. Mr. Wulff hooked a salmon and we quickly got in the right place with the boat and the battle was on. He got up as far as he could in the bow and he would make signs to me whether the salmon was coming or going.

"Now we had to play the fish very carefully as we were using a 4 pound leader and the hook would break after about a pound and a half of pressure. We had to be very careful and Mr. Wulff had lots of patience. After about thirty or thirty-five minutes the salmon was coming closer to the boat and I could almost reach him with the net. And Mr. Wulff would say 'Easy does it, easy does it' and finally—in the net he went. And my heart went out to him—for to see how happy he was, was worth all the time and effort."

While, technically, Lee caught his salmon on a #28 hook, it was not exactly a #28 fly. He tied a fly on a leader—without a hook in it—and just ahead of the hookless fly he let dangle a bare #28 hook. He reasoned that with the tiny hook buried in the feathers of the fly it could never be exposed enough to hook anything.

Joan and Lee then spent a few days on the Grande Cascapedia—one of Lee's favorite rivers—but they did not have much success. Following that they went back to Alaska and stayed with Mike Cusack at the King Salmon Lodge, where they went almost every year in September for the rainbow trout on a fly. Lee went alone down to Santee Cooper Reservoir the following month with the *Metropolitan Rod & Gun* Editors and enjoyed some fine bass fishing as the year moved into fall.

As a fitting windup for the year they attended the annual dinner of the Atlantic Salmon Federation at the Plaza Hotel on November 21st.

Joan's first book, *Joan Wulff's Fly Casting Techniques,* was selling steadily and she was working regularly on her new one—*Joan Wulff's Fly Fishing,* which was due to be published by Stackpole Books. Lee's manuscript about his early flying days, *Yellow Bird,* was roughly finished and he had been working hard on a book for his friend, Nick Lyons. It was due to come out in early 1986 and was a well-done treatise on trout fishing—from A to Z. It was called, *Trout On A Fly* and Lee expected it to sell well to novice fly rod anglers.

He had been doing a regular fly fishing column for Silvio Calabi, Editor and Publisher of *Fly Rod & Reel,* as Editor-at-Large and Joan had regularly been writing a casting column complete with line drawing illustrations for the same publication.

New Salmon Frontiers

Lee and Joan went down to Tallahassee, Florida to write and get away from the cold shortly after the first of the year, courtesy of their old friends Neil and Connie Marvin. After that they spent a week in Boca Paila, Yucatan trying for bonefish and permit.

Their 1986 tour started out with Lee and Joan participating in one show of Ed Rice's International Sportsmen's Exposition. They did casting exhibitions and instructional shows for the show.

The June 1986 meeting of the North Atlantic Salmon Conservation (NASCO) adjourned on an unexpected and positive note in Edinburgh, Scotland. In sharp contrast to the previous year's negotiations, which had broken off without any resolution to establish a quota for Greenland's commercial salmon fishery, the NASCO delegations quickly proceeded to set guidelines and restrictions within the West Greenland and North American Commissions: Greenland (WGC) agreed to hold its commercial salmon catch at 850 tons for a two-year period, and Canada (NEAC) introduced October 15th as the latest date for closure of the Newfoundland fishery.

As the spring wore on the school opened and they were delighted to have all the classes filled and people turned away at the last minute. Joan did most of the teaching, but Lee was always available for lectures, classes and fly-tying demonstrations. School over, they went to fish at Porter Brook Camp on the Miramichi River in New Brunswick—as well as the Restigouche again. They spent a few days in the summer on Martha's Vineyard and were able to fish in the surf with Nelson Bryant for stripers.

Lee had a chance to fish for salmon on Anticosti Island, but it hadn't rained in months and the rivers were too low and clear for good salmon fishing. He saw a lot of salmon though, unfortunately most gathered in schools and lying still and black on the bottom of the pools awaiting the first rain and a rise in the stream level before moving up to the spawning grounds.

For a change they got to spend a week in early fall on the Copper River in British Columbia to fish for steelhead.

Trout On A Fly was published by Nick Lyons Books and the initial sales were good. On November 24, 1986 Lee wrote Curt Gowdy.

" . . . See you on TV now and then and hope to see you in the flesh one of these days, perhaps to fish together again. We'll probably be coming to Florida for a month next February and perhaps we can cast for a bonefish.

"Incidentally our fishing in British Columbia for steelhead was good. We helicoptered in on the Copper River and caught fish from nine to fifteen pounds on surface flies. Joan was very impressed with the beauty of the place and we'll probably go back. Are you interested? We plan to go back to King Salmon Lodge at Naknek, Alaska in early September. The BC lodge was somewhat spartan as to cuisine, but King Salmon is luxurious and, of course, it's fly-out fishing."

Howard Brant wrote a long column in the Newark *Star Ledger* about Lee's injection-molded fly bodies which he had developed in the 1950s and continued to push as the flies of the future. The column was a good one for Lee and Brant was lavish with his praise.

"Wulff's "Flies of the Future" do reveal his usual nature for creating and developing something other than the conventional or traditional, specifically geared to enhancing angler expertise and to making fishing more pleasurable for the average sportsman.

"Flies of the Future are injection-molded body flies on which hair or feathers are attached by simply dissolving portions of the molded body and fastening the hair, feathers or other materials. In other words, no tying thread is used. The assorted feathers, hair, etc., are actually glued to the plastic body.

"One of the most important features of these flies is that you don't have to be an experienced fly-tier to dress them. Actually little or no experience is required to produce outstanding flies and a variety of new and exciting patterns."

Though there was no doubt Lee's plastic flies were well-made and perhaps really were the flies of the future, he continued to run into resistance from trout and salmon fly tiers who were traditionalists and liked to tie flies the old way.

Lee was delighted to read that Canada seemed, finally, to realize the value of recreational fishing license fees for salmon.

During the course of the eighth biennial National Recreational Fisheries Conference, held in Toronto in October, Canada's Minister of Fisheries and Oceans, Tom Siddon, said that the sport fishing industry in 1985 had brought in $4.7 billion dollars in income to the country.

"Given this performance and opportunity, it's time to think not just about preserving the status quo, but about going on from there to grow more fish, to restore more habitat and to develop new fishing opportunities."

What Siddon was doing was to announce a new fisheries policy—the first in Canada—and to acknowledge the need for a new funding mechanism that would aid in the restoration and enhancement of fisheries and fish habitat.

Siddon also announced his intention to propose to the Cabinet significant changes in fisheries law, among them, the designation of Atlantic, Pacific and Great Lakes salmon, and sea-going trout, as game fish.

"What took them so long?" Lee asked Joan.

Reaction from the ASF—which included 10 regional councils—was positive, but cautious. Most knew the power of the commercial fishermen block.

As 1986 moved into 1987 and the schools started up, Lee was saddened to learn that his older sister Lillian Fitzpatrick, who was 83, had died in San Diego. Over the years Lee had not communicated much with either Lillian or his younger sister, Audrey McGowan—who also lived in San Diego. An argument that dated back to the death of their father, Charles, in the 1930s, had kept them from remaining close. Lee had felt that the sisters should have contributed more of their share of their father's estate to the care of their mother rather than using it for themselves. He had turned his share over to his mother.

Lillian had been a school teacher and lived in San Diego for 68 years. Audrey also lived in San Diego, as had their mother until her death.

The news of Lillan's death had no sooner reached Lee than they were notified of the death of Joan's father—the well-known and popular New Jersey outdoorsman Jimmy Salvato. Salvato had given up an accounting job in his twenties to become the proprietor of the Paterson Rod and Gun Store. In addition to running his lucrative outdoor shop, he also wrote an outdoor column for the Paterson *Morning Call* and helped to found most of the conservation clubs in northern New Jersey over the years. Personally involved in tournament casting, he was responsible for Joan becoming interested in competitive fly casting. She won her first casting championship in 1938. Lee was also fond of him as were most outdoor people in the New York-New Jersey area.

That same spring the Atlantic Salmon Federation opened its new U.S. headquarters in Ipswitch, Massachusetts. Located on the banks of the Ipswitch River, the office consolidated ASF's New England office in Hanover, New Hampshire, and its development office in New York City.

The new headquarters would enable the ASF to contribute more to the salmon restoration on New England's historic salmon rivers and to the conservation and enhancement of salmon in Maine. Millions of dollars had already been spent and the outlook for salmon in that region was encouraging.

There were a lot of volatile issues facing the future of Atlantic salmon in New England and it was up to the new office to spearhead plans in that direction. Issues such as acid rain, riverbank development and hydro power were extremely important.

According to John Phillips, executive director of the ASF (U.S.) the 58 dams throughout New England slated for re-licensing in the upcoming years represented the premiere salmon habitat issues. Since re-licensing is a complicated and lengthy regulatory process, local salmon clubs needed to be involved early on to ensure the vital interests of salmon were protected.

It was the responsibility of the ASF to keep local clubs informed on the upcoming dam actions, to provide advice on how to properly deal with the regulatory process and to ensure that the local clubs received the right advice on how to deal politically with such issues.

When the school let out that summer both Lee and Joan went to Ashford Castle in Ireland to conduct several schools on fishing, casting and fly-tying. The weather was good, but the fishing slow.

Lee made a solo trip to Texas to fish for bass with Homer Circle and a number of other friends, but was soon back east for a number of salmon meetings—such as the three-day symposium held in Portland, Maine on "The Future of Atlantic Salmon Management."

The ASF was one of eight sponsoring groups responsible for providing administrative support and organization of the symposium. The gathering was a highly professional collection of salmon experts and was chaired by Hal Lyman, publisher emeritus of *Salt Water Sportsman* and a longtime conservationist and salmon fisherman.

A number of papers on new salmon management were presented and Wilf Carter was chairman for the session on international salmon management issues. The prime minister of the Faroe Islands, Atli Dam, presented the Faroese point of view on interception and Britain's Lord Moran discussed Britain's new management policy for salmon. Representatives from

Norway and Iceland also gave papers and the problems of acid rain, agricultural erosion and hydro-electric development were discussed by Canadian scientist Dr. Walton Watt.

Though Lee was on the Management Committee of ASF, and was a director of both the Canadian and U.S. branches of the Federation, he was not always in total agreement with his peers. Nor were his peers always in agreement with Lee. On the question of making the Atlantic salmon a game fish, a great many committee members and directors thought that was putting the cart before the horse.

Wilf Carter, although a longtime friend of Lee's, was dead set against the plan and thought it might upset the delicate balance of the negotiations between ASF and not only governments, but the commercial fishing interests.

A number of other directors—all friends of Lee—were of the opinion that the scientific approach to aquaculture and the ASF commitment to the scientific program going on at the Federation's headquarters at St. Andrews, New Brunswick was a lot more important than Lee's pet project. Joe Cullman, for example, though a longtime friend of Lee's, was convinced research at the St. Andrews facility, was far more important than the salmon game fish issue.

After a meeting at Joe's Runnymede Camp on the Restigouche that year, Joe wrote fellow management committee member Roger Baikie:

"We discussed at length major problems facing the Atlantic Salmon Federation, both in the U.S. and Canada, as they relate to current problems of the councils and of succession.

"I would like to strongly suggest that you make a visit to St. Andrews and see for yourself what we have done there. Having been a founding member of the Salmon Foundation since 1968, I feel that the St. Andrews facility gave us a credibility that was invaluable and that still is valuable. As a result we have received active and financial participation, also confidence and interest from contributors, and it has not been a drain on our overall operation."

Lee had never been enthusiastic about the scientific approach to salmon management. His theory was that the salmon was right there in the river and why try to change it by fooling around with gene research and the like. He could see no great reason to develop new strains of salmon to feed the world. Salmon as he knew it seemed perfectly all right to him. The St. Andrews project was almost completely concerned with the commercial raising of salmon for food and Lee considered it a waste of time. As a result his tirades against net size and for the game fish status much of the time fell on deaf ears. This did not amuse him.

"Dear Joe," he angrily wrote Joe Cullman that year, "When our ASF (U.S.) Board of Directors passed my motion it went on record in favor of game status for the Atlantic salmon and directed Wilf to press for it at the then upcoming meeting of the Management Committee. I wonder how hard he pressed for it considering word reaching me that he was in strong opposition and voted against it.

"I think you'll agree that the normal rule of bargaining is to ask for what you want (or a little more) and settle for what you can get. If you don't ask for something you don't get it.

"It is pretty obvious that if nets are still legally in the water when the salmon come back in great numbers as a result of the vastly increased spawning of the last two years there will be heavy pressure by commercial fishermen to expand the number of the nets remaining and we'll be fighting the expanding nets all over again. Only game fish status will give us security. I do not see who or what can hurt us for asking for what we want."

It was putting Cullman in a spot—caught between what he professionally believed was the correct course and his respect for Wilf Carter and his research—and his friendship and regard for Lee.

Lee's 80th birthday party: Left to right: Stepson Douglas Cummings, daughter-in-law Ginger McGuffie and son Allan Wulff.

Lee wrote to Mike Cusack, proprietor of the King Salmon Lodge after he and Joan had returned from another trip there in September.

"Enclosed are the twenty White Wulff's I've tied up. I promised one to each of the guests and to each of the staff. This number, with the three tied at the lodge, should make it. If not, please let me know and I'll make up those needed.

"We're beginning to catch up and I've had time to spend a few afternoons with the chain saw and dozer getting some trees out of the forest and headed for the wood pile. I need the exercise and never get enough of it. No matter how determined I am to get several afternoons of exercise a week it never seems to happen.

"We certainly enjoyed our stay at the lodge. The best ever. I can still see those three beautiful char in the sunshine and the drop-off at Ugashik. The ones that either wouldn't take the #28 or wouldn't get hooked on it. Even though I failed to get one of them it was the highlight of the trip for me . . .

"The fall foliage is at its peak right now. We've had a few beautiful days and are starting to shiver today, with a taste of the wintry winds from the north."

Lee was beginning to slow down—almost imperceptibly. He was taking more time to observe things like the foliage, the river flowing by and the rolling field below where his Super Cub was tied down. He still flew, but only occasionally. And when he did he waited until a quiet, sunlit day arrived and he would slowly circle the valley—enjoying the calm feeling of flight and the play of sunlight and shadows on the hills below. He found himself looking forward to visits from his grandchildren and talks with old friends.

"The wealth of old age," he wrote in an issue of *Outdoor Life*, "comes in having past reality to reflect upon instead of future uncertainty to dream about. It lies in knowing firsthand instead of relying on the word of someone else to make decisions. It comes from having done most of the things you really wanted to do at least once and knowing those you enjoy most and want to do again and again. It lies in wisdom, which can only come from experience. Knowing is something youth may have as well as old-timers. Wisdom comes from testing mere knowledge and being able to use it effectively.

"Fly casting, like many other things, is a matter of skill and timing—of easy rhythm rather than power. Such things can be enjoyed all through life and perhaps most of all in the more relaxed years of age. Paddle easily. Climb slowly. Choose the right places from the experience of other days, and enjoy the view to the fullest . . .

"There is a wealth in having sat around many campfires in a multitude of camps. It lies in the friends you make. When you have lived with them on the waters and in the woods and time has seasoned the friendship, it is far more secure and satisfying than those that develop casually, each person showing the other only a part of what he is. It may be that the greatest wealth of all lies in our friends.

"Old friends can wade a trout stream together or walk a woodland cover and encounter not just the fish or the game of that day but also the memories of other days and other places. They've taken the bitter with the better and found it all rewarding.

"The years beyond fifty have been by far the best of my life. I've had the physical capacity to do a great many things and to do them better than ever before. I haven't had to do anything I really haven't wanted to do during those years. I know I put my heart fully into each effort. Because of maturity and depth of interest in what I do, whether writing, making films, or playing a fish, each thing I do should be more complete and better than the things I did in my energetic youth.

"It is good for the young to realize how rewarding the over-fifty years can be—years when the mind has sorted out the things of greatest value. When I look back, it seems I spent my youth and middle age preparing to enjoy my final years."

Lee's friends Gene Hill and Ed Zern. Dick Anderson photo.

Advancing Years

Lee wrote his old friend, Tap Tapply, on February 18, 1988—usually his first long letter of each year.

"Time to leave off my business for a bit and bring you up-to-date. Just finished the manuscript for my book on the flying and fishing explorations in Newfoundland and Labrador. Now need a publisher and have a feeling I'll find one . . . probably Nick Lyons again.

"My ankles bother me, but I get around. Deer hunt but climb more slowly and don't drag or carry them very far anymore . . . ATVs are a help there. I have a Trackster . . . like a little tank with rubber grousers that goes almost anywhere. Grouse are scarce where we live so don't bird hunt much . . . occasional game farm expedition. Envy you the smallmouth fishing but I manage to get some salmon fishing and a week in Alaska with wading but not too much walking. It's nice to still be around, even though the fishing isn't as good as it was.

"Bill must be a great pleasure for you. Allan has come back to flying. He was my best pilot at the camps when he was sixteen and seventeen. We've had the Super Cub fixed up with Loran, transponder and new flying instruments. Year before last Allan took the ship for a trip to Newfoundland with his wife, visiting his old flying grounds and having a fine time. Since we don't live near a lake I keep it on wheels in our meadow and it takes time to change over. Will probably put it on floats again next year and Allan will probably make another bush trip . . . and I may get some float flying in.

"Barry is in Connecticut at Willamantic where he heads the biology department. He's writing about mushrooms and lichens and things. He's on various conservation committees but isn't involved with hunting and fishing. He has two girls 14 and 17.

"Writing the book took me back to a lot of old memories. It's probably the last fishing book I'll write. If I do anything more it is likely to be a stab at spoofing our political or national thinking. I always was a misplaced news analyst I'm afraid. That would be fun and I may try to get it off my chest.

"We have a lot of memories too. I can still taste the apple sauce cake Muriel made for us when we hunted grouse in New Hampshire. Better than a hot loaf-end with honey butter . . . "

In the long days of winter Lee constantly tied flies and played with new ideas for flies, rods and reels. That winter he was busy with some new ideas for the plastic-bodied flies. His latest was a fly with a plastic body with a stub or post projecting from the body around which a hackle could be wound and embedded in or cemented to the post. He hoped to get a patent.

Later in the winter—experimenting with flies for big saltwater game fish—he came up with a way to use the plastic fly head or base on nylon leader material. This meant he could make a shock leader 12 inches in length, or more, with the fly attached and a free-swinging hook. Lee never stopped thinking about new ideas whether it was for fishing or anything else. At an age when most older fly fishermen are thinking of better ways to be comfortable while catching trout or bass, Lee was figuring better flies to catch sailfish and marlin. The huge fish seemed to be more of a challenge to him as he grew older. It may have been because he had caught nearly everything worthwhile on a fly and was seeking new horizons.

In March Tom Pero of *Trout* magazine wrote Lee with an idea he had to make a video of fly fishing for steelhead in the coming summer.

Lee thought it was a fine idea and had a few suggestions:

"Martin Schmiderer has a fine camp (on the Copper River) and fine fishing. His place would be good and, of course, the publicity would be great for him. He specializes in surface fly fishing which is good. A week is a minimum time, I think, because rain, flood or other natural disturbances can cut the number of days on the stream . . .

"It is my feeling that BC steelhead fishing may well be the best trout fishing in the world. I hope they take good care of it. It's not half a world away and the guides (and everyone else) speak English."

Pero did a fine 12-page photo story on the Wulffs fishing the Copper

River and Lee's catching a 9 pound steelhead on a #28 dry fly.

"We're still snow covered and there's snow in the air. Spring is slow in coming but we did have a good mid-winter thaw so there won't be ice jams in the run-off. The maple sap is running and the hatches and the good days can't be too far away . . ." Lee wrote to Tap.

The good days did, indeed, come finally and the school was ready to open. Lee loved to fly fish for shad in the brief period in which they entered the rivers each spring. He wrote Nelson Bryant in May:

"Yesterday we fished the Delaware and caught some shad. Your friend the country clerk, Joe Purcell, was fishing there, too. We were with Mel Eck. Everybody caught a few shad with me catching the fewest. But they were big, active fish and it was good fun.

"I enclose a couple of flies in the hope you'll be a field tester and some-time throw them at bluefish or stripers. I'd like to know whether the tail hook is a better rig for bluefish than the tarpon-type hook at the head.

"I hope you'll be coming up this way one day to fish. Hatches have been good lately and fishing reports are good. Spring has been slow in coming and we're still a week or more away from apple blossoms. The schools have been going well and we're filled with waiting lists. We're harried but healthy. Yesterday was the first time we've been fishing this year . . ."

They had a chance to fish the Upsalquitch and the Restigouche again in the summer and Lee wrote Joe Cullman:

"We had a good time on the Upsalquitch in spite of the warm and low water," he wrote. "Our party was Bill Brewster, Dwight Lee, my son, Allan and his wife, Ginger and Joan and I. We caught 25 fish, I believe, all grilse although there were a couple of salmon hooked.

"We had a pleasant day on the Restigouche—at Runnymede—with Nan (Joe Cullman's sister). Joan caught a grilse and while I had two rises from salmon I didn't hook either one.

"We hope you'll keep us on the list for the Upsalquitch. It's such a beautiful place and such a fine camp. The water won't always be low and even if it is we always enjoy our stay there. It is the highlight of our fishing season."

Both Lee and Joan attended the Federation of Fly Fishermen annual conclave at West Yellowstone that summer and had a chance to fish the Big Horn in Montana. Unfortunately it was crowded with fly fishermen, Joan said—as all the conclave attendees found that the perfect time to fish the surrounding rivers. They also had a chance to fish the smaller creeks like Depuys Spring Creek where Lee loved to catch the tiny native trout on minute dry flies.

On the way back from the Montana trip they went to the Fly Tackle Dealer Show in Denver, put on each year by *Fly Tackle Dealer* and *Fly Rod &*

Reel magazines. It is strictly an industry show and the public does not attend, but the turnout by those members of the industry look forward to it each year.

Joan's mother had come down ill and Joan flew back to New Jersey rather than attend the Denver show. But Lee was plenty busy, meeting friends and keeping up with the latest developments in the field. On the first evening, after the welcoming cocktail party, Lee and I were standing talking with veteran West Coast fly fisherman Cam Sigler when two young staffers from *Fly Rod & Reel* joined up. They were Jim Butler, managing editor, and Brad Jackson, an associate editor.

Lee suddenly turned to us and said he was starving and why not go get something to eat. Cam had to leave to join his wife, Sue, so the three of us went downstairs in the hotel to the dining room. I looked at Butler and could see the two editors were in shock at the thought of dining with the great Lee Wulff. Normally, when Joan is with him, their schedule in generally set well ahead of time.

The dinner lasted at least two hours and the editors sat fascinated while Lee talked about everything from his early days in Newfoundland to catching sailfish and marlin on a fly.

"I remembered very little about that dinner," Jim Butler said a few years later, "except that I realized what a privilege it was to spend that much time with him . . . and just sit and listen to someone who had seen that much. And I also realized . . . as opinionated as he was, when you said something he didn't agree with, he didn't make you feel like an idiot for saying it. He had the reputation," Butler went on, "of being a sort of flinty curmudgeon, but I found him to be gentle, accommodating and friendly."

Jackson, too, was a bit startled to find him quite human. He was amused also to hear Lee admonish Butler at one time for ordering a diet cola. He was amazed at the way Lee's mind worked. "He was just such a common sense guy," he told me. "Here Jim ordered a diet drink and Lee looked at him and said: 'What are you ordering that stuff for?' When Jim said it had lower calories, Lee just looked at him. 'Yes, but there's no substitute for sugar. Drink the stuff with the sugar. God knows it's good for you and it's not man-made.'"

"My other impression was," Brad continued, "you know, for a guy who had received so many accolades and had done so many things—at his age—he was so interested in everybody and every thing! I think his mind worked differently than most people. He would sort of turn things over and look at them from every angle. I guess that's why he was so innovative."

A lot of people found Lee's reasoning fascinating. Steve Sloan, a trustee of the IGFA and a world-class saltwater fly fisherman, was having dinner with Lee in New York with his wife Nancy, and Joan.

"It was during the oil crunch of the early 1980s," he wrote. "Naturally the subject of oil, and the oil shortage was the main topic of conversation. For once a national topic took precedence over local salmon and trout fishing. Lee said 'I could cure the oil crisis overnight.'

We all looked at him and asked how he planned to do it.

"'It's ice,' he said. 'Do you know how much energy we use just to have cold sodas and iced drinks? If we drank our ale warm, our scotch tepid; and all the rest without ice, we could save enough energy to be independent from imported oil.'

"It was a startling remark," Sloan said, "an interesting concept. It just showed the depth and perception of Lee's universe. It did not end at the tip of a fishing rod."

At the end of September Lee and Joan returned to Lew Beach from another week at the King Salmon Lodge. They had a group of Russians coming to see the Beaverkill and would try and entertain them at the school for a day or so.

There was a meeting of the ASF in Bangor, Maine, but Lee was unable to make it. It may have been a good thing he had made another previous engagement as he was very annoyed at some of the members. In a few weeks Wilf Carter was due to retire as president of ASF and was to be succeeded by David Clark.

"Dear Joe," Lee wrote. "It was good to talk. I'm sorry I won't be able to make the Bangor meeting, but I certainly endorse Mr. Clark for the job.

"As you know I've been trying to get the ASF to work to get the mesh size of salmon nets reduced. Inasmuch as the anglers (except in Quebec) are putting back the big fish in order to correct the damage in the average size of

Lee's friend Nelson Bryant.

the salmon in the runs, it seems only fair that the commercial netters should make some sacrifice in this direction. We put back all big fish. They should at least reduce the size to save some of the biggest and best for the spawning beds. A reduced mesh size would do it.

"I cannot understand the opposition to this. It has been years since I started the suggestion. Last executive meeting of ASF (U.S.) I brought the matter up again and thought a motion or a consensus was reached to set a task force on the proposition. I've just received the ASF's long-term management policy for the Atlantic salmon and the mesh reduction is not mentioned. It was the commercial netters manner of taking only big fish by mesh size that caused the reduction in the average size of the runs. Why shouldn't they make a similar sacrifice?

"It would seem that we not only are doing their genetic research (God does the best genetic research for anglers with the salmon in the rivers) but are looking the other way while they continue with the same policy and fishing methods that caused the problem in the first place while we look the other way. We do need a task force to publicize this obvious failure of the commercial netters to do their fair share. Making the public aware of the situation ups their support and with that we can force the issue.

"Can you find out why we are letting the netter off the hook?" Lee certainly had a point.

Unfortunately, he was far outnumbered by members who had other interests and agendas. He had no more luck with his efforts to have the salmon named a game fish, in spite of continued pressure.

Joe Cullman had written him earlier on the game fish status:

"I gather from Wilf that your proposal was fully discussed and that the group unanimously decided that the designation at this time would be detrimental to the Atlantic Salmon Federation's primary goal which should be conservation of the species . . .

"I hope you will not consider this action as one which is in strong disagreement with you on long-term goals—it is not. As I mentioned at lunch, I think that what we are really talking about here is not just policy but longrange planning and strategy. After hearing the discussion at the Management Board on Saturday (prior to the consideration of your letter), I was convinced that to push too hard now for the designation which you seek would be a mistake and would involve us in political controversy that would not enhance our primary goal of bringing back the Atlantic salmon in sufficient numbers to assure its availability as a game fish."

Cullman, as President of ASF (U.S.) and Vice Chairman of the Management Committee, carried on his shoulders a lot of responsibility. He told Lee he was sure they were on the right track and enumerated four reasons why:

"The economic value of the Atlantic salmon as a sport fish is being understood and accepted," he wrote. "This value will be protected by all sensible governments.

"Farm-raised salmon will continue to reduce the market demand for wild salmon.

"Commercial fishing pressure on netting salmon has declined and will continue to decline.

"NASO has begun to make progress in limiting interception on the high seas."

Joe Cullman also had a point.

At the end of December, 1988, the first President of the Atlantic Salmon Federation, Wilf Carter, retired and was succeeded by David Clark. ASF had grown from a staff of 1 1/2 employees to one of 38, and its budget from $93,589.00 to $3 million. Its members lived in 10 Canadian provinces, 50 states in the United States and in 431 countries worldwide. Its conservation programs stretched throughout the North Atlantic, wherever salmon were important in the lives of people.

Wilf was given a retirement party on November 16th in New York at which nearly everyone interested in salmon fishing attended—Lee and Joan included. Wilf was given the Lee Wulff Award for outstanding contribution to the conservation of the Atlantic salmon.

On December 31st—the official day of his retirement—Wilf wrote:

"Dear Lee:

You know that I am retiring today after serving for twenty years as Chief Operating Officer of the Atlantic Salmon Federation. During that time I have watched the fortunes of the Atlantic salmon reverse—from almost certain disappearance in most major river systems around the North Atlantic to an almost unbelievable resurgence and strong, sure recovery. From restoration of salmon to New England's rivers to international control of high seas fisheries—from breaking new research frontiers to bringing the excitement of the salmon's amazing life cycle into our school classrooms—ASF has provided leadership and direction to the private sector conservation community, and we have spurred governments into positive action.

"If the Atlantic salmon's survival is more secure today than it has been in decades—if the magnificent rivers which are home to the salmon are more productive, and if the salmon's ocean feeding pastures are safer, it is due in no small measure to the generous support you have provided.

"With your help ASF has succeeded in performing a modest conservation

Lee's tying bench. Jack Samson photo.

miracle—we have not solved all the salmon's problems yet, but we have created a momentum of positive change which can only increase the salmon's chances of surviving—and prospering—long after you and I are happily casting our favorite flies over distant celestial pools . . ."

"P.S.," he added. "If this letter sounds as though I expect to leave for those distant pools at the first light tomorrow, that is not my intention. I hope to continue helping ASF with fund development, government and international relations—and to fish as many days and as many different rivers as my allotted time permits.

"You and Joan have been such good, staunch friends of the salmon for so long.

> "All the best wishes for health and happiness in '89.
>
> Wilf"

Lure of the Tropics

It was cold and the snow was deep and Lee was anxious to get away to the south. On January 12, he wrote to his old friends, Mike and Thelma Crammond in British Columbia.

"Busy, busy, busy! We're about to take off for a week or so in South Carolina to work and look around for a place to buy and work in future years . . . then more of the same at Tallahassee where we'll hole up without a phone and write. Joan has a book to do on fly fishing for women . . . it should be interesting . . .

"We had the Russians here (we gave them a one-day school) and fished in a "contest" and all went well. TU sponsored it and it was good "PR." We're supposed to go to Russia to fish for salmon on the Kola Peninsula next fall which sounds fairly interesting although I doubt if it will be comfortable or if the fishing in that hungry country will be as good as we have over here. More exciting is that we've been invited to fish in South Africa. Can you imagine Joan hooked to an elephant on her back cast? Two weeks for trout and sessions and then a few days for tigerfish."

February 10th was Lee's 84th birthday and he was pleased to get a nice long letter from Barry while they were in Tallahassee.

"Happy birthday! I hope you are enjoying yourself on this day and during your entire stay in the warm weather environs. We think of you casting for bonefish from a skiff in the emerald waters of the Caribbean . . . "

Barry, in Connecticut, was hardly warm.

He reported to Lee that the grandchildren were well and busy. Sabrina, the oldest, was back at Smith College and was a B student—majoring in business.

The youngest granddaughter, Tasha, was becoming interested in mountaineering—which pleased Barry as he was a world-class mountaineer himself and conducted international travel tours to such places as Norway and New Zealand to hike and climb. His wife Ella May, was a musician and most of her free time was spent with the Hartford Chorale—preparing to do Brahms' German Requiem.

A letter from Allan told them he and Ginger were headed for Utah to ski for a week then planned to spend a weekend in San Francisco.

The sun was warm, Lee was making progress with his Newfoundland flying manuscript and Joan had nearly completed her second fly fishing book. It was pleasant staying with their old friends Neil and Connie Marvin.

Some of Lee's Atlantic salmon fly patterns: Haggis, Cullman's Choice, Lady Joan, and Black Bottom.

Lee and Joan made another trip to Boca Paila for bonefish and permit and then traveled to the ASF annual meeting in Montreal before returning to Lew Beach in early April. It would only be weeks before the school was ready to open again.

Lee was still fighting to get game fish status for the Atlantic salmon, but running across roadblocks at every turn. On April 10th he wrote Joe Cullman:

"A couple of years back you suggested that if I felt strongly about game fish status for salmon I should write my view for the (Atlantic salmon) *Journal*. The previous editor requested a piece "How it was and May Be for Salmon" for the 40th anniversary issue. I wrote one but the section on probable eventual game fish designation was deleted by the new editor.

"So I wrote an article on the subject of game fish status and submitted it. After three months I called to see where it stood. I was told it was a question of policy and there was, after discussion, a promise to take it up with the policy commission. Now, after three more months, I received a letter saying the piece will probably be published in 1990. Could this be delaying with the hope that I'll pass on soon as the mortality rates indicate so the problem will go away?

"I think our members should know that the redfish whose commercial take was greater, I'm sure, than that of the Atlantic salmon, is a game fish in Texas and it is about to become one in Florida and that the snook, a former commercial fish, has been a game fish in Florida for a score of years. Even more important the Quebec representative at our recent management board meeting said he favored game fish status for salmon . . . "

Lee was fighting an uphill battle, he knew, but he never quit trying. The opposition to his crusade was substantial, but, because of his long tenure in ASF and his status as a salmon conservationist, that same opposition was strictly behind-the-scenes. What Lee did not know was that though the editor of the *Journal*, Terry Davis, had promised Lee his story would run in a 1990 issue, he did not establish policy. Those who did made sure that equal time was given to the opposition in the same issue. In a double page spread, Lee's story "Game Fish Status a Must" ran and on the opposite page was a story entitled "Or an Illusory Panacea" by Wilf Carter. The two stories were scheduled to run in the Spring 1990 issue.

Lee sent his *Yellow Bird* manuscript to longtime Knopf Editor Angus Cameron for an opinion. In the past Angus had proven invaluable when it came to advice on how to handle books.

I had invited Lee, on behalf of Billy Pate, in early 1988 to compete in the first International Invitational Billfish Fly Tournament to be held at Flamingo in Costa Rica the first week in May. Thirty-two saltwater fly fishermen from all over the world—Japan and Australia included—had signed up for the competition that was sponsored by Pate's World Wide Sportsman, Inc. in Islamorada, Florida. Pate, who would be tournament chairman, was the first fly fisherman to catch both Atlantic and Pacific sailfish and four species of marlin on a fly.

Lee, who was becoming more and more interested in fishing for sailfish and marlin on a fly, had thought he could make the tournament and had originally planned to go, but had to cancel at the last moment.

Lee had succeeded, finally, in persuading some influential people to support his stand on game fish status for the Atlantic salmon. He received a letter from Perry Bass, an immensely wealthy Texan and a man largely responsible for gaining game fish status for the redfish off the Texas coast.

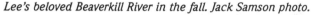

Lee's beloved Beaverkill River in the fall. Jack Samson photo.

"Dear Lee," Bass wrote Lee on June 21st.

"When I was fishing on the Restigouche with Joe Cullman the 11th-14th of this month, he let me read a copy of your article for the *Journal*; which he assured me would be in the winter issue. My congratulations to you. It took a long time, but your perseverance and sound logic finally won out . . .

Warm regards, Perry"

Bass also enclosed a copy of a letter he had written to David Clark, President of ASF. Among other things, Bass discussed redfish and salmon:

"As you may know, I have been instrumental in trying to protect our redfish in the Gulf of Mexico. It was during my tenure as Chairman of the Texas Parks & Wildlife Commission that we managed to pass legislation prohibiting the sale of Texas-caught redfish. Since that time, there has been additional legislation to further tighten the regulations, and just this last month, the Texas Legislature passed a bill that I was pushing that would prohibit any nets within 500 yards of our saltwater.

"Since that time, redfish have achieved game fish status in all the Gulf states except Mississippi, which has a very limited quota and a slot-type size limit. All of the Gulf states have a maximum size limit to protect the spawners and a limit on the number of fish that a recreational fisherman may possess. During the last two years this protection has spread up the East Coast through Georgia, South and North Carolina, which now includes all the Atlantic range of the redfish.

"It's time for the Atlantic Salmon Federation to demand game fish status for the Atlantic salmon and we can springboard on the Norwegian actions while what they have done is fresh on people's minds. If we dally around, we will miss an opportunity that is currently available to us and may never happen again.

"The great effort that Wilf Carter and Joe Cullman have put forth during these past years has brought to the realization of the Canadian office-holders the overwhelming importance of the recreational industry versus the netting industry. With the groundwork that they have laid, the next step of game fish status is timely.

"I know our friend Lee Wulff has been a voice in the wilderness for years saying that the Atlantic Salmon Federation was negligent in not demanding game fish status for Atlantic salmon. Now is certainly a time that we can follow through with that. There is certainly enough pen-raised salmon to meet the market demand, so you would have no consumer resistance, and there is certainly more people involved in salmon aquaculture than there are in the netting of salmon. Now is the time that we can have political numbers in our favor. I think that the Atlantic Salmon Federation should go after this with the main thrust on a national basis, but on a provincial basis as well . . .

"I would like to see an article in the next *Atlantic Salmon Journal* concerning the feasibility of our demanding game fish status for Atlantic salmon. I think the response would be overwhelmingly favorable."

Bass may have had considerable success in Texas—and along the Gulf—but he was not a resident of Canada. They do things differently in the provinces—unfortunately for the salmon.

Bass had been referring to conditions in Norway where after the buyout of the entire NASCO salmon quota for the Faroe Island, spearheaded by ASF's board member Orri Vigfusson of Iceland, salmon populations in Norway's rivers already were increasing.

With the school out Lee had a chance to fish the Upsalquitch and Restigouche Rivers, but the waters were still low and the fishing slow.

On September 25th Lee wrote John Randolph, Editor of *Fly Fisherman.*

"We're delighted and very grateful for the line review (Triangle Taper) in your most recent issue. It tells the thing we want to be told.

"Fishing has been either flooded or bare bones, hot or very cold. We've had only desultory fishing for bass and in the Beaverkill. Now that the water is back up to a good level we may have better results but we've about run out of time.

"We're due to make the trip to South Africa on the 12th of October and are, belatedly, getting the necessary shots. We're looking forward to it. Joan hasn't been to Africa and it will be great for her to see the game. We're off on our own for a week in Botswana to catch tigerfish. Then two weeks with the invited group to fish the various streams at established lodges for trout. That should be fun . . . along with the day in Krueger National Park.

"This winter I think we told you we'd be in Islamorada, however we'll have a week at Casa Blanca, Ascension Bay, and will spend a week with the Mako group at Golfito in Costa Rica for sails, etc. That should be interesting as I want to try out some of the new types of flies I've worked out. Like the pike flies I sent you. Enclosed is a tarpon fly integral with a 100 pound shock leader that is integral. I'll also be trying out some wire shock leaders which would be (are!) finer than the 100 pound mono and more resistant to abrasion. A 60 pound new type wire is very light and flexible and has plenty of strength for a 15 to 20 pound class leader section. Would you like a few flies for sails or other saltwater fish to try?"

The trip to Africa was a wonderful experience, especially for Joan. They fished in Botswana for tigerfish, but were only able to catch a very few on flies. Both were impressed with the ferocity of the game fish and the set of formidable teeth they possessed. After that they traveled east to the Krueger

Lee fights a Pacific blue marlin on a fly off Golfito, Costa Rica at age 85.

National Park, with which both Lee and Joan were thoroughly impressed.

After that they fished a number of small streams that had been set aside for trout fishing. Trout were not native to Africa and had been established by the British, particularly the upper class, back in the colonial days. Both Lee and Joan were struck by the beauty of the land near Himeville where they found some good brown trout fishing.

But they both were happy to be back home after the long, tiring trip. They had been accompanied by some British outdoor writers and several American ones, Gary Borger and Jim Casada. They had been hosted on the trip by Neil Hodges of Durban and the Fly Fishing Club of South Africa.

Both Lee and Joan went down to New York for the ASF salmon dinner and stayed overnight with Lee's longtime friend, Mac Francis.

As the year came to an end Lee received a long letter from Angus Cameron who had read Lee's *Yellow Bird* manuscript. Angus was of the opinion that Lee should re-do the book and put in a lot more salmon fishing. The manuscript was mostly about Lee's learning to fly and his early flying experiences in Newfoundland and Labrador.

"I could say at this stage that in writing this particular manuscript you have written the wrong book. But this is only partly true; a lot of what you wrote is just what your readers feel they can expect from you. I refer primarily here to passages that evoke the scenes of the rivers and the wilds.

"But what they expect from you that you are not offering here is much, much more on the salmon and on fishing for the salmon."

Angus always critiqued Lee's manuscripts when asked, but at the end of his letter he asked:

"P.S. Do you want to do me a favor? Send me a White Wulff and a Surface Stonefly tied by Lee Wulff."

Thinking it over, Lee agreed with Angus on the approach he should take to the book and vowed to begin on a revision.

Eager to try his new saltwater game fish flies, Lee was excited as he and Joan left for Golfito in extreme southern Costa Rica on a Mako boat trip planned by his longtime friend, Bill Munro, Public Relations Director of Mako. Lee was anxious to set a new 8 pound test record on billfish.

They fished in open center-console Makos that were maneuverable, if slightly under-powered, and had a fairly long run each day out to the billfish grounds. Lee hooked a blue marlin of several hundred pounds on one of his new flies and fought the big fish for an hour and a half. Joan, standing in the small boat as Lee stubbornly battled the big marlin, was concerned that he might be doing too much physically. She needn't have worried. Lee was as excited and intense with the billfish as he had been with his first salmon. The marlin made a number of jumps close to the boat and Munro managed to get some excellent photos of both the fish and Lee. When the leader finally broke and the huge fish sank slowly into the depths—swimming tiredly—Lee bowed his head briefly then smiled slowly, nodding at the fish.

"Beat me fair and square," he said softly to the departing marlin.

This was not to be a trip of great triumphs, though none of the fish that got off were of Lee's doing. The next day he hooked a large Pacific sailfish on one of his new flies that Munro said would have been a world record had he landed it. After a series of magnificent jumps the sailfish settled down to a stubborn, deep battle and Lee fought it for about six hours before the hook pulled out. Lee was tired, but happy. He really didn't mind losing the fish. It was the taking of the fly, the hooking of it and the fight that counted.

"I learned to work with static pressure," he wrote in an article for *Outdoor Life* "so that the boat traveled on the same course at the same speed as the fish as often as possible. The line neither comes off the reel nor is reeled in, so that maximum strain can be put on the fish with a minimum of effort. I learned to break down the fish's will to resist."

He and Joan went to Florida prior to Lee's 85th birthday party being given at the Waldorf Astoria Hotel in New York, February 10th.

217

On February 1st he wrote to a friend from Islamorada where he and Joan had gone to write:

"We're here in Islamorada working on books. Joan works on a fly fishing book for women and I'm working on my bush flying salmon exploration in the 40s, 50s, and 60s. We'll sneak out for a bit of fishing as we have a new boat, a 17 foot Mako which we are learning to run. We still don't have it rigged out with a radio, Loran, depth finder, etc. and will have to get used to operating it. It's a little heavy and deep of draft for the bonefish flats and a little small for offshore fishing, but we can manage some of both with it.

"We have new computers and are just learning how to use them. It's been pretty puzzling, but they make writing a lot easier . . . mainly because it's so easy to correct mistakes and I sure make a lot of them, I'm a lousy typist.

"We'll be going north for my birthday party of course. I hope they raise a lot of money for the Catskill Fly Fishing Center. It should be a fun party.

Catskill Fly Fishing Center. Jack Samson photo.

The Big 85th

Planners could have made a lot more money for the Center had they not decided to do the party in such a grand manner—celebrating it at the Waldorf Astoria Hotel in New York City. The turnout was impressive—more than 300 friends and admirers. Dan Rather of CBS, a fly fisherman himself, was scheduled to be the master of ceremonies, but South Africa's Nelson Mandela was let out of jail after years of incarceration and Dan had to leave for Africa. Bob Schieffer, another longtime CBS anchorman substituted for Rather and did a good job. Among the speakers were Curt Gowdy and even Lee's son Allan said a few words about his father, causing a tear to run down Lee's weathered cheeks.

Expenses for the gala party at which Peter Duchin's popular society dance band played were very high. Food, corkage fees and general expenses per person were about $150, so only about $10,000 was raised for the Center, but no one seemed greatly concerned. It was a great party, Lee said afterwards.

Lee was almost shocked to realize he truly was 85 years old.

Like most men, when he looked into the mirror each morning before shaving, he saw the face of a rugged, handsome man—an outdoorsman. True, the hair was now pure white, but the tanned, seamed face could be that of any man who had spent his life in the outdoors. There were a lot of aches and pains that weren't there before, but how did he get to be 85 so quickly!

He and Joan spent a week at a new bonefish and permit spot on Ascension Bay, Casa Blanca, not far from their old haunts at Boca Paila. There were a number of bonefish flats though the bonefish, for the most part, were small. There was one very good permit flat, Esperanza, that stretched for miles, a pure white coral sand flat that curved like a cycle against the emerald shallows of the Caribbean coast. Though they saw a number of permit— and had a few follow flies—they did not catch any.

The ride back to the comfortable lodge from Esperanza is about a 45-minute run in 14 foot wooden open skiffs. When the wind comes up each afternoon the trip back is a tortuous ride across the choppy bays. When Lee returned home, he wrote a letter to Brett Schwebke, of Mako Boats.

"We've just come back from a week of bonefishing at Ascension Bay in Yucatan. It was fairly windy and we had to make long runs in the 14 foot bonefish boats. As in the past, they are rough rides. Riding in the middle of those boats, banging down on the waves endlessly, is one of the most uncomfortable experiences I've ever had and I've had to do it on occasions since the early fifties. Often I've had to worry about camera equipment to keep it from damage. Everyone was complaining. I believe the whole thing is unnecessary if the guide can sit or stand in the center of the boat and the anglers can sit in the back, one on each side of the motor. All that takes is a little rigging of the motor consoles. A small center console wouldn't affect the fly casting as the whole forward area would remain untouched.

"Wouldn't it be smart to make flats boats that would be run like that so the young, tough guides could take the pounding and the less tough, paying customers could ride in relative comfort? . . . It amazes me that nothing has been done about making such long runs over the chop more comfortable in all the years that it's been going on. Maybe I'm crazy but I think some boat manufacturer is going to make such a boat and that it will replace a lot of the boats now in use."

Lee never stopped thinking of a better way to do things—fishing-wise. On April 12th he wrote his old friend from Garcia days, Dick Wolff.

"I'm looking out the window at snow flakes. The trees are bare . . . quite a change from Florida. We left just as all the old-timers were coming back . . . Stu Apte, Rick Ruoff, and others. We saw Bill Curtis on a day of fishing and George Hommell at his operation.

"We never seem to have time for leisurely travel and always rush to wherever we're going and back. Joan will fish in the One-Fly Tournament at Jackson Hole in September. We'll fish for salmon for a week on the Upsalquitch and I may go up to Minipi for a film for the Newfie government after that. Which will probably keep us from going to the FFF Conclave in Eugene.

"We're healthy, we think, allowing for the aches and such that I don't remember having before . . . Still have my Super Cub and will go get it from its winter hangar in a few days when I get a chance. Our Lab died a year ago and we're without a dog. We miss her.

"As I look around I see stuff piled on top of stuff . . . dozens of boxes of transparencies . . . not even looked at and not filed away. It would take months to get this office in order and I'm afraid it's going to get worse before we quit everything else and spend a month reorganizing.

"I hope you're both in good health and that your house is neat and easy to live in . . . "

On April 27th Lee received a letter from his old friend Wilf Carter that affected him deeply:

"Dear Lee," he wrote,

"I am sitting in my den overlooking the Bay of Fundy on this beautiful spring evening, wondering how far away the returning schools of salmon are, and thinking how lucky I am to be alive and well, and dreaming of the fishing that is to come this season.

"I am thinking too of you—and selfishly of me—and wishing that as we are growing older that we were growing closer instead of farther apart, because I have sensed, as I am sure you have too, the disagreements we have had on some important salmon conservation issues have influenced our personal relationship, and I deeply regret that this has happened . . .

" . . . Perhaps we may never agree on some things, and I do respect your right to a differing opinion, for as I grow older too I realize that my view is not the only one, and not necessarily the right one either.

"No one has made a greater contribution to fisheries conservation and to the salmon's cause in particular than you have, and generations of fishermen will always be indebted to you for your leadership, dedication and yes, for your stubborn adherence to ideals in which you strongly believe. But the salmon world is bigger now than it was even a decade ago, and there are many more players in the game. It isn't so easy now for any of us to influence events, and we have to subscribe to a consensus more often than we like, but that is the new way of moving ahead in today's democracy. You made many of your greatest contributions when it took the most courage to be innovative, and different. You haven't changed, although society has, and I think you will continue to foster innovative change and common-sense conservation long after others have given up in despair, because above all you are not a quitter.

"I really wish we could be good friends while still respecting each other's right to hold differing opinions. In our separate ways we can each claim to have made significant contributions to conservation—yours far outweighing my own. That is the way I shall always remember you, and respect you—for the tenacious determination with which you have so steadfastly pursued goals which you sincerely believe, despite the odds.

"Perhaps, if I am lucky, I will live to be 85 too, but I will never live long enough to even approach the record of your enormous contribution to the welfare of our beloved salmon.

Maybe we can fish together sometime soon.

With warmest personal wishes.   Sincerely,
                                                                  Wilf"

Lee, touched, knew it took a big man to write what Wilf had written.

Donald O'Brien, a vice president of ASF (U.S.) wrote Lee in June asking him to continue to serve as a member of the Management Board. Also, other board members wanted Lee to serve as a member of the Scientific/Research Committee.

Atlantic salmon. Jack Samson photo.

"I also talked to Livvy, David Clark and Joe Cullman about your interest in having ASF take a hard look at the issue of sinking lines and lower river spawning. The suggestion was made that these are issues which should be referred to the Scientific/Research Committee.

"I understand that you are disappointed about the apparent lack of interest in having the Atlantic salmon receive designation of game fish status. However, I hope that you can take some comfort in the fact that you have been ahead of your time on almost all conservation issues concerning the Atlantic salmon and that many of your victories were only attained after years of hard struggle. This, I am sure, will be the case with the game fish issue . . ."

Wilf Carter was right. There were more players in the game and the rules were changing too.

I was deeply involved in trying to catch all of the marlin on a fly in August of that year and had been corresponding with Lee off and on about new type flies.

"Dear Jack," he wrote, on August 11th.

"Enclosed are a couple of the flies I make for saltwater fishing. These are for sailfish and marlin but, of course, will work for other species. They have certain advantages.

"The shock leader is an integral part of the fly and is easily attached with an Albright or similar knot. It doesn't have to be tied to a class (tippet) and can be changed quickly. The hook which is back in the best position but isn't a long-shanked hook which is a handicap in playing fish because of the leverage of a long shank. The hook swings free and easy. The fly is welded (not glued or epoxied) to the plastic base which is attached securely to the shock leader itself. These flies are practically indestructible and take all kinds of abuse from toothy fish like barracuda, pike, bluefish, etc.

"I hope you have some fun with them. If you'd like more just holler. If you have some special fly you favor over the others send me one and I'll see if I can have it duplicated. Joan joins in our best—house to house. Good Fishing . . . "

I used them in Costa Rica and caught several Pacific sails on them. On returning I wrote to thank Lee for the flies and to send him several of my own which had caught billfish. I told him I was going to Venezuela in October to try for a white marlin on a fly, having just returned from Townsville, Australia where I had taken a black marlin on a fly.

"Dear Jack," he answered, "Many thanks for your newsy letter. It's great that you've gotten deep into the marlin on a fly. Wish I could have wangled or afforded it. It's good to see one of us making big tracks—even though you aren't an 'average guy' because of your media stature.

"Too bad the rod broke (on the black marlin—though it was still landed) I guess that keeps it out of the record books. But just hooking and playing it must have been exciting. It is a great challenge and I wish you all the luck in the world.

"We're going to Venezuela in October too—Las Roques—and while it's primarily for bonefish, we may go out to the white marlin area. Will you be there at that time? We're off now—for some fishing in Wyoming—culminating in the "One Fly" contest . . . then down to Denver for the Fly Tackle Dealer Show.

"I'm grateful for your flies. I'm sure they work well . . . I think our Venezuela trip is late in the month . . . good fishing,

Lee"

Later in the month Lee heard from Keith Gardner, editor of *Fishing World* with both good and bad news.

"Many thanks for the tigerfish piece, which I have vouchered for $600. This is more than we pay elsewhere, but you and McClane should have all we can afford.

"I assume you heard that A. J. (McClane) had a heart attack last month out in Ennis. They took him to Missoula for a triple bypass and installed a pacemaker. He is back at their summer place in Ennis and when I last called, Susie had to go get him. He was outside on the lawn practicing fly-casting."

McClane—one of the icons of fly fishing—had been fishing editor of *Field & Stream* for more than 30 years and had pioneered flats fishing for bonefish and permit in the Bahamas and elsewhere.

Both Lee and Joan fished in the One Fly and enjoyed it immensely though Lee did not expect to like competitive fly fishing for trout. He found—as did others who fished the annual event put on by Jack Dennis of Jackson Hole—that it was pure fun and not too many people took it that seriously.

Lee wrote Dennis when he returned to Lew Beach:

"Finally getting settled. I've written a column on the One Fly and I enclose the first draft. I've already made some changes and need to have our guide's last name. Is he from Jackson?

" . . . Don't forget the information on the money we owe you. All our stuff you shipped is here and we're very grateful. We sure had a good time and appreciate you taking care of us in spite of all the running around you had to do at the time . . . "

On October 19th Lee wrote his longtime friend, Jim Chapralis, who publishes the *PanAngler*—a fishing newsletter in Chicago.

"We're planning to go south January 15th and stay south until the first week in April. I plan to fish for sails with a fly and would like to go to a place where there isn't the long run of two hours each way to the grounds as there is at Golfito . . . is this a trip you'd like to make? . . . Any ideas during the winter period?"

Chapralis—a veteran saltwater fly rodder—recommended they fish at Quepos, Costa Rica and planned to accompany them himself.

On November 29th Lee wrote Bill Brewster:

"Allan and I have decided to make a trip to Labrador and Newfoundland instead of the Upsalquitch this (upcoming) year. We'll put floats on my Super Cub and it will be a real memory trip. I want to go to Minipi where I opened things up and the fishing was fantastic back in 1957 . . . The fishing is still amazingly good. One friend took an 8 1/2 pound brookie two years ago and last year one of his party took a 9 pound 6 ounce fish. It's one of the few success stories of my efforts up there."

Lee wrote on December 4th:

"Winter season is moving in on us. Deer season opened on the 19th. I shot a 7-point buck the first morning. Haven't been out since . . . My hands get cold quickly . . . I went fishing on the no-kill section of the Willowemoc near the end of November and had cold hands there too. Water temperature was over 40. We caught a few trout on #24 midges, but it wasn't much fun. I think we'd move south if we didn't have so much stuff and love this place— except in winter.

Gardner Grant, who fished with Lee that day, remembers the trip.

"Both of us noticed a fish rising tight against the bridge abutment on the far bank. I tried for it, but the water was too deep to get any closer than about 50 feet and the confusing currents made it impossible to get the needed drag-free float with that long a cast.

"Absorbed in my own fishing, I didn't notice Lee wade out of the water, cross the bridge upstream from us, and walk down the opposite bank to the bridge abutment. I watched in amazement as he crawled under the girders of the bridge, and ended up in a crouch on the concrete cap of the abutment, about 10-12 feet above the river. Then he fashioned what I can only describe as 'the Lee Wulff underhand, backhand, upstream sling' for trout. The fish continued to sip, unaware, directly below him. On the third pass, the trout sipped once more and Lee had him. He played the trout into the abutment and started to lift slowly. I couldn't wade close enough to help, and I knew Lee couldn't lift a thrashing, 12-inch trout vertically, 10 feet up in the air on a 7X leader.

"Lee, what are you going to do?" I asked, "You'll break it off when you lift."

"That doesn't bother me," Lee laughed. "It's your fly."

Lee was delighted to get a letter from Perry Bass saying he was prepared to fund a study on net mesh size for Atlantic salmon. Lee wrote Bass:

"I'm delighted that you'll help in getting a fair shake for the mesh size deal. They've done everything they can to avoid the issue so far and when Dr. Parsons in his report took John Anderson's report as gospel and said 'the chances are it won't work' I took issue and said he had no information to back up that statement. Fortunately on the research committee, there is a Dr. Vaughn Anthony and he said I was absolutely right . . .

"So if you could make your donation for the purpose of 'making the Lee Wulff net mesh size test' with Dr. Anthony directing and participating for the ASF, I believe we'll come out with the truth about the mesh size. We can be certain that the commercial interests will do their best to discredit anything that will take any big fish away from their catch, but I believe the right mesh size will let us get the bigger fish through the interception zone and home to their native rivers.

"Without your help in this matter I am sure it would be delayed ad infinitum. The salmon and I will be deeply in your debt."

Lee catching a small permit on a fly at Boca Paila in Yucatan.

Perhaps Lee's insistence on putting his name on the study was what did it but, true to form, the offer somehow was deflected and lost in a maze of policy discussions by ASF board members.

At the end of the year, still fighting, Lee wrote Joe Cullman:

"I may not have made clear the situation on one of the faces of our policy I find illogical. We had a survey made to find out the comparative value of net-caught and angler-caught salmon. We found it was almost 40 to 1 more favorable for fly-caught salmon in dollars to say nothing of the recreational benefit. Obviously the best thing for the salmon and the country would be to have all salmon taken by rod and reel. Therefore that should be our goal. I hope you don't disagree.

"When we join up with the commercial fishermen in jointly saving the salmon, instead of independently seeking our logical goal, we create a difficult situation. We are their allies in getting back for them a traditional major share of the total take and they assume that we agree to that. As long as they have a share they will try to make it as great as possible and we, as their partners in bringing the salmon back, will be expected to help them get it. Our position, right from the start, should be that we want what is best for Canada and for the salmon's security which, to our pleasure, is angling only . . .

" . . . The commercials will never be our buddies and we should not be theirs. Our basic ideas are in conflict. Doesn't independent action for ASF make the most sense?"

As the year came to an end, Lee was rightly angry at the tactics of some in the ASF. One softening note came from a friend, Jack Fallon, a Massachusetts angler and writer who had just finished reading a passage from one of Lee's stories.

"Lee:

'. . . and the river whispering its muted song of the lower, slower flows of summer.'

Millions of words in print and you still manage to mint such melodies. May you go on forever . . . Happy Christmas."

The Long Journey

By the first of the year Lee realized the Perry Bass offer was probably not going to be accepted by the ASF and he wrote Perry:

"Dear Perry: The mesh business has become very cloudy and confused. According to Livvy's letter things happened which I do not believe occurred. I was not at the meeting in April, but I know that at the November meeting it was not stated that the DFO had been contacted to make the mesh size study or I would have objected . . . sorry this has gotten into such a mess but I hope with all my heart that we can get a fair study and get it soon."

On January 7th Lee received a long, involved letter from David Clark, president of ASF, in which he tried to set the record straight on the Newfoundland net mesh issue. At the end he wrote an interesting and encouraging paragraph:

"As a side bar, it is interesting to note two recent phenomena, one the consequence of the other. Following up on the introduction of enforceable quotas for the commercial fishery in Newfoundland, the fishermen have, in apocryphal response to quotas, begun to ask the government for a license buy-out program. As of last week, the government of Canada shot opening salvos of buy-out discussions with the Newfoundland government. The signals from Ottawa indicate reductions of the quotas in 1991. That should produce a heightened plea from fishermen to be bought out. My guess is we are witnessing the death throes of the commercial fisher for salmon in Newfoundland, and I predict it could happen as early as 1993. If events unfold as predicted, the results of a mesh-size study will prove to be of academic interest only in so far as the harvesting of salmon is concerned."

It would be a development Lee had wished for for decades, but he was not yet ready to give up on his net mesh study—just in case the Newfoundland commercial fishermen changed their minds.

In typical hard-nosed Wulff language, Lee wrote Clark, ending with:

"As to the net berth buy-outs, I'm certain we should insist on an all or nothing deal. We buy them all out on a take-it or leave-it basis or we let them stew in their falling markets. If we don't . . . if even a few nets are still legal, it is a foothold that can be used by their powerful lobby to expand again to get their share. Our economic survey shows that the best thing for Canada is for them not to have a share."

Weary of his battling with people in the ASF about the net mesh and the game fish status for salmon, Lee wrote Joe Cullman on January 12th, ending with:

"I bring the wisdom of years of salmon conservation experience and a fine track record of integrity and judgment. I'm sorry it has not been more valuable. Within the scope of my beliefs I will continue to help all I can— even though, as I am sure you realize, it had been quite discouraging at times."

A couple of events in late January cheered him considerably and he was looking forward with great anticipation to going down to Costa Rica in about a month to fish for sailfish and marlin on a fly.

The Wings Club in New York sent him a letter expressing thanks for his long participation in their activities as a pilot since 1955 and informing him that he had been made a Golden Eagle member. Such an honor only occurs when a member's age added to the number of years of continuous membership equals 120 or more points.

Lee received a letter from Thomas Humphrey, president of the Salmonoid Council of Newfoundland and Labrador, adding the Council planned a tribute to Lee Wulff on Thursday, November 21, 1991 in St. Johns. Lee was touched. He had doubts at times whether the salmon anglers of those provinces had really appreciated his years of devotion to their salmon fishing.

From March 5th to the 7th, Lee and Joan and Jim Chapralis fished from the port of Quepos in Costa Rica for billfish. They had chartered the 31-foot Bertram *Marlin Azul* and Lee was equipped with some of his new flies.

Winston Moore, a longtime saltwater fly rodder and an angler who had caught more than 100 Pacific sailfish on a fly, called Chapralis on the phone before he left Chicago.

"Find out what Lee uses to stay as young as he does. When you find out, we'll bottle it, some some for you and me, and sell the rest."

It was a source of constant amazement to other big game anglers that Lee at age 86 was still going strong.

Sailfish were scarce and not many came up the first day. The second day off Quepos was as calm as a lake and in the afternoon it was broiling hot. Looking at the mirror-like sea, Lee remarked that it looked like dry fly conditions on a pond which gave him an idea. He would tie up a big creation—to resemble he knew not what—and try to interest a billfish in a big dry fly.

That night he rigged up a weird-looking, fan-winged creation—brown hackle for the body and white calf's hair for the wings and tail. The wings were about 6-inches wide.

The following day—as it always happens in fishing—the sea was rough, not calm. Nevertheless, a sailfish came up to one of the teaser baits and Lee cast the huge fly out and let it "float" on the rough surface. To his, and everyone aboard's, surprise, the sailfish took the fly like a trout taking a Royal Wulff.

Chapralis said the sailfish dove for the depths after the take and Lee settled down in a folding chair for a long battle. It was blistering hot and Jim said he repaired to the shade of the bridge with a cold Coke. Joan stood behind Lee as he battled the big sailfish—a black, long-billed cap shading his eyes. The boat skipper, Raphael, kept the *Marlin Azul* in slow gear as he peered down through the clear water trying to follow the direction of Lee's line. Carlos, the mate, perched on the cabin roof, his legs dangling down.

One hour and two hours passed. The heat was sweltering. "Is he O.K.?" Chapralis quietly asked Joan.

"He's O.K.," Joan assured him.

By the three hour mark, the crew was getting bored as they always do during a long fight with billfish on a fly rod. They are used to taking out anglers who hook and fight 100-pound sailfish on conventional boat rods and 50-80 pound mono. The fights usually only last about 30 minutes before the fish are hauled aboard.

Shortly after 3 p.m. the sailfish came in, jumped a number of times close to the boat and Carlos reached out with a gloved hand and grasped the sailfish's bill. It had been a great fight and Lee was exhausted but happy.

It was not until after I had written the account of Lee's dry fly sailfish that I realized the Bertram on which he caught his last billfish was the very same boat on which Joe Hudson and I won the first International Billfish Fly Tournament in Costa Rica years before—with the same crew. The *Marlin Azul* is a lucky boat.

Later Lee wrote of his trip:

"We caught sails on our new flies . . . and I caught one on a dry fly . . . about as big as a swallow. I wonder what the sail thought it was. It's a silly thing, but a dry fly sailfish gives me something to write about."

Home again, Lee wrote John Randolph at *Fly Fisherman* and mailed him the story of the sailfish. He had also written an account of it for his column in *Fly Rod & Reel*—assuming the two magazines were not competing. He had second thoughts about that in his letter to Randolph.

"I must tell you I wrote a piece about the dry fly fish for my column and I enclose it for you to look at. No conflict in my mind as far as stories go . . . only that they are about the same fish. The one for you has much more clout. Had I known I was going to write it, I could have held off on the column . . . Anyway I hope you'll see fit to take it. If not rush it back so I can send it to *Salt Water Sportsman*."

Lee was now thoroughly immersed in his fly fishing for billfish and was already making plans to go after more. He had been thinking about a number of things connected with billfish on a fly and wrote Jim Chapralis that month:

"There has long been discussion on the length of the shock leader. Most record-holders who have had to use the 12 inch length are against any length-ening. They feel they had to do it the hard way and it shouldn't be made easier for future anglers. I'm one old record-holder who doesn't feel that way. I think it makes very little difference whether the shock leader is one foot long or three or even five. It will still take a lot of skill to bring a sailfish or marlin in to the side of the boat and when he does if the mate can reach out and take a strong leader, it will save a little exhaustion of the fish (and a better chance of survival after release) as he can be billed and released sooner."

In Lee's letter to Randolph, Lee wound up with:

"We plan to spend a week at Lac Beauchene in western Quebec for small-mouths and then fish Anticosti for a week. May go down to Minipi to make a film for Labrador, taking my plane down so it can be in the film. Allan will fly with me, if the deal goes through, as I'm not strong enough anymore to handle it on a rough shore in high winds. I get old-age aches these days.

"Spring finally seems to (be) arriving and my friends are saying come on with me . . . I'll show you lots of Blue-Winged Olives . . . Haven't found time yet to go . . . "

Sunday, April 28th, was a warm and calm day and after giving a lecture on wading to the fishing school students Lee kissed Joan lightly on the cheek and strode down to the meadow to where the Super Cub was tied down. He was due for a routine check ride at a nearby Hancock, New York airfield to re-qualify for his pilot's license. He took off and 30 minutes later let down

231

and landed at the club-owned grass field where he was to meet Max Francisco, his FAA instructor.

Most of the pilots were making coffee in the small operations shack as Lee and Max climbed into the Super Cub—Max in the rear seat. There was a gentle five mph breeze blowing from the south as they taxied out and began the pre-flight take-off check.

"As we lifted off," Max said later, "I saw someone standing beside the runway taking our picture as they often did at our airport. After some slow flight and a few turns, I suggested that we do some take-offs and landings. As we approached the north end of the runway at about 75 feet (altitude) and on a heading of about 215 degrees for runway 17, he failed to turn left and added power. At that I thought that he was going to go around to land on runway 35. If this had been a student pilot I would have questioned as to his intentions, but when do you start to question someone who has been flying airplanes for 44 years?

Lee's Piper Super Cub 102LW.

"He was still on the controls and there was no indication of anything wrong. After we passed the end of the runway he again closed the throttle and it was now clear to me that he was not in control of his actions and we were due to land in trees of about 60 feet tall.

"At this time I applied power and he suddenly reduced it. The airplane stalled and dropped the right wing. At this time I instantly grabbed the stick and shook it violently to free it from him. Now we were in a gully that runs perpendicular to the runway with a heading of about 350 degrees and a hill about 200 feet higher ahead.

"Just as I had it flying again I saw tree limbs passing by the windows. After hitting the trees, the airplane nosed down and came to a violent stop. I do not think I was unconscious at any time. The top and right side of the airplane were completely torn away. I felt for the seat belt and unlatched it and sort of fell to the ground. I tried to stand up, but with a broken bone in my left foot, a broken toe on my right foot—along with five compound fractures and six lacerations from my upper lip to my eyebrows—it was no use. One glance at Lee and I knew that no one could be of any help to him."

Francisco—covered with blood and losing it rapidly—lay on his back and pushed with his legs through the dried leaves, trying to reach a nearby road. He probably fainted a number of times on the way. The pilots back on the field began looking at their watches. It had been too long a time since the plane had passed the field. One man turned on a hand-held radio to 121.5 and they suddenly heard the automatic distress signals put out by the transponder on the downed plane. Taking off in two planes they soon saw the wreckage. Returning quickly they called rescue crews and an ambulance.

By this time Max could no longer see, but had heard the planes pass overhead. He was carried on a litter to a pickup truck which took him to the airport. He was picked up by a medical helicopter and flown the 40 miles to a hospital. He was more than six hours on the operating table, but finally recovered and is now back to flying again.

About the crash, Max says:

"I will always believe that Lee's death was the cause of the accident—rather than a result of it."

The long journey had come to an end.

Epilogue

The fishing world was shocked to hear of Lee's death. It was inconceivable that he was gone.

On Sunday May 5th, Charles Kurault, host of CBS's "Sunday Morning" network TV show said of Lee:

"Lee Wulff was to fly fishing what Einstein was to physics."

On the same day, Nelson Bryant's obituary of Lee appeared in the New York *Times*.

"Lee Wulff was possessed by a furious desire to refine the art of angling and was extraordinarily successful in that quest, right to the end of his 86 years.

"The refinements were not only in techniques and tackle; a half century or so ago, he became the first major exponent of the catch-and-release philosophy. He helped to persuade subsequent legions of anglers that wooing, playing and ultimately releasing a splendid game fish was often more pleasurable than killing it, that such fish are too valuable to be caught only once.

" . . . Although he was often dogmatic and unbending and had no fear of treading on anyone's toes, most of those whom Wulff encountered soon understood that his fundamental concern was for the salmon, that he had no other ax to grind. He was the conscience of the Atlantic salmon restoration effort in North America."

Lee had bequeathed a sum of money in his will " . . . to celebrate my long and pleasant stay on earth."

Friends by the hundreds came to his "Happy Party" at the New York Anglers' Club Tuesday, June 25, 1991.

Trout and salmon fly fishermen ate and drank and talked and thought of Lee until far into the night.

Ed Zern had earlier written a tribute to Lee which speaks for all who knew him:

"There seems to be a universal human desire for immortality, a common wish for some kind of survival through eternity. But for some of us, acceptance of the conventional notions of afterlife is difficult. We can accept, though, the concept of the word "immortal" as it's used by the French National Academy, which designated its members as "The Immortals," and with good reason. So long as there's civilization, Flaubert and Racine, de Maupassant and Dumas, Voltaire and Gidet will live and be influential.

"We're here tonight to honor a friend who has already achieved that special kind of immortality. For as long as men and women fish for sport, and for an opportunity to experience through angling a one-ness with what we call Nature, for as long as anglers think first of the well-being of the species they fish for, and of defending the habitat that's essential to survival of those species, and only then think of catch (or the catch-and-release, most often), for that long will Lee Wulff's name be known and honored by anglers the world around. Not just for the Wulff fly and its almost infinite variations, although that alone would guarantee a well-deserved niche in the pantheon of angling. Not just for innovations in technique and tackle. Most importantly, Lee's name will continue to stand, as it does today, for the concept of game fish as too valuable and too precious to be caught only once.

"And so we salute this pioneer, this explorer, this adventurer, this innovator, this artist, this conservationist, this film maker, this author, this realist, this defender of sport's best traditions, this iconoclast of obsolete traditions, and above all, this great American sportsman.

"Lee, we are not going to say we hope you will live forever. We know you're going to, and we rejoice."

On April 15, 1991, an agreement was signed between private interests and the Faroe Island commercial salmon fishermen, endorsed by the Faroese government, to buy out the high seas Atlantic salmon fishery of the Faroe Islands.

In the spring of 1992, one of the oldest dreams of the Atlantic Salmon Federation—and salmon anglers throughout North America—at last came true. It was the shutting down of Newfoundland's commercial salmon fishery—one of the world's largest.

And in July, 1993, negotiators signed an agreement in Copenhagen,

Denmark that Greenland's native netsmen will be paid $800,000 to forgo catching Atlantic salmon in 1993 and 1994 and an additional $50,000 when negotiations re-open on a compensation package to extend the moratorium through 1997, Art Lee reported in the December, 1993 issue of *Fly Fisherman*.

And some day—perhaps not soon, but some day—the great schools of Atlantic salmon will return to their native rivers around much of the world each year to be caught only by recreational anglers. Untold thousands of children as yet unborn will learn the joy of salmon fishing with rod and reel.

And Lee Wulff will rest easier.

Lee's watercolor painting of a feeding bluefin tuna—circa 1940.

Lee, salmon and his second float plane—a Super Cub—in 1955.

Lee and skipper Larry Cronin on Notre Dame Bay, Newfoundland.